Democracy in Europe

LARRY SIEDENTOP

Democracy in Europe

COLUMBIA UNIVERSITY PRESS

NEW YORK

Columbia University Press
Publishers Since 1893
New York   Chichester, West Sussex
Copyright © 2001 Larry Siedentop

Library of Congress Cataloging-in-Publication Data

Siedentop, Larry.
Democracy in Europe / Larry Siedentop.
p. cm.
Includes bibliographical references and index.
ISBN 978-0-231-12376-1 (cloth)
ISBN 978-0-231-12377-8 (paper)
1. European Union.
2. Representative government and representation—Europe.
3. Democracy—Europe. 4. Federal government—Europe.
5. Constitutional history—Europe. I. Title.
JN30 .S47 2001
320.94—dc21
00-065576

Columbia University Press books are printed
on permanent and durable acid-free paper.

Printed in the United States of America

For Daryl

Contents

Preface

Through three sweltering Philadelphia summer months in 1787, fifty men talked, argued and reflected. They were the delegates of thirteen states which had only a few years before liberated themselves from British rule. Unfortunately, the intervening years had seen the loose Confederation which bound them together stagger from crisis to crisis. These crises ranged from disagreements between the states about reciprocal obligations, through problems arising from paper currencies, indebtedness and domestic rebellion, to foreign problems such as the imprisonment of American sailors by Barbary pirates. Public opinion in the former colonies, and not least among their élites, had become convinced that something had to be done. A stronger federation, a more effective central power, seemed imperative.

Yet these fifty men were by no means agreed about how that goal should be achieved. Some were nationalists who did not mind overly if the construction of a central government, acting directly on individuals rather than negotiating with member states in the fashion of the Confederation, involved the erosion of the states' 'sovereignty', while others remained suspicious of any executive power that recalled the British Crown, and wished strictly to limit the delegation of authority and power to the centre. Fortunately, the habit of public discussion and government by consent which had roots in more than a century of considerable *de facto* American autonomy prevailed in Philadelphia. The influence of older men of prestige, such as Washington and Franklin, joined to the abilities of James Madison and Alexander Hamilton, enabled the delegates to find a way forward through a series of compromises.

By September 1787 those compromises resulted in a document

which the Convention recommended to the states for adoption. That document became, of course, the Constitution of the United States of America. But its adoption by the states at the end of September 1787, as the weary delegates left Philadelphia on horseback or by coach, was by no means a foregone conclusion. Anti-federalist agitation had already begun in many of the states. For some of the compromises reached – such as that giving equal representation to states in the Senate or Upper House, which in effect reduced the influence of the largest and most populous states such as New York, Virginia and Massachusetts – created opposition, not least among current state office-holders.

A great public debate thus got under way. It was carried on in tracts, pamphlets, sermons and newspapers. The quality of the arguments put forward varied considerably. But at its best the debate involved contributions which rank, in subtlety and depth, with the most important works of European political thought. That best took the form of a series of short articles written by Madison, Hamilton and Jay for New York newspapers and signed 'Publius'. These articles were widely republished and dispatched abroad, and probably made a crucial difference to the outcome in the various state conventions organized to consider ratification of the proposed Constitution. Collected together, these articles even now have a claim on our attention as *The Federalist Papers*.

I tell this story because of the contrast it suggests with Europe today. Western Europeans have been taking part in a great experiment for more than four decades, and are now faced with proposals for an even more radical degree of integration, monetary and political, to reinforce the Single Market. These moves, associated with the Maastricht Treaty and its revision, amount to a major step towards creating a federal state in Europe.

It might be supposed that such proposals, with all their profound implications for nation-states with far longer histories than those of the former American colonies in the 1780s, would have created another great debate – a debate at least as far-reaching and profound as that which raged through the American states in the last months of 1787 and through much of 1788. It might be supposed that the desire to advocate or to oppose change would have created by now in Europe the counterparts of Madison, Hamilton and Jay.

But it is not so.

Why not? Why is there nothing which has seized the imagination of European peoples about the direction of their own development, about their own fates? Does it matter? And what does the absence of a grand debate suggest about the condition of Europe at the beginning of the twenty-first century?

These are the questions which have prompted me to write this book. The men who rode to Philadelphia in 1787, who took part in the discussions of the Convention and later defended its work, were men of means and leisure, gentlemen. Some were even slave-holders. But however rooted in the past in these respects, they also shared a sense that what they were doing was of decisive importance for the future – that the possibility of self-government in a democratic society hung on the outcome of their deliberations. Nor were they wrong. The 'compound' republic which Madison sought to create, and did finally help to create, provides the crucial point of reference for the attempt to create a European federal state today. Any evaluation of the prospects of that enterprise should begin with American federalism.

Are we such pygmies that we cannot rise to the occasion? I refuse to believe it. And we ought not to believe it.

What follows is an attempt to stimulate a debate. This is a book of reflections and, I hope, provocations to argument. In thinking about the future of Europe, I have been much influenced by my earlier encounters with nineteenth-century French liberal thought, especially with Tocqueville's truly incomparable *Democracy in America*. But I also owe something to the living! First, I must thank Nick Robinson, who suggested I write the book – though there have been a few moments when I have wished he had not done so. Next I want to thank those whose comments on particular chapters have greatly assisted me: Roger Boden, John Burrow, James Griffin, Dennis Nineham, Paul Seabright, Robert Skidelsky, Edward Skidelsky, George Richardson and Anthony Teasdale, and, for the publisher, Stuart Proffitt and Daniel Hind. Of course, they are not responsible for any remaining faults. I also want to thank Denise Battisby, who has valiantly coped with successive revisions of the manuscript.

Larry Siedentop
Keble College, Oxford

I

Democratic Liberty on a
Continental Scale?

Democratic legitimacy in Europe is at risk. In many respects European integration is now an accomplished fact. A single market and, for most member states, a common currency have arrived. But what remains uncertain is the political form the European Union will finally take. That is why a great constitutional debate has become indispensable. Such a debate is needed to establish the goals of European political integration, the limits which such integration ought to respect and the means by which new powers and institutions can be made accountable to the peoples of Europe. Only by means of such a debate can the peoples of Europe once again become involved in their own fate.

A great constitutional debate need not involve a prior commitment to federalism as the most desirable outcome in Europe. It may reveal that Europe is in the process of inventing a new political form, something more than a confederation but less than a federation – an association of sovereign states which pool their sovereignty only in very restricted areas or to varying degrees, an association which does not seek to have the coercive power to act directly on individuals in the fashion of nation-states. Or, it may reveal that even if federalism is the proper goal for Europe, such a goal must be pushed well into the future – for the immediate need is to firm up or create democratic political cultures within member states as a preliminary to creating such a culture on a Europe-wide basis.

Only a debate which explores all of these options can begin to create among Europeans the sense that what is happening in Europe today is not merely the result of inexorable market forces or the machinations of élites which have escaped from democratic control.

But how do we begin? At the outset a bit of history is essential. For centuries it was an axiom of European political thought that a really large territory could only be governed in one way – despotically. That axiom was repudiated in the course of the nineteenth century. But before understanding how it came to be repudiated, it is important to understand why so many European thinkers long believed that, once a state exceeded a certain size, it could only be governed in a despotic or tyrannical way. For their doubts must raise an initial question about the project of creating a pan-European state.

What were their grounds? The easiest way to understand those grounds is to consider arguments put forward in the mid-eighteenth century by the French jurist Montesquieu, the first European thinker to identify a bureaucratic state as the distinctively modern form of despotism. Montesquieu argued that any self-governing community or republic depended on civic virtue, and that such virtue in turn required the full participation of citizens in public discussion and decision-making. For that reason, he concluded, a self-governing republic was only possible in a very small territory – small enough to permit all citizens, at least in principle, to attend the sovereign assembly.

Of course the trouble with that argument was that it seemed to relegate self-government to antiquity, to the world of the ancient city-state. That world survived in modern Europe, if at all, only in the form of the little republics such as Venice or Geneva. But what of the national monarchies or nation-states which were the dominant political form in modern Europe? Could they only be ruled bureaucratically and despotically? Was there no hope for self-government in modern Europe?

Montesquieu did not quite despair. Two things gave him hope – first, the aristocratic structure of post-feudal society in Europe; and, secondly, the example of England. Montesquieu argued that what he called 'moderate' government in anything as large as a nation-state – by which he meant the dispersal of power and the rule of law – depended upon European aristocracies preserving a role in local government. For that role prevented a dangerous concentration of power in central government.

The development of the French state in the seventeenth century, under Richelieu and Louis XIV, illustrated, in Montesquieu's eyes, a danger threatening every European monarchy or nation-state. For

Richelieu and Louis XIV had deprived the French nobility of their role in local affairs and substituted for them civil servants accountable only to their masters in Paris. The whole of French society thus became subject to the 'tutorship' of bureaucrats. Local interests could be ignored, local opinion dismissed.

It was to oppose this centralizing of power in the name of political liberty and the rule of law that Montesquieu made so much of the example of England. For England offered the example of a government in which elected representatives governed in the name of the people. But not only that. It was a form of government in which, formally through the House of Lords, and informally through the House of Commons, the aristocratic structure of European society was both reflected and reinforced. England offered the precious model of a political system in which legal authority was centralized, but power was decentralized. For the English aristocracy, which dominated both Houses of Parliament, had no interest in allowing its local role to be subverted by bureaucratic rule of the kind that had made such headway in France.

That is why Montesquieu concluded that the rule of law and avoidance of bureaucratic despotism in European states depended upon an aristocratic social structure – upon status differences, which meant that one section of society had a vocation and vested interest in defending local autonomy and the dispersal of power. Their 'honour' depended upon it.

Living up to one's status or living honourably in a society with distinctions of rank was thus identified as the chief means of preventing the development of bureaucratic despotism – especially if reinforced by representative government on the English model, which gave the aristocracy an important role, not only in local government, but in central government as well. In retrospect, this model of political liberty can plausibly be described as 'aristocratic liberty'. For it assumes that self-government in a nation-state requires government by social superiors, by a class set apart by custom and wealth, if not by legal privilege. And the reason for making such an assumption is not hard to find. Association is always the key to dispersing power, and an aristocratic society creates powerful local associations. It sorts people into two roles. Either they play leaders or they play the led.

3

In an aristocratic society, habits of leadership and deference provide a basis for association which does not depend upon 'natural' sympathy or choice. The assumption of social superiority on the one side, deference and gratitude for patronage on the other, creates groups or corporations accustomed to acting together and, if need be, resisting. They thereby become effective brakes on the centralizing of power, while requiring only a limited kind of sympathy among those associated – sympathy limited, that is, by the assumption of social inequality.

But what if European aristocracies failed to perform their traditional role in government or were ousted from it? Then, Montesquieu believed, the outlook for political liberty in Europe was grim. How could he be so sure? Montesquieu believed that there was a simple way of testing his argument. It was to look at what happened in the very largest political units, empires on a continental scale. Empires were collections of diverse nations which lacked a coherent superior class or aristocracy able to defend the dispersal of power.

What was the result? In empires, government by strangers tended to replace government by social superiors. The Turkish and Chinese Empires offered, in Montesquieu's view, examples of the kind of political system which seemed unavoidable in states on a continental scale. They were what Montesquieu called 'immoderate' states, lacking the rule of law, states in which power was so concentrated that a person's status and privileges depended upon the whim of the ruler and his acolytes. They were states in which a kind of equality reigned, it is true. But it was an equality of fear. No corporation or social class with deep local roots offered a permanent barrier to the sovereign's will or caprice, in contrast to European monarchies properly so-called.

Thus, government by strangers came to be identified as the central technique of despotism. It is the technique which Montesquieu feared might destroy moderation and political liberty in Europe. It is the technique which, he feared, could turn European monarchies into something not much better than 'Oriental despotisms', subjecting them to bureaucratic rule from a remote centre.

But why were European states on such a slippery slope? Why was there such a threat to the traditional dispersal of power in Europe? Montesquieu perhaps only half understood or only half wanted to understand the social mechanism which underlay the threat to political liberty in Europe as he conceived it. For that threat sprang from a deep challenge to aristocracy in Europe, from growing and justified resentment against forms of social privilege which had survived into post-feudal Europe.

That resentment created a social mechanism which opened the way to despotism. For once the aristocratic organization of society is challenged, the jealousies excited by social privilege can be turned by distant rulers into the means of depriving localities of political influence – that is, by playing off one section of local society against another, and introducing the rule of strangers. To a greater or less extent, that mechanism has played an indispensable part in the creation of European nation-states – paving the way for political unity by destroying feudal jurisdictions, along with the radical social inequality and localism they sustained. It led the French communes, for example, to acquiesce in the growth of royal power, in order to escape from the hateful oppression of local feudal lords. That was the positive side of this social mechanism. But it also had a negative side. For class conflict can survive its sources and contribute to further centralization. By undermining local solidarities, class conflict reduces local resistance and makes it easier for a central power to rule through its own agents. And the larger the territory, the easier this technique of rule becomes. For rulers can then employ as agents people who may even have a different language or a different religion.

The psychological basis for this mechanism of despotism is pretty clear. Differences in language and religion make it more difficult to enter the minds of others, to identify their wants and discontents and sympathize with them. But that kind of sympathy is the necessary source of local influence in a society no longer organized hierarchically or in ranks – in the fashion that Montesquieu, as late as the 1740s, still took for granted in European states. As we have seen, in an aristocratic society habits of leadership and deference provided a basis for association and resistance which required only limited sympathy. The kinds of leadership and association provided by aristocratic social conditions may now look morally dubious. But they were long an effective way of dispersing power.

Let us now accept, however, that a social revolution has taken place in Europe – that a society without formal differences of rank has developed, a society in which everyone is equal before the law and enjoys the same basic rights. Let us suppose further that such a society has also weakened the importance of many informal sources of social stratification – by the growth of a 'middle' class which means that income is more evenly distributed, education more widely spread, with increasing social opportunity and mobility. The consequence is that there is no longer a more or less permanent political class on the model of the old aristocracy, a class which is in a position to defend local autonomy and limit the centralization of political power.

Then Montesquieu's famous constitutional precautions against tyranny appear less convincing. Drawing on the example of England to urge the separation of powers in central government, Montesquieu took aristocratic social conditions for granted. The separation of powers into executive, legislative and judicial branches was designed not only to prevent too much power accumulating in the same hands, but to open a crucial function of central government to local leaders. Such a separation of powers was for Montesquieu the means, above all, of reinforcing the aristocratic structure of society by giving the aristocracy an important legislative role in central government.

But we have now imagined away such an aristocracy. What, then, are the means of preventing a central government, which claims a sovereign right, the unlimited right to make law, drawing all power to itself? Equal subjection to a sovereign agency – which is, after all, what we mean by a 'state' – then conjures up the threat of an indefinite centralization of power. Is there any way that a society which lacks an aristocratic or privileged class can successfully combat the centralizing of power?

Today this argument ought to give us pause. For if Montesquieu's model of aristocratic liberty is correct, then the dangers arising from the absence of a distinct political class are acute – and far greater for a pan-European state than for older nation-states such as Britain and Holland, which have a residue of aristocracy in their political classes. Can Europe enjoy political liberty without aristocracy? Montesquieu thought not. I think he was wrong. But there is a case to be answered.

By the 1820s one state in Europe had developed in a way that confirmed Montesquieu's worst fears. By that time France was governed in the fashion that, for Montesquieu, empires on a continental scale had to be governed. France had become a bureaucratic despotism. For Napoleon had reinforced the bureaucratic character of the state machine inherited from the *ancien régime*, completing the destruction of regional and local autonomy. Although only a nation-state, France had become the caricature of a continental empire. It was ruled from the centre by civil servants and their agents, who in most cases were not locals.

Ironically, it was this development which led some French liberals to begin to take an interest in American federalism. American federalism thus first seriously impinged on European political thinking, *not* as the model for a European federal state, but as a model for reforming one nation-state which had taken the despotic form of a continental empire. A young French aristocrat, Alexis de Tocqueville, decided that once the aristocratic structure of European society was largely destroyed and society 'levelled', then Montesquieu's formula for dispersing power by reinforcing the local role of the aristocracy and bringing that class into central government was no longer adequate.

For Tocqueville, such a 'democratic' social revolution meant that the terms of political debate had to change. For if the new democratic form of society resembled Montesquieu's empires in so far as it lacked a hereditary political class or aristocracy, then the political threat facing it was also similar. Would it be possible to set limits on the concentration of power in central government? Or could a balance be found between central power and local autonomy?

These questions drew Tocqueville's attention to the United States. By the 1830s the United States had succeeded in governing itself in a decentralized way for half a century. Yet – contradicting Montesquieu's vision – it was a quasi-continental state without a privileged class or aristocracy. American federalism seemed to offer a new means of combining central government and local autonomy in a levelled or democratic society. With its formal division of sovereignty between centre and periphery, American federalism seemed to represent a new form of the state. Might not such a form of the state be more instructive for France than the aristocratic British form which Montesquieu had endorsed? Suspecting so, Tocqueville managed to find an excuse to travel through the United States in 1831–2.

In the United States, Tocqueville soon felt his hunch was vindicated.

American federalism *did* represent a new form of the state, one which could foster political liberty and the dispersal of power in the absence of aristocracy, and that even on a quasi-continental scale. Enjoying the sovereign right to act directly on individuals *in certain spheres*, American federal government did not suffer from the weakness of earlier confederations such as the Holy Roman Empire and Switzerland – which, depending on the member states to execute orders, had either come to be dominated by the strongest member or had become impotent. By contrast, the American federal government did not rely on the states to enforce its writ.* Yet, at the same time, the states and local government had their own independent spheres of action. Observing expecially the vitality of New England townships, and the way local self-government gave an extraordinary impetus to civil society by fostering self-reliance and the habit of association, Tocqueville became convinced that the American form of the state offered a better model for reform of the French state than did the English Constitution.

* In order to understand the 'discovery' in America that enabled Tocqueville to distinguish between federalism properly so-called and confederations, it may be useful to recall his words in *Democracy in America*: 'In all confederations previous to that of 1789 in America, the peoples who allied themselves for a common purpose agreed to obey the injunctions of the federal government, but they kept the right to direct and supervise the execution of the union's laws in their territory. The Americans who united in 1789 agreed not only that the federal government should dictate the laws but that it should itself see to their execution. In both cases the right is the same, and only the application thereof different. But that one difference produces immense results.

'In all confederations previous to that of contemporary America, a federal government appealed to the particular governments to provide its needs. Whenever one of these disliked the measure prescribed, it could always avoid the necessity of obedience. If it was strong, it could appeal to arms; if it was weak, it could tolerate resistance to laws of the union . . . Consequently, one of two things has always happened: either the most powerful of the combined states has assumed the prerogatives of the federal authority and dominated all the others in its name or the federal government has been left to its own resources, anarchy has reigned among the confederates, and the union has lost its power to act.

'In America, the Union's subjects are not states but private citizens. When it wants to levy a tax, it does not turn to the government of Massachusetts, but to each inhabitant of Massachusetts. Former federal governments had to confront peoples, individuals of the Union. It [American federal government] does not borrow its power, but draws it from within. It has its own administrators, courts, officers of justice, and army.' (*Democracy in America*, Vol. 1, 1835, Part 1, Chapter 8)

Tocqueville did not suppose that nineteenth-century France could become federal, dividing sovereignty between central government and the provinces. But other features of American federalism could be adopted. American federalism had, for example, created a new political role for the courts, which, through judicial review, were able to defend the separation of powers and protect individual rights. Nor was that all. The American legal system provided a way of ensuring the accountability of elected local officials, without embedding them in a single bureaucratic hierarchy. It showed that the rule of law did not require rule by civil servants.

The apparent success of American federalism transformed liberal constitutional thought in the course of the nineteenth century. But what began as a model for reforming one over-centralized state in Europe was bound, sooner or later, to suggest a possible model for wider European political union. If the 'new Europe' across the Atlantic could create a successful federal state, why should not 'old Europe' follow suit – thereby finding a way beyond the national rivalries and wars which had for so long marked its history? Of course, unifying 'projects for peace' in Europe had a very long ancestry. But they had always remained speculative. In the twentieth century that began to change. After two catastrophic wars in Europe – what has been called the European 'civil war' – the attraction of federalism became far more potent.

No sooner is the project of constructing a federal Europe put forward, however, than it brings crucial questions in its wake. These are questions which even now have not been adequately addressed. Yet they must be addressed if the federalist project in Europe is to be anything more than dangerous adventurism. What extra-constitutional conditions made possible the success of American federalism? Were there not a number of informal or cultural conditions crucial to its success? And, if so, can they be matched in Europe today?

American federalism, unlike Jehovah's creation, was not created *ex nihilo*. It was not simply the result of constitutional rules adopted by the men who gathered in Philadelphia in 1787. Rather, American federalism drew on established habits and attitudes, some of which dated from the earliest days of the colonies. Just what were those pre-existing habits and attitudes? In *Democracy in America* Tocqueville

9

identified at least four informal conditions which he considered pre-requisites for the success of American federalism: the habit of local self-government; a common language; an open political class domin-ated by lawyers; and some shared moral beliefs. Are they also prerequi-sites of the success of European federalism? Are there others? We must find out.

Arguably, the first major difference between the former English colonies at the end of the eighteenth century and European nation-states is one which Tocqueville – unbothered by any serious project for European federalism – did not explore. Yet it is an important difference. Before their revolt the American colonies had never enjoyed complete sovereignty. Although they had enjoyed very wide *de facto* autonomy, they had also been subject to the British Crown. That recollection of a common subjection, as well as the habits of association springing from it, contributed to the sense of a common need for political union in Philadelphia in 1787. There was tacit agreement among the delegates that some functions of the British Crown, especially those to do with foreign policy and military matters, were only temporarily in abeyance – waiting, so to speak, for a central authority to take them over once again. In that sense, what might be called the *ghost* of the former Imperial government was present throughout the deliberations of the Constitutional Convention in Philadelphia. It was a ghost which had considerable influence on the deliberations.

Here, the contrast with Europe today is striking. It is true that since the end of the Second World War Western European nations have ceded important rights to shared enterprises, beginning with Nato and the Coal and Steel Community. They have in that way had to come to terms with a practical abridgement of their sovereignties. None the less, not one of them has renounced national sovereignty. Formally, Europe still consists of proud nation-states with political cultures largely shaped by and attached to their sovereign rights. Puzzling as it may seem, not even the acceptance of a European jurisdiction superior to national legislation and national courts has changed that pattern as yet. It has taken the Maastricht Treaty and its aftermath – with the rush for monetary union and its implications for national control of fiscal policy – finally to bring the issue of national sovereignty to boiling point.

Will European nations whose identity was long shaped by, and is still so intimately bound up with, the claim of 'sovereignty' be willing or able to abandon that claim formally? It remains to be seen. The risk of nationalist reactions to the project of federalism, reactions of a kind which were never really plausible in the former English colonies, remains only too real in Europe today.

That brings us to several other informal pre-conditions of the success of American federalism, pre-conditions which *were* identified and explored by Tocqueville. One was the habit of local self-government which the settlers of New England had brought from their mother country. The English settlers were used to managing their own affairs locally. Local liberty was, so to speak, their inheritance. Self-reliance and the habit of association were the crucial offshoots of local liberty, and helped to give civil society in America its peculiar dynamism. The habit of self-government had gradually shaped a civic culture upon which those who drafted the American constitution could draw. Indeed, there is a sense in which American federalism was simply a formalizing of long-standing habits and attitudes of the English colonists. It was their free *moeurs* (as French observers enviously described them) which led the English settlers to create townships first, state governments later, and only after the Revolution, with the disappearance of British sovereignty, a federal government.

Of course, the English colonists' habit of managing their own affairs was closely tied to their having a common language. That is the second informal prerequisite of the success of American federalism which Tocqueville noticed. The importance he attached to it emerged especially two decades after the publication of *Democracy in America*. By the 1850s Tocqueville, like many liberal European observers, viewed with mounting anxiety a new flood of European immigration into the United States. These were immigrants who did not come from countries with the habit of local self-government, nor did they have English as their language. Could immigrants who did not initially possess the free *moeurs* of the settlers of New England, or English as their first language, be successfully assimilated into the American federal system? Or, would such immigration gradually undermine free institutions in the United States, creating social conditions which led either to the destruction of the Union or to the centralization of power?

By the end of the nineteenth century these questions were mostly answered. The United States had proved capable of assimilating not only the Germans, Dutch and Scandinavians who arrived in the mid-nineteenth century, but also Southern and Eastern Europeans, especially Italians, who began to arrive in increasing numbers towards the end of the century. These new immigrants came from countries with little or no experience of self-government or representative institutions. Yet the experience of self-government offered by American federalism, together with the civic education it gave to newcomers (at least in principle), proved capable of creating in the new settlers something like the free *moeurs* of the original English settlers. Thus, despite new pressures introduced by immigration, urbanization and industrialization, American federalism seemed to have established that self-government on a continental scale was possible, and that the old axiom, which assumed that extended territories could only be governed tyrannically, was now outmoded. New Europe across the Atlantic seemed to offer that political lesson to Old Europe.

Yet it is important to notice that this successful assimilation had involved the new settlers adopting English as their first language. The American experience might reasonably be understood as establishing that a shared language is a prerequisite for a workable federal system, providing an indispensable civic bond. The extent to which Americans deem this to be the case has emerged in recent resistance to multiculturalism whenever it seems to threaten the established role of English. Could the United States long survive without a shared language? Many students of American government doubt it. For that reason the example of American federalism raises a serious doubt about the prospects of European federalism. The experiences of federal states which have attempted to combine different 'official' languages are far from reassuring. Canada and Belgium spring especially to mind. In each of those countries, the question of whether political union can survive linguistic and ethnic differences is now moot. Nor is the example of Switzerland really a convincing counter-example. For the success of Switzerland as a federal state has probably depended more upon the unity engendered in a small nation by powerful and dangerous neighbours than upon anything else.

In the United States, a major contribution to the process of assimilating immigrants to both constitutional and linguistic norms was made by lawyers, who, Tocqueville noticed, came early to dominate the political class. A legal education was relatively easy to come by and provided the means not just of economic advancement but also of cultural adjustment – adjustment, in particular, to a Common Law and jury system which defended the importance of local custom. That led many immigrants into the mind-set of a form of the state utterly different from the ones they had known in continental Europe. Continental states had often been created from the 'top' downwards, with rulers relying on a Roman Law tradition which regarded regional and local units of government as mere appendages of central government. The Roman Law tradition did not, that is, give the habit of local self-government a primordial value. In part that was due to the greater difficulty of state-making on the continent, where recalcitrant regions and cities were often subdued finally only by force or ruse. Even today the inhabitants of some areas of Italy, France and Spain look upon the inhabitants of other areas as 'foreigners' to an extent that makes the Scots' suspicion of the English seem rather pallid. But such an inheritance makes the formation of a political class on the American model – with local liberty successfully joined to social and geographical mobility – far more difficult to achieve.

The fourth informal prerequisite for the success of American federalism identified and explored by Tocqueville was shared moral beliefs. Tocqueville noticed that in the United States there was a remarkable consensus about what justice required, which derived from an interpretation of Christianity almost universal among the settlers of America, an understanding of Christianity as authorizing 'equal liberty'. That is to say, Christianity in America was given a liberal interpretation. Civil equality and political liberty, and the range of choices they permitted, were understood not as the enemies of religion, but rather as sanctioned by Christian moral beliefs. This was perhaps a controversial interpretation of Christianity. It certainly could be described as a Protestant interpretation, placing emphasis on conscience and voluntary assent rather than authority and obedience. But its importance in the United States remains fundamental. For the United States still offers the example of a nation in which avowed Christians remain in the majority, accepting strict limits on the public role of religion in the name of a liberty sanctioned by that religion itself. By sanctioning a private sphere of choice, moral consensus in America set clear limits on the sphere of legitimate state action, limits which were formally written into the United States Constitution as a Bill of Rights. Nor was that all. The consensus over moral equality and equal liberty also made a crucial contribution to the success of American federalism because it worked against the kind of class-consciousness which had intensified social conflicts in Europe, creating powerful centralizing mechanisms within each state. That, in Tocqueville's view, had been the sad story of France from the fifteenth to the nineteenth century. The bureaucratic form of the French state was its offspring.

How do these considerations of moral belief apply to the project of a federal state in Europe today? If the moral pre-condition of self-government in an extended territory is interpreted negatively – that is, as the absence of social conflicts rooted in class-consciousness – then there can be little doubt that Western Europe has made enormous strides since 1945. The withering of earlier class identities resulting from prosperity, wider educational opportunities and social mobility has helped to create a social scene which more closely resembles that of the United States. The recent marked decline in the appeal of socialism in Europe reflects these changes. For socialist ideology derived much of its appeal from class-consciousness, from an 'us' against 'them' attitude which socialism sought to reinforce.

But this pre-condition for federalism can also be interpreted in a stronger sense, as requiring the existence of a moral consensus. And the question of whether such a consensus exists in Europe today is more difficult to answer. It turns on one issue especially. What is the moral residue of Christianity in Europe? Have some values survived the apparent collapse of Christian belief and the decline in church-going? Indeed, what is the relationship, historically and logically, between Christianity and liberalism? These are momentous questions which I shall explore more carefully later. For the moment I will simply say that the answers depend upon how the tenacious European belief in human equality, and the requirements for justice which follow from that belief, are interpreted.

The difficulty of interpreting moral egalitarianism and the resulting sense of justice as Christian-inspired is that in some European countries anti-clericalism continues to play so important a role – associating the Church not with 'equal liberty' but with intellectual oppression. Here the contrast between Europe and America remains extreme. Whereas in Europe the Church, especially the Catholic Church, was caught up in the struggle between social privilege and protest – becoming identified as an instrument of social control 'used' by the upper classes and thereby losing some of its moral sway – in the United States the Church has in the past made a crucial contribution to moral consensus. There, what was understood as Christian morality provided a theory of justice which has permeated American society, helping to prevent the development of a class-conscious politics, with its centralizing potential. That is why the socialist movement in the United States failed to become important.

Has the Christian Church in Europe ceased to be divisive and become instead a unifying force on the American model? It is doubtful. Certainly, there remain important differences between the Catholic and Protestant versions of Christianity. One way of looking at the changes associated with the Second Vatican Council (1962–5) is to see them as representing an important effort by the Catholic Church to shed its earlier divisive social role in Europe and claim liberalism – in the form of representative government and the defence of human rights – as a Christian inheritance. If so, it was an attempt to accept responsibility for 'modernity', to endorse a narrative about European development which no longer interpreted 'progress' or the cause of human rights as a decisive break with the Christian past. But of course the papacy of John Paul II has in some ways called any such enterprise into question, apparently again casting doubt on any narrative which seeks to establish a deep, intrinsic connection between Christianity and modernity. To that extent, it is far from clear that contemporary Europe can match the degree of moral consensus that Tocqueville identified as sustaining American federalism.

In reviewing these informal, cultural pre-conditions underlying the success of American federalism, we have found some important convergences between America and Europe. But we have also found important differences, especially with regard to sovereignty and national identity, the habit of self-government, a shared language and moral consensus. Perhaps we should simplify the test. What is it that these informal conditions contributed to in America? What sort of political culture did they help to shape?

What the American experience establishes, I suggest, is that the success of representative government on a continental scale will depend upon creating and sustaining a culture of consent. That is a culture marked by a willing suspension of disbelief – a culture in which cynicism about the law-making process is kept in abeyance by a kind of confidence in the law which springs from a conviction that the law can be changed if it does not adequately represent popular will. In the longer run, the practice of self-government, when it is not a mere sham at the centre of society but obtains at all levels, generates such a confidence in the law. Its polar opposite is a cynical view of the law as the self-interested plaything of élites.

Such confidence in the law has a remarkable effect on national identity and on the character of patriotism in any nation. Perhaps the most telling historical example of that is the case of England, and of what might be called the strange feebleness of English nationalism. For the English pattern is by no means accidental. It is a result of the fact that England has been a self-governing nation longer than any other. Representative government has had a continuous history of more than 700 years. The tradition of parliamentary government and local liberty has created a diluted form of nationalism in England, a nationalism diluted by idealism about the 'proper' form of government. In the nineteenth century that emerged even in the English attitude towards Empire, where – apart from religious convictions – the belief in a civilizing mission was framed in terms of preparation for self-government. And the early creation of dominions such as Canada and Australia showed that this was not entirely a pretence.

Such a 'diluted' form of nationalism also sprang from the political system created by the English settlers of North America. For it can be argued that American federalism is in some respects simply the eighteenth-century Whig constitution which England never quite got around to giving itself – formalizing a decentralized state, with the addition of a division of sovereignty between the states and the federal government, as well as entrenched rights and judicial review. Certainly the political culture which shaped the thought of Madison and Hamilton was essentially English – though it was an England understood partly through the eyes of the Frenchman, Montesquieu, and thus incorporating fears of centralized power of a kind more typical of France than of England.

The diluted or idealistic patriotism engendered by American federalism meant that 'democracy' – at least as understood on the model of the American political system – became inextricable from national identity and national pride. That is what made the spread of American power and influence in the world in the twentieth century so ambiguous. What to hostile observers looks almost like the growth of an American empire, looks in American eyes simply like the spread of democracy – that is, of the institutions of self-government and a free market, founded on respect for human rights.

But it is not only the English and American political systems which created this idealistic and ambiguous form of nationalism. It was also, for a time, true of France. In the years after the 1789 Revolution, the spread of French armies outside France and the overturning of governments in Italy, Holland and elsewhere did not at first arouse widespread popular opposition in surrounding European nations. The reason is clear. French expansion in the 1790s was widely seen as the expansion of an idea – the spread of a vision of a society founded on civil equality and crowned by representative government. It was therefore welcomed as a kind of liberation. Only when French republican government gave way first to military dictatorship and then to empire, did French expansion begin to arouse the patriotic hostility of Germans and Spaniards, who now saw the invaders as motivated by mere greed or dynastic ambition rather than by the idea of civil and political liberty. Beethoven's famous volte-face over Napoleon, while composing the 'Eroica' symphony, symbolizes the disenchantment of a whole generation of continental Europeans.

Why did France so readily abandon self-government, falling prey to a military dictatorship? Indeed, why did many continental nations find it difficult to establish representative government in the nineteenth and the early twentieth century? Here we again come upon a moral factor, the destructive role of the class-consciousness which survives in societies once founded on privilege. In its morally defensible form, nationalism should be seen as the form of democratic honour, the honour appropriate to a society founded on the principle of civil equality. Yet there is also a pathological form of democratic honour, a more extreme nationalism which sacrifices the universalizing aspects of democratic principle to tribalism and envy. That extreme nationalism is far more likely to develop in a society ravaged by class-consciousness and unused to self-government.

The absence of class-consciousness surviving from an *ancien régime* made it far easier to establish self-government in America. For social equality shaped American attitudes from the outset. In Europe, however, one of the things that social levelling often involves is that formerly inferior classes develop – instead of the fear and deference which once shaped their relations with local members of a superior class – a peculiarly bitter jealousy and cynicism about the claims of their former 'betters'. A kind of disenchantment seizes them. They are deeply unwilling to consider their former hereditary leaders as candidates for membership of a new open and democratically chosen class of leaders. Recollection of a social subordination, which they now deem to have been a form of oppression, leads them into an attitude which poses serious problems for creating a new political class with strong local roots and ready to defend local autonomy – the kind so familiar from the United States.

What is that attitude? People would rather be oppressed by strangers than by people they know. The recollection of social inferiority works against the habit of association and paves the way for government by strangers, by servants of a remote central power. Thus, in European societies which have an aristocratic past, there is available long after the abolition of social privilege a mechanism which can play into the hands of a centralizing power. Nor is that all. The mechanism which within a locality can throw power away from locals into the hands of strangers also operates between localities and between regions. For the rivalry between two villages may make government by someone who comes from neither village more acceptable than government by those who come from either village or both. And between regions similar rivalries can easily lead to similar results. Government from London may seem less threatening to the people of Lancashire than government from York.

Such mechanisms have played an important role in the formation of most European states. I do not for a moment want to suggest that there was not enormous gain to be had through the process of centralization. The rule of law, the definition and protection of basic human rights, regularity and efficiency of administration, limits on local eccentricities and parochial opinion – all of these benefits attended the creation of European states from the fifteenth to the nineteenth century. But the price paid for these benefits was a high one. For the process of state formation was, especially on the continent, essentially a despotic one. It involved the creation of instruments for government from above – government by lawyers, bureaucrats and 'experts' – at the expense of local and regional means of deliberation and action. France epitomized this process. Germany and Italy remained to some extent exceptions until the nineteenth century, when they too passed through the process of centralization to become nation-states.

Today, the largest issue raised by the project of European political integration is in a sense simple. The issue is whether European unification must, like the usual process of state formation on the continent, pass through a more or less despotic phase – that is, a phase in which, whatever the gestures towards representation and accountability, European rules and decision-making will be made by a central bureaucracy with political control provided, if it is provided at all, by one or two of the most powerful member states. Probably some will shrug their shoulders and accept that such a despotic phase, though deplorable from a moral standpoint, is a necessary phase in the creation of a larger political entity in Europe – an entity which they suppose will bring benefits analogous to those brought in the early modern period by the nation-state itself.

Others – among whom I count myself – believe that civil society in Europe has now developed to the point where further European integration need not involve the despotic phase analogous to those of earlier nation-state formation. In their eyes, the struggle against social privilege or aristocracy has now receded sufficiently into the past to weaken if not remove the social mechanisms which previously underpinned a tyrannical form of the state.

This assessment imposes an obligation on us. It taxes our liberty by laying on us the burden of seeing that power remains dispersed within the European Union and that Europe does not create a new Leviathan. Yet even those who are determined that this should be so must not lose sight of the profound obstacles on their path.

One obstacle follows from the legacy of class conflict in Europe, a legacy which even the apparent triumph of market ideology should not lead one to dismiss out of hand. The renewed emphasis on 'laws' of the marketplace in neo-liberal thinking does not prevent and indeed may be contributing to the emergence of a new underclass in advanced capitalist societies. Will that underclass gradually become conscious of itself as a class? If so, there is little reason to suppose that such an underclass will not be vulnerable to the kind of appeals which in previous centuries led both the bourgeois and the working classes, feeling themselves oppressed, to centralize power in order to combat what they perceived as privilege. The way such mechanisms survived into the twentieth century can be illustrated only too easily from the history of Eastern Europe. For, after 1945, the Communist Parties of Eastern Europe were able to impose a despotic control of the state, not just with the help of Russian power, but by means of a demonology which threatened ordinary people by insisting that the only alternative to communist rule was the return to power of their previous 'bourgeois' oppressors. Thus, residual hatred of social privilege acted as the means by which people became their own oppressors. That is the sad story of post-war Eastern Europe.

Clearly, the development of a new self-conscious underclass as well as the legacy of oppression in Eastern Europe (part of which, it should be remembered, is now incorporated in the most powerful European state, Germany) could still seriously jeopardize the optimistic scenario for dispersing power, while continuing the process of European integration.

But the residue of class-consciousness in Europe also makes far more dangerous two other circumstances which foster the centralizing of power in every modern society – economic crisis and war. Thus, even the United States witnessed an enormous expansion in the power of the federal government as a result of the Great Depression of the 1930s and the Second World War. No political system can be made invulnerable to such powerful crises. None the less, an important difference remains between the United States and Europe. Once the immediate crisis had begun to pass away, the habits of American federalism reasserted themselves. A battle of attrition against central-ized power resumed in the later 1940s, bringing together good and bad motives under the slogan of 'states rights'. By contrast, in Europe, the pressure to decentralize power was much weaker. For example, in many respects the British state retained its war-time form well into the post-war period. A kind of instinctive association of social reform with centralization was widespread.

The American Founding Fathers themselves underestimated the importance of that association. One of the principal objects of Madison's 'compound' republic was to reduce the threat of power becoming concentrated at the centre through the operation of the majority principle, to forestall anything like the tyranny of a majority – especially of the poor over the rich. That was why Madison sought not only to divide sovereignty between the states and the federal government but to reinforce Montesquieu's separation of powers with checks and balances as well as judicial review. The multiplication of jurisdictions promised to make it far more difficult to muster a coherent national majority over any issue.

Yet Madison underestimated the centralizing potential of minorities acting to defend their interests or assert their rights. Probably no eighteenth-century thinker could have anticipated the extent to which the achievement of civil equality and representative government did not satisfy all claims in justice but instead raised the expectations of previously disadvantaged groups – leading to demands for government intervention on behalf of women, blacks, the physically disabled and homosexuals, among others. These claims are made on the basis of a theory of justice formulated in terms of basic human equality and therefore requiring something like equal opportunity.

Here a sad truth emerges. Perceived injustices can easily become motors of centralization. For it is usually the most remote and general agency of government that is appealed to – on the grounds that it is best placed to overcome local or regional prejudice, defining higher standards of conduct or provision, and enforcing them in a uniform way across the political system. But of course that move carries with it a tremendous centralizing potential. It put the constitutional safeguards of the United States under enormous strains in the twentieth century, tilting the balance of power away from the states and towards the federal government. Thus, the multiplication of jurisdictions in a 'compound' republic has in a sense been matched by the multiplication of minority causes with a centralizing potential. But that is not all. Uniformity can easily become a kind of God, worshipped in its own right and quite apart from its role in sustaining claims founded in justice.

We then find ourselves back facing Montesquieu's risk – the risk that a central agency can draw all power to itself by playing off one region against another, one group or culture against another. In the absence of a common language, a widely shared political culture and a coherent political class – all of which could be taken for granted by the delegates to Philadelphia in 1787, and which underpinned the American federalist experiment – the danger of European federalism subsiding into a bureaucratic form of the state should never be underestimated. Whether such a tyranny could long survive, or would itself break up in a contentious and perhaps even violent way, is another matter. But even if the latter were the case, such an outcome would not obviously contribute to democratic liberty in Europe.

In fact, there is an even deeper and more perennial threat to the dispersal of power in Europe. That is one facet of human nature. In a society where everyone is formally equal, there is a powerful urge to resist the claims to leadership of anyone who is local and familiar. There is a strong temptation to think it less humiliating to choose for leadership someone unknown over someone known. For surely such a person must be free of weaknesses, faults of character or intellect, which can be seen in those whom we know. That inclination or temptation to prefer strangers, to prefer someone unknown to someone known as a candidate for leadership, caters to a deep weakness in our nature. Yet it is both politically and morally dangerous to give in to this weakness in ourselves. It is dangerous politically because such an inclination is ultimately subversive of the dispersal of power. It is dangerous morally because it disguises, while at the same time reinforcing, a distrust of ourselves. It is as if in order to feel contempt for ourselves we have to become contemptible.

A decentralized Europe is important, then, not just on political or constitutional grounds. The dispersal of power is fundamental to the development of human character. For that dispersal breeds emulation, self-reliance and humility. These qualities are infinitely preferable to the fear, sycophancy and resentment bred by the centralization of power. After all, we do not merely want to make a Europe safe for bureaucrats.

There is a sense in which the dispersal of power, through local autonomy and maximizing opportunities for political participation, forces the issue of character. By giving individuals not only basic civil rights, but the experience of exercising political rights – the experience of addressing issues of public policy and bringing knowledge and judgement to those issues – a policy which disperses power helps to change the nature of the relationship between the state and civil society. Instead of being merely the passive bearer or recipient of rights or civil liberties, the citizen becomes an active agent – one who seeks to identify the public welfare for him or herself, learning to strike a balance between advantage and disadvantage when considering public policy proposals. The active citizen is thus led insensibly to combine theory with practice, ideals with facts, and in doing so his or her judgement is refined and knowledge extended, and the moral expansion of the agent through citizenship derives from a constant confrontation with the needs or wants of others.

Clearly, this process does not merely yield knowledge. The citizen's judgement is refined through the need to estimate the character of others and, in particular, the claim of those who seek to lead. Active citizenship is not only anti-utopian in its effect therefore, obliging the mind to consider the duties which correspond to rights, the 'hard' cases which limit or qualify the application of rules. It also constantly draws attention to the role of character in political life, and works against the assumption that 'strangers' are to be preferred – that public policy is the domain of others, more or less expert.

The willing suspension of disbelief which I have already described as a prerequisite for a political culture of consent – a belief that the law can be our own parent and child, insofar as its norms both shape our intentions and lead us to identify defects in the law which can be remedied – is in fact the most important constituent of a sense of community. It makes possible an almost familial relationship with the law, a relationship which stands in contrast with the view of law as a remote and alien thing, something imposed by 'others' at one's own expense, something to be foiled or circumvented whenever possible.

For that is the irony of *étatist* political cultures, political cultures shaped by a bureaucratic form of the state. On the one hand, such cultures foster a view of law and public policy as the domain of experts, of 'strangers' who, almost by definition, have an advantage over locals. To that extent, locals are expected to be submissive and passive, mere spectators of the political process. On the other hand, by neglecting the active dimension of citizenship, *étatist* political cultures store up trouble for the future. For the passivity and patience of any population are not unlimited, and so such political cultures are tempered by violence – by outbursts against the state which is seen merely as an external agency, a physical and coercive force. Such sporadic violence can easily become a kind of revolutionary tradition, which, at intervals more or less frequent, interrupts orderly constitutional life.

In fact, both sorts of political culture have in the past adhered to different forms of the state in Europe. They have fostered very different types of political ethos and psychology. But if that is so, then the question which confronts us today is what kind of political culture and political psyche is likely to develop as European integration proceeds. And, beyond the question of fact is that of desirability. What do we really want out of Europe in these respects?

When we ask such questions, it quickly becomes clear that uncertainty about the future shape of Europe, about what shape for it is truly desirable, coincides with a deep-seated uncertainty in liberal political thinking at the moment. Indeed, what might be called the crisis of European integration – the issue of democracy in Europe – is at the same time a crisis of liberal political thinking.

It is to that crisis that I shall now turn.

2

Where are our Madisons?

Our object should be to create a culture of consent in Europe. But if such a culture is difficult to achieve in a nation-state, how much more difficult it must be in a federal state on a continental scale! Two dangers immediately spring to mind. The first is that conflicts between and perhaps within nations will act as springboards to the transfer of power to the centre in Europe. The second is that the losers in such competitions will take refuge in atavistic national or regional pride, looking upon a European state as a remote foreign oppressor.

Only a culture of consent in Europe can begin to keep such dangers at bay. Yet the obstacles to creating such a culture are formidable. When the question of creating a federal state in Europe is posed in this way – that is, how to foster a particular kind of political culture – it draws attention to several crucial issues. Why should we seek to supplant existing nation-states with a federal state and on what terms, if any, can national political cultures in Europe be successfully fused? To what extent can a constitution contribute to that fusion? And what form of constitution is most likely to strengthen liberal democracy in Europe?

The rule of law, the protection of basic human rights and represent-ative institutions are, of course, well-established liberal democratic goals. These have been, broadly, the achievements of the existing nation-states of Europe. Yet already, in arguments put forward by Montesquieu and Tocqueville, we have encountered two other values which are central to liberal democracy – the dispersal of power as well as the building of human character and self-reliance. Both of these values can be promoted by a form of the state which opens the way to active citizenship by guaranteeing local and regional autonomy.

Would a European federal state do more to promote these values than existing nation-states? There is one reason why it might. Federalism provides a formal sanction for local and regional autonomy, thereby inhibiting the development of an over-centralized or bureaucratic form of the state. Federalism, properly understood, works against uniformity becoming a fetish.

By creating different spheres of public authority, and withdrawing from central government the power to alter those spheres unilaterally, federalism promotes still another value closely related to the dispersal of power and the building of human character. That value is diversity. For it is especially important that a political system serving an extended territory should seek to foster diversity. It is important because such a political system must, on the one hand, remain sensitive to a wide range of geographical, climatic and social differences and, on the other hand, encourage innovation and experiment within the broad limits established by justice.

It has often been observed that, in the ancient world, competition and emulation between city-states made an important contribution to the rapidity of Greek cultural development. But, in modern Europe, competition and emulation between nation-states, both large and small, has been just as important and creative. Now at first glance a federal state in Europe would seem to offer the advantage of formalizing a relationship between the nations and regions of Europe in a way that secures the advantages of competition and emulation, *without* the disadvantages which marked the world of the Greek city-states and the world of early modern Europe – namely, incessant war and instability. Unfortunately, those advocating a federal Europe recently have often seemed to be more concerned with promoting uniformity than with fostering diversity.

Nor is that all. Today, many European federalists seem to have lost sight of the central traditional argument for federalism – namely, that federalism is a political system which makes it possible to combine the advantages of small states and of large states, without at least some of the disadvantages attaching to each. Tocqueville was especially clear about that. He saw that small states tend to be inward-looking, well-ordered and resistant to tyranny. For the range of interests in small states is limited, ambitions are more restrained, and the attention of people is turned towards material prosperity rather than glory or conquest. Corresponding to these advantages, however, are the disadvantages of a small state, especially narrowness of mind, parochialism and vulnerability to aggression. By contrast, the advantages of a large state are that it broadens minds and excites ambitions through an extended range of interests and the multiplication of ideas. But the drawback is also plain. 'The ambition of private persons grows with the power of the state; the strength of parties with the importance of the goals they adopt; but the love of country which must struggle against these destructive passions,' Tocqueville wrote, 'is no stronger in a large republic than in a small one.'

In principle, federalism should offer a means of combining the advantages of different scales of political organization – offering small nations the security and strength of a large state, while dispersing interests and ambitions in a way that works against an excessive centralization of power and anything like majority tyranny. That is why James Madison, the most profound of the American Founding Fathers, described his federalist project as the project for a 'compound' republic.

Questions about the dispersal of power, building human character and the fostering of diversity were at the heart of the subtlest constitutional thought in eighteenth- and nineteenth-century Europe. But they are seldom addressed openly or adequately these days. Just why is that? Why has Europe failed to generate a debate which approaches, in range and depth, the debate which developed around the drafting of a Federal Constitution for the United States? Where are our Madisons?

The answers to these questions are not reassuring about the intellectual and moral condition of Europe today. At first glance they seem to reveal an extraordinary impoverishment of political language. Of course it might be argued that one reason for the mediocrity of recent European debate, in contrast to America in the late 1780s, is that Europe is not in crisis. Hence, the argument might go on, there is no sense of urgency concentrating minds in Europe. But that is a bad argument. For the truth is that there *is* a crisis in Europe. It is a delayed crisis resulting from German reunification. For it is the French response to German reunification – the determination to bind the new enlarged Germany into a far closer union – that has led the French political class suddenly to accelerate the process of European integration. They have decided that a *Europe des nations*, long the French model for European development, must now give way to a European federation. That is the import of the Maastricht and Amsterdam Treaties and their aftermath.

But what justifications for this sudden acceleration are on offer? The arguments which have marked recent public discussion about European political integration have scarcely gone beyond the following ones:

1 European unification is necessary to prevent war in Europe – that is, to prevent anything like World War Two happening again.

2 European unification is necessary to complete and sustain the Common Market and a single currency, providing the political scaffolding for the larger market which will make Europe richer.

3 European unification is necessary to control and restrict German power by giving others some part in the government of Germany.

4 European unification is necessary to enable Europe to become one of the world's major power blocs, able to hold its own with the United States and emerging Asian economic powers.

But none of these arguments – with the partial exception of the third – says anything about desirable constitutional arrangements, about the proper distribution of authority and power within a European federal state. None of them really addresses the question of democracy in Europe.

So it is easy to feel dismay about the post-Maastricht debate. For running through it is a dangerous confusion. Two issues – national sovereignty and self-government – have become hopelessly embroiled and confused. Sometimes people speak as if these issues were one and the same. Yet, in fact, they must be separated, if we are to think clearly about the pros and cons of European political integration. And it is self-government which matters most. A truly self-governing Europe must be our goal. Arguments about the location of sovereignty are secondary.

Representative democracy or self-government can exist when sovereign rights are united (as in the United Kingdom) or when they are divided (as in American federalism). But neither form of the state guarantees self-government. I suspect that the middle ground of European opinion – both those who with some reluctance feel it is best to move towards a federal state and those who unhappily conclude such a move should be opposed – is concerned primarily with the issue of self-government rather than sovereignty. Those who reluctantly support federalism fear that they may be sacrificing self-government to the development of the Community, while those who oppose federalism fear that their concern with self-government may be misunderstood as blind nationalism, as turning away from Europe on the simplistic ground of preserving national sovereignty. And both sections of middling opinion are right to fear what they fear.

The future of representative democracy in Europe, understood as requiring the dispersal of authority, checks and balances and significant local autonomy, ought now to be the issue. Until the eighteenth century, as we have seen, it was an axiom of European political thought that the larger the political unit, the more likely it was to be governed despotically. Only with the help, first of the British model of government and then of American federalism, was that axiom overturned by liberal constitutional thought. But that does not mean that the causes which had for so long led political thinkers to take a dim view of the prospects of self-government outside relatively small communities have ceased to operate. In fact the democratic political cultures of European nation-states today are fragile enough to raise serious doubts about any easy pan-European extension.

Yet in recent decades politicians have become almost cavalier about the constitutional dimension and political culture of the European Union. Take, for example, the casual way in which the population of Eastern Germany was absorbed into both a reunified Germany and the European Union. For sixty years some seventeen million people in Eastern Germany had been subject to despotic government, first of the right and then of the left. Can anyone doubt that the habits and attitudes formed under such regimes survive or that a prolonged education in representative government and constitutionalism may be needed to root out authoritarian attitudes? Recent examples of violent reaction to immigrant workers and foreign visitors suggest how strong an undercurrent of opinion bred by repressive regimes remains. The attraction of the extreme right to younger people in Eastern Germany amounts to an inversion of the previous communist order. It is the liberal centre which may not hold.

French leaders have evidently concluded that the best response is to bind the new Germany to the rest of Europe by creating a more centralized decision-making authority, which – whatever its name – resembles nothing so much as the unitary French state. Doubtless the French hope that such a structure will preserve their *de facto* domination of the Community, despite the increased size, population and economic power of Germany. It was the urgency of this French design – pursued by the Brussels Commission under the presidency of Jacques Delors, a former French civil servant – which led to the Maastricht and Amsterdam Treaties, treaties which do not address seriously enough the need for a proper constitutional settlement.

Such issues were scarcely identified, let alone addressed, by European leaders at Maastricht or Amsterdam. How were they able to avoid them? One reason looms larger than any other. In recent decades the language of economics has largely driven out the language of politics and, in particular, the language of constitutionalism in Europe. Yet the latter was the great achievement of European liberal thought in the eighteenth and nineteenth century. It was directed especially at solving one problem: how authority and power can be dispersed in a political system so that tyranny is prevented, without making efficient and just government impossible.

But that has not been a recent preoccupation in Europe. Instead, the pursuit of economic integration has resulted in a curious outcome. A European Union inspired by liberal democratic principles has increasingly acted on quasi-Marxist assumptions, assuming that when economic progress has been achieved, other institutional improvements will follow 'inevitably' or as a matter of course. But that is a vulgar form of economic determinism which has been discredited both intellectually and practically. The state, whatever its form, is not the mere scaffolding of a market economy. Adam Smith never suggested that it was. Only, perhaps, Karl Marx.

A vulgar Marxism has been noticeable in the most unexpected places and in the most unlikely people. Even that scourge of socialism, Britain's

Mrs Thatcher, fell victim to this fashionable subordination of political to economic issues. When she helped to prepare and sign the Single European Act in 1985, it is clear that she did not consider the political commitments it contained to be of any real importance compared to the practical, 'bread and butter' economic agreements designed to extend and reinforce a single market in Europe. Later, that neglect of political institutions came back to haunt her – leading her to believe that Jacques Delors and the Brussels Commission had hidden an unacceptable political agenda behind the economic provisions of the Single European Act. In her memoirs Mrs Thatcher scarcely mentions her own role in the preparation of the Act or her acquiescence in its terms. Her embarrassment is obvious.

Mrs Thatcher's neo-capitalist idiom – the idiom of 'balancing the books' and the family budget – had provided her with powerful weapons in combating what she saw as creeping collectivism in Britain. But that idiom did nothing to alert her or her audience to the profound political issues raised by what became Delors' project for Europe. When she had to face them, she fell back feebly on what was essentially a legal category, the defence of national sovereignty. But it was not a category which, in itself, could foster serious, innovative thinking about democracy in Europe.

Nothing better reflects the way that the domination of economic language has impoverished political thought than the hasty way European leaders have put forward the 'subsidiarity' principle, whenever they have to deal with popular fears about the centralizing of power and weakening of democratic accountability. For what does subsidiarity mean? Is it merely a tactical principle, so that any outcome is by definition compatible with subsidiarity, since there are no clear criteria governing the distribution of power? Or is it a truly constitutional principle? But if it is the latter, then subsidiarity implies a full-blown constitution for Europe, with some agency – presumably the European Court – being vested with the right to settle conflicts of jurisdiction and protect different spheres of authority. And if so, what should be the terms of reference for the Court? What framework would be adequate both to guide its decisions and to legitimate them?

Liberal constitutionalism in the eighteenth and nineteenth centuries sought to deepen our understanding of such questions. Its most celebrated prescriptions – federalism, the separation of powers, checks and balances, entrenched rights and judicial review – were means to that end. To suppose that a summit meeting of European leaders or a quick tour around European capitals to reach a consensus on 'how subsidiarity works' is enough, represents an intellectual regression which could have dreadful practical consequences in the longer run. Curiously, and perhaps ominously, the legal tradition from which the principle of subsidiarity was suddenly plucked is that of Catholic Canon Law. Yet it is far from clear that the principle has been effective in preventing the centralizing of authority in the Roman Church. If the papacy of John Paul II is anything to judge by, rather the contrary is the case.

Subsidiarity provides merely one example of the denaturing of political language in our time. Many other examples such as 'Europe plc', 'economic sovereignty', 'Super-state' and 'rationalization' could be cited. If the language in which the European Union identifies and creates itself becomes overwhelmingly economic, then the prospects for self-government in Europe are grim indeed. Are we creating Europe merely in order to have a larger supermarket?

It is as if the problem of governing Europe has been superseded or passed into other hands. And perhaps that *is* our perception of the way things are. If so, in an uncanny way it resembles the vision of Europe's future projected in the nineteenth century by an eccentric French aristocrat, Henri de Saint-Simon. Saint-Simon predicted that governance as known in recent centuries would give way to the administration of society by bankers, industrialists and scientists. 'The government of people will be replaced by the administration of things,' he argued. Saint-Simon strongly approved of this development, arguing that it amounted to the substitution of positive knowledge and skill for the self-serving rhetoric of the traditional politician. It amounted to replacing prejudice and ignorance by rationality.

But was he correct? Today there is little doubt that the political classes in many Western European nations are viewed with cynicism, if not contempt. Interest rates, fiscal policy, investment levels – a whole range of questions crucial for economic growth are now widely perceived as being understood and controlled by figures who are not politicians, people whose understanding of economics makes it possible and perhaps necessary for them to manipulate the political system and politicians in the name of ever greater productivity. For economic growth has become a kind of god, the god whose commands override other considerations. Nor is the goal of making the largest number of people richer an ignoble one, though 'richer' and 'better off' are too often used as if they were synonymous. The language of economics and the utilitarian philosophy which underpins it have displaced an older political language in which questions about controlling public power, ensuring accountability and political participation were central. And, by and large, the political classes of Europe have connived in this development. It is as if they acknowledged, privately, that public policy is now a matter for experts rather than the people and their representatives.

It is, of course, true that the democratizing of European society and the substitution of economic growth for earlier goals such as dynastic or national glory are closely related. The growth of a global market since World War Two, with the astonishing increase in prosperity it led to, has also contributed to the subverting of the traditional language of politics by that of economics. These days international meetings of bankers and economists often do seem more important than the gatherings of elected political leaders. Who is the statesman now?

Let us call these developments 'economism'. Economism has deep roots in the European project. It can be traced back at least to the idiom of Jean Monnet and others who helped to create the European Coal and Steel Community shortly after World War II. Faced with the urgent need to reconstruct a West European economy devastated by war and threatened by Soviet power in the East, such figures, though in fact often convinced European federalists, did not and could not make federalism central to their agenda. Instead, a kind of Saint-Simonian modernization of Europe became their appeal. They left political institutions and democratic accountability largely to one side. At the time, the semi-pariah status of the post-war West German state made closer political union almost unthinkable.

Yet we are now paying a high price for that subordination of constitutional concerns and neglect of issues touching political culture. For economism has made it easier to avoid the most difficult questions. How and at what pace can different national political cultures be fused, while fostering a pan-European culture of consent? The truth remains that, to the extent that they exist at all, democratic political cultures in Europe today are closely tied to and dependent upon nation-states. The real danger, seldom discussed, is that a sudden movement towards European political integration might simply mean further weakening of democratic constraints on market forces.

A generation that has witnessed the development of a global market is especially likely to succumb to the fallacy of scale. Having been bombarded with arguments about economies of scale, we are prone to believe that a larger political organization, regardless of differences in national political culture, must be the appropriate response to increasing economic interdependence. Thus, it is often assumed that an increased scale of political organization will automatically lead to more effective democratic control of capitalism, especially in the form of multi-national companies. Indeed, the regulation of such companies is often cited as a primary justification for a European state. But this is dubious. The first result of creating a federal state in Europe could be an even greater democratic deficit. For the new political authority created might be chiefly concerned to establish its own legitimacy, unwilling or unable to embark upon controversial reforms.

So are we simply making Europe safe for bankers, consultants and managers? Has the West seen off the communist challenge only to fall victim to an unelected élite, in its own way as arrogant and exploitative as the communist élite, though relying on a different rhetoric and managing in a different style? Somewhat exaggerated in form, these are none the less important and urgent questions.

There is another way of looking at these developments. Economism and the triumph of economic language over political discourse in the public sphere have involved the substitution of one role for another, the role of consumer for that of citizen. Now, ostensibly, no particular conception of the conditions of human flourishing has governed the project of European political unification. But that is only superficially true. For the absence of a searching debate about European integration – a debate which would bring to the surface underlying assumptions about human well-being – is itself symptomatic of a crisis in European beliefs. For it is hardly too much to say that there is today a crisis of identity afflicting European liberalism. Liberalism, the dominant ideology of our time, has been dangerously distorted by the impact of economism. It is that impact which has knocked the citizen off his pedestal and replaced him with the consumer.

Thus, while no conception of human well-being overtly presides over proposals for European political integration, that does not mean that no such conception is to be found. The actor is there, but he is offstage. Alas, when the conception of human well-being implied by so much discourse about European unification is brought onstage, it appears crudely one-sided. For it presents humans as passive rather than active. It presents them as having wants or preferences. It also presents them as benefiting from rights, especially civil rights and welfare entitlements. But about political rights, and the active sense of duty which the exercise of political rights can foster, little or nothing is said. Thus, the prevailing conception of well-being does not hold out a framework which can, at the individual level, suggest a means of integrating rights (with the duties they imply) and wants. It does not, that is, understand the potential of a liberal constitutional framework for changing wants and forming intentions.

These failings are by no means accidental. They provide, in fact, the clearest evidence of the nature of the current crisis in Western political thinking. Economism has created a kind of liberal schizophrenia. A split personality has emerged within the ideology which has reigned virtually unchallenged since the death of communism.

Two versions of liberalism have come into competition. Each invites the individual to imagine himself into a different situation – the first offering the hedonistic delights of a supermarket, the second offering the grave reassurances of a law court. These competing versions of liberalism invite us to choose, in effect, between seeing ourselves as consumers or as litigants. Yet something is missing. Should we not also see ourselves as citizens? Neither of these versions of liberalism conjures up the vision of a public assembly in which citizens argue about the common good and help to make law. Neither pays enough attention to the *form* of the state.

There is something profoundly unsatisfactory about the choices on offer. In the modern world we can, typically, act in three ways: first, we can pursue our own interests within the marketplace, by working and perhaps drawing interest on capital; second, we can claim our legal protections and entitlements from the state; and, third, we can help to decide what rules are to govern the marketplace and the state. Unfortunately, the most recent versions of liberalism focus on the first and second types of action at the expense of the third. And this has very damaging consequences for the way liberal democracy is now perceived – that is, for the way we perceive ourselves.

So let us look more closely at these recent competing versions of liberalism. The first is a version decisively shaped by the marketplace and by market relations of exchange. Its focus is on existing human wants and their satisfaction, which is why I have described this version as a 'supermarket'. Utilitarianism, which is its philosophical form, calls upon us to maximize the satisfaction of individual wants. Utilitarianism does not seek, at least in the standard form which shaped economics, to criticize or reshape those wants. From a political angle, this can be seen as a populist form of liberalism in so far as it puts forward a form of the majority principle as the criterion of public policy. The resolutely democratic aspects of this version of liberalism are its assumption that everyone is the best judge of his or her own preferences, and its understanding of the market as an instrument which both co-ordinates wants and disperses power widely. The market is thus portrayed as democratic in a way that a command economy can never be democratic.

In contrast to utilitarian liberalism stands another form of liberalism which relies on the language of law, insisting that basic or fundamental human rights ought to constrain the operation of the majority principle and calculations of utility. In its concern with justice and the equal distribution of basic rights, this form of liberalism – which I have dubbed the 'law court' – tends to look upon utilitarianism as a liberal 'heresy'. That is because, while utilitarianism takes individual wants as the basis of its calculations, it does not really protect the autonomy of the individual by insisting – in the fashion, say, of the United States Supreme Court – that basic rights should serve as a criterion for law. Instead, utilitarianism regards law as the criterion of rights and wants or preferences as the criterion of law.

In the eighteenth and the nineteenth century, when liberal constitutionalism flourished, no such radical conflict between the marketplace and the law court, the principle of utility and the defence of basic human rights, was envisaged. And that, I think, provides us with a clue about how the current crisis in liberal thought can be superseded. It may also provide a clue about how the current crisis came about. For the factors which have contributed to the impoverishment of constitutional thought in our time are the same factors which have contributed to the onset of liberal schizophrenia.

The professionalizing of intellectual life in this century has taken a heavy toll of liberalism. At first glance the separation of philosophy, economics and political science into distinct 'subjects' has brought to them far greater precision and sophistication, and nowhere more so than in the development of economic theory. But it has forced liberalism into a mould utterly different from the one in which it emerged, a mould which combined questions of moral philosophy, history and economics with legal issues. It was that combination which originally made liberalism so exciting. Liberalism at the outset was a vision of the conditions of human flourishing – of the way in which guaranteeing a set of basic human rights fostered not only prosperity but moral autonomy and responsibility, providing social conditions for the self-government needed to complete a virtuous circle of self-respect.

We have strayed far from such worries about the conditions of self-respect. The professionalizing of intellectual life has fostered a widespread fear about straying outside one's subject, outside the discourse of any profession. But, that, in turn, has meant that constitutional thought has become more technical and descriptive, less morally combative. Those concerned with the nature and operation of political systems – 'political scientists' as they are now called – have by and large ceased to operate with any conception of human well-being or flourishing. They shun passion. That is most obvious in the case of psephology, the study of electoral behaviour. The sources and goals of political activity are neglected in favour of analysing observable trends. It is a bit like studying the sexual act without any reference to love or desire!

This withering of the ambition of political thought has paved the way for the domination of economic language in discussions of public policy. As we have seen, an economic idiom has become the habitual idiom not just of economists and civil servants but of politicians and commentators. Sometimes it seems as if economic growth is the *only* criterion of public policy. One reason for this is plain enough. Economic growth is less contentious than other object goals of public policy, even though ecological concerns are mounting and the Green lobby is becoming more important in most countries. As long as the cake is getting larger, conflicts over its distribution are eased. In that sense issues of social justice can be postponed. Satisfying wants – and few do not wish to be richer – and maximizing satisfactions seems a straightforward goal when compared with the almost metaphysical problems raised by pursuing social justice as a goal. For the latter may require changing wants rather than merely satisfying those that exist.

So it is little wonder that politicians have come to rely upon economists for advice to an enormous extent. Economists have become the witch-doctors of the modern world – performing rites and intoning formulas which make it possible, at least in the short run, to keep the demons of social injustice at bay. Economists have been encouraged to take on this role because they are perceived as drawing upon a body of highly sophisticated and reliable economic theory.

Yet the refinement of economic theory has carried with it, if only tacitly, an important philosophical commitment. For, as we have seen, the history of the development of economic theory has been in part the history of the elaboration of utilitarianism. That is why some philosophers have recently mounted such a fierce rearguard action, championing rights as constraints or 'trumps' on public policy. But just as utilitarianism fails finally to provide an adequate place for justice, so these recent rights-based theories of justice fail to find an adequate place for social facts. They suffer from timelessness and a lack of context, through an excessive reliance on legal language.

So we are confronted by competing theories in which justice is detached from social reality (the law court) or social reality is freed from an adequate theory of justice (the supermarket). We are, as I have said, almost obliged to choose between seeing ourselves as consumers or litigants.

Now, at a formal level, I do not think that theories founded either on wants or on rights can ever be fully reconciled or merged. In that sense the search for a unified theory will probably fail. And there is a reason for this. The differences between any theory which takes human wants as given, as so to speak irreducible, and a theory seeking to change or shape wants spring from moral and epistemological differences so profound that a single framework of argument cannot contain them.

But that is where constitutional forms enter. For it is the point of such forms that they offer a practical means – through creating spheres for active citizenship – of negotiating the difference between a language of wants and a language of rights, of reconciling, at least up to a point, taking wants as they are and as they should be. Here I only claim that such forms can begin to negotiate the difference, if they are carefully designed to do so. For constitutional forms are able to direct action and thereby shape intentions.

Constitutional forms, and the intuitions they generate, can lead a people sometimes to deny its own immediate impulses. The attitude of the American people – usually a deeply moralizing people – to the revelations about President Clinton's sexual misconduct provides a striking recent example of this. Heavily influenced by the Constitutional definition of 'high crimes and misdemeanours', a large majority of Americans resisted the campaign to remove the President from office. A strong sense of Constitutional propriety thus prevailed over both prurience and moral disapproval. The United States Constitution kept populist instincts at bay.

By setting limits on the sphere of public power, dispersing authority and fostering participation, constitutional forms can have a decisive impact on the way we conceive of our own interests and thereby shape our conduct. This conjures up a decidedly different version of liberalism. Liberal constitutionalism presents itself as a process rather than an outcome. It is a liberalism which fastens on to the active rather than the passive side of human nature, drawing out the fact that justice is an active virtue, the virtue of a citizen. Active citizenship or participation in the process of government can be the means of changing wants and altering intentions. No exact formula about the outcome is held out. For the process – the means and climate of government – is considered to be more important than any particular policy outcome.

For liberal constitutionalism, the most important thing that can be achieved through government is a climate of consent. Yet that fact, clear enough to Montesquieu and Tocqueville, has been obscured through the development of utilitarianism and its child, economic theory. For it is important to notice something here. Even the recent use of rights to limit the impact of utilitarianism on political thinking perpetuates utilitarianism's chief characteristic, its emphasis on the outcome rather than the process of decision-making. In that way this train of thought has also unwittingly contributed to a dangerous reorientation of personal identity in the liberal West. Increasingly we have come to understand ourselves as consumers of justice rather than active citizens.

This near obsession with the end rather than the means of public decision-making has done much to discredit liberalism in our day. For at the moment when economic liberalism and a market model of society seem to have triumphed over socialism and perhaps even the welfare state, there is no doubt that the words 'liberal' and 'liberalism' have become pejoratives.

It is a paradoxical development. What is its source? I suspect that the reason why a broader or social liberalism has come in for so much criticism, while economic liberalism or *laissez-faire* has become almost sacrosanct, springs from the excessively passive view of the conditions of human well-being just described – from the fact that even in its rights-based form, liberalism has succumbed to consumerism. The consequence is that, increasingly, social liberalism has ceased to sustain our idealism.

Faced with the glaring inadequacies in our societies – with crime, promiscuity and the abuse of welfare provision – conventional wisdom now holds that social liberalism undermines human responsibility. Liberalism does this, it is suggested, by emphasizing rights at the expense of duties, inflating the currency of rights until it is almost useless. Social liberalism has thus come to be identified with permiss-iveness and greed, with a dangerous lack of self-control and a disregard for others. Yet at the formal level this account is simply absurd. For the rights privileged by liberalism necessarily lay obligations or duties on others. 'Equal liberty' is the heart of liberalism, and so respecting in others the rights one claims for oneself is absolutely central. Liberalism does not assert the priority of rights over duties.

What recent critics of liberalism seem to deplore at bottom is what they see as the excessive individualism encouraged by liberalism, an individualism which they see as being not very different from mere egotism or selfishness. Yet, curiously, as we have seen, such critics often focus on the rights-based version of liberalism rather than the market model when making their attack. Why is that? The reason should now be clear. The inflation of the language of rights in our time has resulted in almost any want being redescribed and asserted as a 'right' – leading in the United States, for example, to a hypertrophy of judicial review, at times to the point of discrediting it. (Should having a television be considered a 'right'?) But that inflation of rights language can itself be seen as further evidence of the suborning of the language of liberalism by the language of economics.

While the claim that liberalism generates selfishness might be plausible if the object of attack were narrow economic liberalism, a *laissez-faire* outlook which legitimates the satisfaction of existing wants regardless of other values, it seems a wildly unfair criticism of a broader social liberalism. For it is precisely the definition of a range of basic human rights, as well as the opportunities in society which such rights presuppose, that can make liberalism the source of an important critique of unadulterated market relations. If, for example, something like reasonable equality of opportunity is entailed by the belief in 'equal liberty', then liberalism can justify a great deal of intervention in the marketplace in the name of social justice. A reformed or 'social' market, which turns on the duties owed to the less advantaged by the more advantaged, then becomes one part of an over-riding liberal commitment.

But it is only one part. Something else is required. That is a liberal doctrine of citizenship, a doctrine which encourages an active sense of public duty. Such a doctrine must demonstrate the benefits of political participation – presenting those benefits in terms of dispersing power, building human character and fostering diversity. Such a doctrine must focus attention on the process of government rather than merely on the outcomes of public policy-making. In that way it can foster pride in the quality of government – understood as a process which *includes us* – and tap our idealism. It is probably the residue of such pride which underpins British doubts about the sudden acceleration of European political integration. For a nation so long used to self-government, and identifying itself so completely with parliamentary sovereignty, it is bitter, indeed almost intolerable to forgo the satisfactions afforded by self-government.

A liberal doctrine of citizenship is a far better way to combat individualism – that is, something approaching mere selfishness or egotism – than the appeal to 'community' which has been made by some critics of liberalism recently. For if any word in our social and political vocabulary is a siren-word, it is 'community'. Unless we are careful, immersing ourselves in the delights of community could become the latest and most dangerous example of an illusion against which even children are warned: thinking that you can have your cake and eat it too.

If we ask ourselves what image the word 'community' brings to mind, it is that of co-operation and harmony. It is the image of a social order in which everyone performs his or her allotted task, because all enjoy doing what is expected of them and more. It is the vision of a frictionless society. But on closer inspection this vision of a frictionless society ought to give us pause. For it suggests a relationship between individuals and the social roles they occupy which is far removed from the modern world. That is, it suggests a relationship in which people have immersed themselves completely in their social roles – *becoming* those roles, so to speak, and scarcely existing apart from them. Yet what happens when the claims of conscience come into conflict with established roles and social expectations? That is the rub.

For just what beliefs and practices are required to create a true 'community'? And what are their implications for the commitment to individual liberty, with the role for conscience it sanctions, a role which is at the heart of liberal democracy?

Communitarians often begin by insisting on the social nature of humans, arguing that humans have no pre-social identity. They argue that, as self-conscious agents, we cannot do without the norms and roles embedded in some language. But it is possible to agree that all human actions depend upon a social (that is, linguistic) context, without having to abandon liberal values. To recognize that liberal values, above all the commitment to human autonomy, have grown out of a particular social tradition, the European tradition, and draw upon the norms of that tradition, does not entail abandoning the liberal value of autonomy. To recognize the individual as in one sense a social construction may draw attention to the moral and sociological pre-conditions of such a role, and in that sense to its fragility. But that does not mean the role of the individual is any less desirable. Autonomy, even if it depends upon social arrangements, may none the less be their proper goal. If so, this argument ought chiefly to make us determined to understand the European liberal tradition, its sources and evolution, better than we do.

A second communitarian argument concerns the content of a social structure rather than its origins. People, communitarians argue, need well-defined social roles, in order to relate to each other satisfactorily and overcome the cupidity and unlimited ambition to which they will otherwise fall prey. Such roles limit and order our desires. Therefore, a healthy society or 'community' is one which provides a very tightly integrated set of such roles.

This argument rests on the twin assumptions that (a) the worst fate for humans is not to know their place in society, not to be given a clear, distinct status or role – uncertainty being the greatest obstacle to human flourishing; and that (b) the best social structure is one in which such roles are related hierarchically so that the outcome is a harmonious whole, ensured by relations of superiority and subordination. But of course the first assumption is deeply subversive of human liberty, while the second is inconsistent with the principle of civil equality which must underpin a society conforming to liberal beliefs. Historical examples of community which best satisfy the two assumptions made above are examples of societies in which status is assigned at birth, in which no fundamental equality before the law is acknowledged.

I have warned that the apostles of community are in danger of thinking they can have their cake and eat it too. We can now see why. They are in danger of wanting both the form of social order characteristic of a pre-individualist society – with permanent social roles founded on assumptions of superiority and deference – as well as the range of choice and forms of mobility which have been the great achievements of European liberalism, with its underlying belief in human equality.

We must not allow those who are pedalling pre-individualist models of society to appropriate the value of social order. That would amount to making the idea of a liberal social order a contradiction in terms. Yet the weight of historical evidence as well as introspection provide decisive objections to any such move. Liberal societies have been able to cope with change in an orderly fashion which is quite outside the reach of pre-individualist societies. We ought not to confuse the degree of publicity in liberal societies, with the constant underlining of social problems that involves, with the submerged oppressions and inarticulate sufferings characteristic of pre-individualist societies. For that would jeopardize what is arguably the chief conviction of modern Western societies: the belief that freedom is a prerequisite for moral conduct. That, it can be argued, *is* the important consensus achieved by the liberal West. And it is difficult to see why it should be excluded as a basis for social order. Of course mere conformity can and in some respects must be enforced in a liberal society. But we do not believe that moral conduct itself can be enforced. Rather, it must spring from conscience.

These assumptions about man and society have underpinned the long-standing liberal attempt to found social arrangements on consent. That attempt, however fraught with difficulty, has none the less turned Western societies into the most progressive known to history. Here we return to our starting point. Is there any reason to suppose that a sense of mutual involvement can be created only by appealing to the idea of community and not by a liberal doctrine of citizenship? I think not. But the passive form taken by both utilitarian and rights-based liberalism recently – their offering only the visions of a supermarket or a law court – have made it far more difficult for liberalism to respond to this challenge than it ought to be. By contrast, the active character of constitutionalism makes it possible for liberals to address this challenge, with the help of an ideal of citizenship which does not rely upon some of the morally dubious arguments defended in the name of community.

Probably what communitarians fear most are the consequences of the increased scale of social and political organization in the modern world. Yet, in identifying and trying to address problems raised by that new scale of organization, the communitarians have made a mistake strikingly similar to that made by eighteenth-century thinkers such as Rousseau who held up the patriotism of the ancient city-state – ancient 'virtue' – as the only remedy for modern conditions. But that was to fall victim to a dangerously anachronistic vision of social harmony, one which flew in the face of the complexity of modern economies and government. In a curious fashion, the communitarian argument plays into the hands of economism – for it too draws attention away from constitutional issues, from the form of the state and its potential for fostering both self-reliance and the habit of association.

What Europe today needs is active citizenship, not unthinking social solidarity or atavistic patriotism dressed up as community. Active citizenship rather than a dream-fulfilment called 'community' offers the best hope of remedying the weaknesses of a liberal social order, of a market economy and the nation-state. The danger of recent attacks on liberalism in the name of community is that they could open the door to a return of nationalist and ethnic excesses. Community, like nationalism, provides no clear foundation for justice, for the definition and defence of individual rights. Nor is that all. Community, like nationalism, removes from the socializing process its universalizing potential, the value of humanity. But that is what a liberal constitutional order can, at its best, provide. It not only incorporates a range of basic rights as 'human' or 'natural'. It also provides a framework of action in which the values of equality and reciprocity help to form intentions and gradually shape character. It is that long-term influence of a liberal constitutional order on character which is the key to creating a climate of consent. Constitutional forms which provide a framework for par-ticipation and engage citizens in the public decision-making process give individuals a 'local habitation and a name' more effectively than nebulous appeals to community. Moreover, the self-reliance and habit of association fostered by citizenship easily spill over into civil society. That, I suspect, is what communitarians are *really* seeking.

In a sense liberal constitutionalism provides a benign substitute for religion, a kind of civic religion which is devoid of the sinister aspects of nationalism. An obvious example is the role of civic religion in the United States, a civic and patriotic fervour which is not quite nationalism in the ordinary sense. Indeed, what might be called the constitutional religion of the United States has assumed great import-ance, in part, because a nation composed of such diverse immigrant groups and traditions needed a focus of loyalty which moved beyond their ethnic and national backgrounds.

The importance of that constitutional religion in the United States should never be underestimated. We can see that by looking at a recent example: its role in the Watergate scandal during the Nixon presidency.

What is striking is how well Nixon fared in the opinion polls *until* the Supreme Court handed down its decision on executive privilege and the tapes. It was from the moment of that Supreme Court decision that Nixon's standing eroded rapidly and resignation became the only alternative to impeachment.

That powerful, relatively sudden surge of public opinion against Nixon was a symptom of what I have called the constitutional or civic religion of the United States. The perception that constitutional order was at risk moved American opinion because the first dogma of that religion is that, finally, the Constitution is the only protection the American people have against themselves. Such must always be the case in a democratic society which is self-governing. In Europe, this truth has been obscured or overlaid by the fact that European nations usually have more homogenous populations, longer national traditions and survivals of an older governing class. If in the future Europe is to govern itself as a federal state, however, Europeans will have to come to terms with this truth about the quasi-religious role of a written constitution.

3

The Dilemma of
Modern Democracy

Today, no state can belong to the European Union unless it is democratic. Just a few years ago democracy was the constant appeal during the dramatic events surrounding the fall of Communism in Eastern Europe. Indeed, throughout the world in recent decades, democracy has become the habitual demand of peoples facing repressive, tyrannical or foreign-dominated regimes.

Yet it is easy to forget how recent this almost universal appeal for democracy is.

Until half a century ago, democracy was a word unknown to most of the non-Western world. Even in the West, until two centuries ago, the word carried decidedly unfavourable connotations. Until then, the role of the idea of democracy was not unlike the role of the *id* in Freud's theory of the psyche – both suggested a dark, inscrutable and fathomless threat from below. The upper classes of European society and the established Churches looked upon democracy as something almost demonic.

What an extraordinary transformation in our time! Appeals to democracy have run from the squares of Beijing, through the streets of Moscow and Bucharest, to *ex cathedra* statements from the Vatican. Now the non-Western as well as the Western world daily invoke this standard.

But what does democracy mean? How coherent is this goal, now invoked almost universally? Can it take the burden which all of these appeals impose on it – a burden which has grown with the waning appeal of socialism and communism? Can the idea of democracy provide clear guidance in sorting out our beliefs or reconstructing our institutions?

Although it is modern Europe which has given the ideal of democracy to the rest of the world, the word and its meaning have far earlier roots – roots in antiquity, in the world of the Greek city-state. But in its modern form the idea of democracy has acquired a more complex meaning. In at least one very important respect, its meaning has shifted since antiquity.

That shift in the meaning of democracy is crucial to the construction of Europe today. Yet it is little understood. And that is dangerous. For it means that Europeans do not really understand how this central component of their beliefs points simultaneously in opposite directions – how the modern idea of democracy introduces a tension into the identity of Europe which could even tear that identity apart.

The modern idea of democracy threatens Europe with a divided self. That threat follows from uncertainty. What scale of social and political organization is required by democracy? On the one hand, democratic liberty or personal autonomy suggests that a large scale of social organization is needed. For market exchanges and the increasing social division of labour obviously enhance choice and help us to lead our own lives. On the other hand, democratic citizenship suggests that 'small is good' because it opens the way to political participation and civic virtue. If we simultaneously entertain such conflicting intuitions about what scale of organization is required to achieve democracy, can we pursue a consistent course through life? Can we find social and political roles, public and private lives, which are compatible with each other? That is the dilemma of modern democracy.

If we are to understand that dilemma, we have to look far more closely at the ways the word 'democracy' has come to be used in the modern world. Only then can we begin to probe the roots of our dilemma and hope to get beyond it. In order to do that, it is necessary, I think, to distinguish between three distinct types of appeal for democracy:

democracy *simpliciter*
democratic government
democratic society

Mostly I shall be looking at the latter two appeals. For that is where the dilemma of modern democracy emerges unmistakably. But first I want to say something about appeals for democracy *simpliciter*.

The appeal for democracy *simpliciter* is a negative use of the word – that is, it is used to identify and reject some form of oppression or oppressor, be it a privileged class, an autocratic party or a foreign colonial power. When used in this way, democracy is a guide to the past rather than a guide to the future. Put in religious or philosophical language, this appeal for democracy tends to be dualist. It divides the world into 'them' and 'us', the friends and foes of the people, the *demos*. This use can also be apocalyptic, suggesting that a sudden 'transformation of heaven and earth' is possible, and perhaps even imminent.

Alas, this negative appeal for democracy does not provide any guidance for the construction of a society or its governance. It is simplistic. And, for the purposes of social and political decision-making, simplistic ideas may be stirring, but they are dangerous. Exaltation, the exaltation of victory, is the emotion especially associated with this kind of appeal for democracy. But how constructive is exaltation? It is not only ideas that can be simplistic. So too may emotions be. Such concepts and emotions cannot, by their very nature, give rise to or sustain social and political institutions. Indeed, they may make it more difficult to develop durable and legitimate institutions.

One of the saddest features of human life is that injustice often breeds ideas and feelings which, when the injustice concerned is diminished or removed, themselves become a new source of injustice – that is, the struggle against injustice or privilege distorts our beliefs and practices.

Let me return to a historical example I have already explored. It is the story of how, in France, a tyrannical form of the state grew out of class conflict, the struggle of the bourgeoisie against the feudal aristocracy. In that struggle the French Crown, through its lawyers and civil servants, became the vanguard of the bourgeoisie, encouraging and justifying their struggle against local feudal privilege. The consequence was that the boroughs of France acquiesced in the transfer of power to the Crown until local autonomy was extinct. Unwittingly, the French bourgeoisie had forged a political weapon – the sovereignty of the Crown – which could be used to oppress them when the feudal aristocracy had been subdued. Out of a hatred of privilege, the French bourgeoisie became their own oppressors, the creators and the victims of a tyrannical state machine. A later example of the same tragic process can be seen in the way Lenin used an autocratic party, a party which claimed to be the vanguard of the proletariat and to represent its interests, to construct a monstrous tyranny over the ruins of the Russian *ancien régime*.

In both cases tyrannical organizations 'fed' on what can only be called a democratic demonology. That demonology suggested that there was one struggle so important that all other issues and values should be sacrificed to it – the struggle against privilege, whether 'aristocratic' or 'bourgeois'. Thus it is only too easy for tyranny to emerge as the unintended consequence of a struggle against injustice. For, as we have seen, people often prefer to be oppressed by someone they do not know rather than someone they know. And that is a formula for tyranny. So the appeal for democracy *simpliciter* must be handled with great caution, even with suspicion. It is usually a guide to the past rather than to the future.

Let us now turn to the two other types of appeal for democracy, appeals to the idea of a 'democratic government' and to the idea of a 'democratic society'. These are far more promising. Yet here too we must be careful. These appeals for democracy rely on very different frameworks of ideas and take us into two utterly different historical worlds. The danger is that if we move back and forth between these two types of appeal for democracy – especially if we do not notice the moves we are making – we risk seriously confusing ourselves.

The frameworks of ideas in which these two types of appeal for democracy are embedded – and the images associated with them – coexist in our minds. We draw upon each, now upon one, now upon the other. But do we realize that appealing to the ideas of a democratic government or of a democratic society requires us to shift the framework of our thinking and imagining? I doubt it.

Perhaps the easiest way to understand this is to look at the imagery associated with each appeal. And here the history of modern European art can help us. For seventeenth- and eighteenth-century European painting offers striking examples of each type of image – images which conjure up quite different kinds of space, the one public, the other private.

Two paintings by the late eighteenth-century French neo-classical painter David conjure up a world which consists almost exclusively of public space, the space of the citizen. *The Oath of the Horatii* suggests a degree and quality of public commitment which seems to leave little or no space for domestic loyalties. David's famous painting of *Brutus Preparing to Kill his Son*, for the sake of the commonwealth, makes the same point even more emphatically. Both paintings stake out the peremptory claims of citizenship, of the public space.

By contrast, seventeenth-century Dutch painters such as Vermeer and De Hooch conjure up a world in which the public space has almost disappeared. Here everything is domestic and intimate. The quiet of personal contemplation replaces the clamour of public oaths and public violence. The same introspective quality can be seen in the work of the eighteenth-century French painter Chardin. Private choices and affections, and the satisfactions and sadnesses they give rise to, provide a subject-matter which seems to make citizenship almost beside the point.

Let us now smash these two (admittedly composite) images of public and private spaces into pieces – into hundreds of small, irregular pieces. They are like the makings of a puzzle. But with this difference. We have in our minds the makings of *two* puzzles, not just one, whenever we appeal for democracy. But often we are not aware of this. And so we try to fit together pieces which do not and cannot form a single image, for they are the pieces of two puzzles.

Our intuitions about democracy are rather like the pieces of these two puzzles. We constantly run the risk of using the wrong pieces when trying to put together each puzzle. So what follows is an attempt to explore the disparate contents of our minds when we appeal to the idea of democracy.

How should we describe these two puzzles, when each consists of pieces of language? Let us call each a tradition of discourse – or, for short, a discourse. If we do that, then probably the best descriptions available are those that emerged in the eighteenth century, when the two traditions first came into close proximity. Then, the appeal for a democratic government was associated with the discourse of 'classical republicanism' or 'citizenship', while the appeal for a democratic society or civil equality was associated with the discourse of 'civil society'. These two traditions of discourse did not merely come into close proximity in the eighteenth century, however. They also began to rub up against each other. The friction which resulted suggests still another analogy – an analogy with the earth plates of our planet which occasionally grind against each other with terrifying results. Something like that destructive potential accompanied the rubbing together of these two democratic discourses. For the different assumptions about equality they embodied could not easily be joined together.

Can a stable, coherent relationship between these two discourses be established? That question first surfaced in Western Europe during the eighteenth century because of growing social equality, the rapid contraction of the status differences which had survived feudalism in Europe. There suddenly developed in Western Europe a quite new sense of the conventional, almost arbitrary nature of inherited status differences. That emerges vividly if Beaumarchais's play *The Marriage of Figaro*, written in the 1770s and the inspiration for Mozart's opera, is compared with Madame de Sévigné's *Letters*, dating from the end of the previous century. When noble ladies of Louis XIV's court wished to speak privately, they spoke of a salon being 'empty' if there were only servants present. In their view, servants did not matter – indeed, they were scarcely human. By Beaumarchais's day, however, the tables had been turned. In his play, Count Almaviva is clearly inferior, morally and intellectually, to his valet Figaro, and is at least dimly aware of the fact. They are presented not as essentially different beings, but as humans to whom chance has allotted different social roles.

This rapid contraction of social distances created a powerful new impulse in parts of Western Europe – an impulse not to be satisfied merely with the goal of civil liberty or equality before the law (a goal which the example of Britain had long inspired in reformers on the continent), but also to seek political liberty, the rights of citizenship and a share in law-making. Thus, the later eighteenth century saw the emergence of a widespread interest in and campaign for self-government.

But just what did self-government involve? There were really only two models available – one drawn from medieval Europe, the other from classical antiquity. Which was it to be? It might be supposed that Europeans would have fallen back on their own immediate inheritance. Representative institutions – such as the British Parliament, the Spanish

Cortes and the French Estates-General – had been the distinctive creation of late medieval Europe, of a society which was corporate in character. But that was now the problem. By the eighteenth century the association of representative institutions with social privilege and exclusivity worked to undermine the appeal of such institutions. It helped to make them seem bastions of reaction and prejudice.

Far more attractive, suddenly, was the vision of the ancient city-state or *polis* – the vision of citizen-heroes assembling together to debate the public weal, to vote on controversial questions, and, if need be, to defend their city as a free militia. It was a seductive vision, a vision which rapidly discredited most of the representative bodies inherited from the Middle Ages. Participation in public decision-making now seemed to be the crux of democracy. Europeans began to anticipate the satisfactions which had led the philosopher Aristotle, two millennia before, to claim that the life of the active citizen was the only life worth living.

That is why the new passion for self-government in Europe came to be expressed, *not* in terms associated with the representative institutions inherited from medieval Europe, but rather in terms of a discourse which had its roots in the world of the ancient *polis* – the discourse of classical republicanism or citizenship.

Invoking the discourse of citizenship created moral ambiguities at first little noticed in modern Europe. Ultimately, however, they became very serious. For the discourse of classical republicanism or citizenship sprang from a social and intellectual setting which was pre-individualist, whereas the discourse of civil society, which had grown out of the Christian Natural Law tradition, was radically individualist in its assumptions. Another way of putting it, as I mentioned earlier, is to say that these two traditions of discourse embodied utterly different assumptions about equality. So we must now explore that difference.

What were the central terms of the discourse of citizenship? The standard for conduct it held up was 'civic virtue' or patriotism, unlimited devotion to the welfare and glory of the city. What were the chief threats to civic virtue? They were threats which this discourse described as 'luxury' and 'corruption'. In its account, the growth of luxury led, inexorably, to the corruption of the city. For the taste for luxury turned citizens away from their proper concern, which was the public weal.

A taste for luxury led them into preoccupations with wealth and its perquisites – consumption, display and pleasure. Such preoccupations weakened the citizens' public ardour, fostering instead a kind of effeminacy and self-indulgence. The austere character of citizens properly so-called – their willingness to sacrifice themselves for the public weal – necessarily declined as their taste for luxury developed. That is why the growth of luxury involved, sooner or later, the corruption of the city.

Often the discourse of citizenship relied upon a contrast between images of masculine hardness and feminine softness. The former was associated especially with the warrior-citizens of Sparta and early republican Rome, while the latter was associated with the more commercial and pleasure-loving societies of Athens and Corinth, where love of display and refinement at times succeeded in subverting civic spirit. From the standpoint of the discourse of citizenship, the masculine ought to characterize public life, while femininity was relegated to the inferior sphere of domestic life, the sphere occupied not only by women but also by slaves and merchants. The citizen hero was expected to distance himself from the domestic sphere by freeing himself from superfluous wants or desires.

It is no accident that nudity figured so much in late eighteenth-century neo-classical European painting associated with the revival of the discourse of citizenship. Images of the citizen stripping for action were meant to convey the need for those truly dedicated to the public weal to abandon superfluous wants. Altogether, these images conveyed the deep distrust of commerce which ran through the discourse of citizenship – a discourse which associated civic virtue with renunciation, with moral and physical self-control. The love of luxury tended, by contrast, to enfeeble the heroic will of the citizen. Luxury turned men almost into 'women', who, along with slaves and merchants, were deemed to be inferior by nature to citizens.

We are now in a better position to assess the discourse of citizenship. The first thing we must notice is that the civic virtue it holds up is clearly not virtue in a modern, post-Christian sense. This discourse does not identify moral principles which obligate every individual as such. Rather, it holds up the virtue of solidarity, of dedication to the group – with very little said or asked about what the group is up to.

The discourse of citizenship does not contain any principle of justice or of equity. In modern terms, therefore, this discourse does not have any moral content.

When, indeed, we look closely at the way this discourse subordinates domestic life and its concerns to the public arena, we can see that it has roots in a radically hierarchical or aristocratic model of society. For domestic concerns are, *ex hypothesi*, the concerns of social inferiors – of women, slaves and merchants. Central to this discourse, consequently, are categorical exclusions from citizenship, permanent forms of social inequality. Citizens are equal, but they preside over a society composed of their inferiors. Ironically, then, the vision of citizenship which excited eighteenth-century Europeans concealed aristocratic assumptions even more radical than those they associated with the representative institutions inherited from medieval Europe.

Once again the imagery associated with the discourse of citizenship provides us with an important clue. There is often something theatrical about the behaviour of the ancient citizen. And that is because the ancient citizen is constantly on parade before his inferiors. The citizen must therefore strike appropriate poses in order to define and emphasize his superior role – if possible by astonishing his audience, moving it to wonder at his courage and single-mindedness. It is no accident that the image of Brutus preparing to sacrifice his own son to what he conceived to be his civic duty was such a recurrent image in eighteenth-century neo-classical painting.

Altogether, there is a vast moral gap between the world conjured up by this discourse of citizenship and the modern world. It emerges in radically different conceptions of liberty. In the discourse of citizenship, to be 'free' is to occupy a superior social rank, to enjoy the status of a citizen. To be free is to enjoy the privileges of citizenship, the privileges of attending the public assembly, speaking and voting. Freedom does not refer to rights enjoyed by all members of society equally. Freedom is therefore not a moral principle, a value to which all can appeal in the modern fashion. The idea of liberty associated with classical republicanism is a sure sign of the absence of that assumption of moral or 'natural' equality which is so familiar to us.

Still another feature of the discourse of citizenship is its unmistakably martial connotations. The reverse side of that coin is its devaluing of work or labour. Here too this discourse carries forward valuations derived from its original context, the world of the ancient city-state, where there was no clear distinction between military and economic activity. How could there be? Part of the point of warfare and conquest in antiquity was the enslavement of the enemy. War was also the recruitment of labour. Little wonder that labour was dishonourable. It was associated with defeat and with permanent social inferiority.

Since the eighteenth century the discourse of citizenship has been purged of the most obvious of these connotations. It has, up to a point, been adjusted to the moral beliefs of the modern world. But even now these resonances remain, resonances which carry forward the values originally embedded in this discourse. First, this way of thinking seems to entail a relatively small, face-to-face society if the potential for participation and civic spirit is to be realized. The claims of the public assembly, the need to assemble together to debate and vote, mark out the appropriate size of the polity, which must be small. Only then can one be seen to do one's duty. Secondly, this way of thinking insists on the primacy of public over personal or domestic concerns. It emphasizes the peremptory character of the claims of public life or citizenship, and implies that self-abandonment, devotion to the public weal, is the *telos* or purpose of man. Thirdly, this way of thinking continues to imply that the only role that counts in society, the role of the citizen, requires a kind of abstinence, an avoidance of luxury or wants which might undermine willingness to sacrifice oneself for the public weal. This way of thinking carries, in consequence, a deep distrust of commerce and the marketplace, as potentially if not actually corrupting.

Let me pass a judgement on this discourse of citizenship, before looking at its rival, the discourse of civil society. What is striking is that the discourse of citizenship can easily serve to discourage would-be citizens because of the totality of its demands, the stringency of the claims it makes for public life. Because of this stringency it can encourage rejection of active citizenship in favour of a far less demanding, consumer-orientated model of democracy. From a moral point of view, moreover, its claims on the citizen seem precarious. The ever-present danger is that this discourse can be hijacked for some purpose or by some agency that is not morally acceptable. In a sense, the attractions of citizenship on the ancient model are aesthetic rather than moral –

the pleasure of self-assertion and social superiority, of cutting a striking figure before inferiors.

Let us now turn to the appeal to the idea of a 'democratic society' and to the discourse of civil society associated with it. The difference is immediately apparent. The discourse of civil society begins not with the group but with the individual. It is founded on the assumption of moral or 'natural' equality, creating a status which all human agents share as such, rather than as members of any particular society. This equal moral standing gives individuals – and here the term 'individual' really comes into its own – weighty claims in justice on each other, claims which ought to govern our social and political arrangements.

The origins of the discourse of civil society are complex. It developed as an amalgam of Greek philosophy, Roman Law and Christian theology. But the question of its origins need not detain us. What matters here is that the assumption of moral or natural equality – which should be seen as a presumption in favour of equal treatment, unless morally relevant grounds for treating people differently can be adduced – has generated a tradition of moral discourse integral to the development of modern Europe. This tradition has passed through several distinct stages. Thus, medieval Natural Law theory paved the way for seventeenth-century Social Contract theory and the eighteenth-century theory of Civil Society, which have, in turn, largely shaped nineteenth- and twentieth-century liberalism. Yet one thing has been constant. Belief in the moral equality of humans has been central to each of these stages in the development of what are now our moral intuitions.

The proposition I want to defend is that this tradition of moral discourse is internally related to the transformation of European society since the early Middle Ages. It has contributed decisively, over the centuries, to what can be called a social revolution. Its assumptions and values have provided the framework for the emergence in Europe of a historically unprecedented kind of society, a democratic society. What is unprecedented about a democratic society is that it eschews all forms of 'privilege' – founding its legal order on the rights and duties of individuals, rather than on the claims of castes, corporations or the family.

Unfortunately, in the nineteenth century, the kind of democratic society which the discourse of civil society has created came to be labelled 'capitalist'. Since then even defenders of a democratic society have come to rely upon the label, which was originally put forward by socialist critics of liberalism. That is unfortunate, because calling a democratic society 'capitalist' obscures the role of the beliefs which have created it. The label 'capitalist' gives away to critics of modern democratic society more than is necessary. It implies a sort of historical materialism, and strengthens the widespread assumption that economic factors are always decisive in historical change. It draws attention away from ways in which belief in the moral equality of humans can continue to provide grounds for criticizing the workings of a market economy, and so stimulate further development in the idea of a democratic society.

If we look closely at the norms associated with this discourse of civil society it quickly becomes clear why three notions – personal autonomy, human rights and contract – are so closely associated with its development. When the right to command and the duty to obey are no longer written into separate social roles, assigned at birth, it follows that liberty is a birthright – a right that ought to be acknowledged in all equally. For, if all enjoy an equal moral standing, then there must be an area in which every individual should make his or her own decisions and be able act without constraint. In that way, the ideal of personal autonomy makes a dramatic appearance with this discourse.

That is why this discourse is closely associated with the notion of human rights. It justifies the assertion of individual rights against others – if need be against the world – by insisting that the protection of human autonomy is a condition of self-respect. Such a notion scarcely existed in antiquity. By insisting on the role of fundamental human rights, this discourse in effect separates a private sphere from the public sphere, the sphere of civil society as distinct from that of the state. This is a sphere in which the pursuit of private ends is no longer treated with the contempt reserved for it by the discourse of citizenship. Henceforth Vermeer's young woman reading a letter need not *necessarily* fear comparison with David's Brutus raising his knife to sacrifice his son for the public weal. Instead, the pursuit of private ends is legitimated and protected, at least so long as they are consistent with justice. Thus, civil society is a sphere in which individuals can exercise choice according to conscience and protected by rights. The crucial role which this discourse gives to human choice is confirmed by its emphasis on the role of contract.

A contractual model of society implies the central role of choice, of social relations governed by equality and reciprocity. The model of contract makes it clear that obligations, to be truly obligations, must be self-assumed. The upshot is that in this discourse liberty ceases to describe a superior social status, the status of a citizen, and becomes instead a moral principle, a principle to which all can appeal. That is why 'equal liberty' is at the heart of modern liberal thinking.

Altogether, the development of the discourse of civil society in early modern Europe involved an astonishing reversal of traditional assumptions. Instead of assuming social inequality to be 'natural' and hence to need no justification, the discourse of civil society assumed that equality was natural. But this reversal of assumptions had a revolutionary impact. For it followed that, henceforth, inequalities of status and treatment could no longer be taken for granted. They had to be justified on moral grounds. Inherited forms of subordination were, so to speak, deemed to be guilty unless proven innocent. By providing means for the critical evaluation of inherited social roles, this discourse became a revolutionary instrument – creating, in due course, an unprecedented kind of society in Europe, a democratic society. Equality before the law replaced privilege as the fundamental principle of social organization.

Another way of making the same point is to say that this discourse brought about a radical change in role-structures in Europe. It did this by introducing a primary role or status – that of the individual, a role shared by all equally – which was distinct from the secondary roles such individuals happened to occupy (husband, dentist, soldier, daughter, etc.). In that sense this discourse distanced its morally equal agents from particular social roles, leading them to see themselves as role occupiers – that is, as individuals whose identity was *not* exhausted by the particular social roles they happened to occupy.

That is the respect in which democratic society in Europe differs from traditional societies. In such societies the terms which ascribed social status or roles also justified them. There was no clear distinction made between description and justification. But the distinction between primary and secondary roles in a democratic society does not only make that distinction possible. It makes it necessary. That is why the development of the discourse of civil society led to an increasingly systematic and subtle critique of inherited inequalities of status and treatment. Given the new presumption in favour of equal treatment, one social distinction after another came under scrutiny. Thus, property as a determinant of civil status was rejected (so that, for example, voting rights no longer depended on a property qualification), paternal authority over children was greatly reduced, the subjugation of women was discredited (so that women acquired a legal status as property owners and voters, equal to that of men), while, most recently, discriminating upon the basis of race or sexual preference has become offensive, often even illegal.

This moral critique of inherited status differences or forms of subjection created what is arguably the deepest European urge, a passion for that equality of status which confirms our dignity as individuals. Yet that passion has had, in turn, an extraordinarily important *unintended* consequence. For the demand to be treated as equals has generated, gradually but irresistibly, a new scale of social organization. It is a scale embedded in the two most characteristic institutions of modern Europe: the nation-state and the market. The nation-state emerged as the agency for creating and protecting individual rights, the instrument of civil equality. And a market economy flourished as a direct consequence of civil equality. For the freedom to move about, buy and sell (including one's own labour) – as well as the *need* to do so – can be seen as the other side of the coin of civil equality. That is why the rejection of so many traditional inequalities of status and treatment has released ever-increasing numbers of market-orientated agents – noticeable most recently with the massive entry of women into the labour force.

Clearly, these institutional developments in Europe amounted to the emergence of a scale of organization far removed from the slave economy which had underpinned the ancient city-state. For the new framework of individual rights and market exchanges underwritten by the assumption of moral equality led to a rapidly increasing social division of labour and economic interdependence – to the weakening of localism (whether urban as in antiquity or rural as in feudal Europe) and to the 'centralization' of political, economic and social relations. Yet although it was an unintended consequence, this new scale of organization sprang directly from the most distinctive European moral urge – responding to and reinforcing the demand for 'democracy' in the form of civil equality or equal liberty. But where did this distinctive European urge towards civil equality and a democratic society leave claims for democratic government or citizenship?

That was and remains the rub. The discourse of classical republicanism or citizenship had long since tied the idea of democratic government to localism, to the ability of citizens to attend the assembly and share in public power. In modern Europe, however, the pursuit of social equality has gradually created institutions of a new scale, the nation-state and the market, which make public debate and decision-making far more remote and elusive. Consequently, the ideal of an equal distribution of power represented by the ancient assembly of citizens has come to look like a will-o'-the-wisp. The very scale of a democratic society makes the model of active citizenship seem virtually impossible to attain. Society has become too complex, political power too centralized and economic decision-making too diffuse.

Yet one side of us continues to want an equal share in public power. For the discourse of citizenship has become part of our conversation with ourselves. We want not only to be consumers, but to be citizens. That is the dilemma of modern democracy, a dilemma with deep roots in our psyche. The pursuit of one kind of equality – civil equality or equality before the law – has generated, as an unintended consequence, a scale of social organization which apparently rules out active citizenship or political participation. But, looking within ourselves, we find that we cannot give up the wish to have an equal share in public decision-making, to be active citizens. Not to have a share in public power is somehow morally offensive.

So, do we simply want incompatible things? A controversial early eighteenth-century writer, Bernard de Mandeville, argued that we do. In his view if we really want citizenship and civic virtue, then we have to accept the consequence, a 'pitiful and frugal' society – a society which does away with the exchanges, the multiplication of wants and advanced division of labour, which mark modern democratic society in the West. If, on the other hand, we decide to encourage commerce and pursue prosperity, then, Mandeville argued, we have to dispense with the ancient ideal of active citizenship, of citizen-heroes.

Is there no way out of this dilemma? Two paths have been explored. The first, which we have already encountered, puts forward the notion of 'community' as a corrective or antidote to the conflicts of interests arising from the multiplication of wants. Different models of community have been proposed, from Rousseau's moral community governed by 'a general will' to Durkheim's intermediate associations and guild socialism. The trouble is, however, that these models of community often seem to jeopardize the civil equality which has been the great achievement of modern Europe. Anxious to remove the 'gap' between civil society and the state by fully integrating individuals into the group or community, these models jeopardize personal autonomy.

Yet there is another way we can try to reconcile participation or active citizenship with civil society and the new scale of organization it involves. That is by means of a more restrained notion of citizenship, a notion which does not require the almost total submergence of the individual in the group demanded of citizen-heroes in antiquity. Instead, we need a notion of citizenship which acknowledges the importance and legitimacy of the private sphere, and accepts that the claims of the public sphere on citizens ought to be limited by justice – justice understood as guaranteeing equal liberty, while at the same time insisting that the form of the state is such that it can mobilize our consent by engaging us actively as citizens at some level.

Modern citizenship requires that the ancient citizen-hero take a cold shower and put on his clothes. A more restrained doctrine of citizenship would take as its subject not the ancient hero stripped for action, but the ambivalent modern, wanting to carry out his or her duties in a committee meeting, while also anxious to get home.

Such a restrained doctrine of citizenship finds its natural place in a devolved form of the state. That is why constitutional forms are so important, and ought to loom very large indeed in discussions about European political integration. Constitutional forms are far the most promising means of reconciling, at least up to a point, the two potentially conflicting urges towards equality which are deep within ourselves. On the one hand, formally entrenching a range of basic human rights reinforces the foundation of civil society, by limiting the sphere of legitimate state action. On the other hand, devolving as much authority as possible to local and regional levels of government increases the ability of the state to foster citizenship. And if a devolved form of the nation-state is the first step, federalism would be its natural extension. Federalism, more than any other form of the state, makes it possible *in principle* to adjust the claims of both citizenship and civil society, of the public and private spaces. It can do this by helping autonomous individuals who are also citizens to take a new view of their own interests, a view which leads insensibly from narrowly personal interests, through local and regional interests, to national interests and beyond. In that way federalism firmly anchors the individual in different layers of association.

That is why in Europe subtle constitutional reform, indeed a new constitutional settlement, is required if we are to begin to overcome the dilemma of modern democracy – which is that we want more from public life than we are prepared to put into it. We want a share in power, but we also want to be left alone.

4

How Britain has Lost its Voice

A vision of the benefits of self-government is what, at all costs, we must not lose. We must not lose it because our self-respect depends upon it. It is no accident that this vision presided over the long, arduous struggle in the eighteenth and the nineteenth century to create representative government or 'free' institutions on the continent of Europe. And that brings us to Britain. At first glance it might seem eccentric to move from general ideas about democracy to a discussion of the British constitution. But there are two good reasons for doing so.

The first is that Britain invented modern representative government, the form of government which has been adopted throughout Europe and spread to much of the rest of the world. In the eighteenth and nineteenth centuries, liberals on the European continent looked upon the British constitution as a prodigy or marvel. It inspired them with hope and defined their political ambitions at home. A vision of 'British liberty' floated over the continent. The Anglophilia of continental liberals was not due simply to British leadership of the coalition against Napoleon or the development of the British Empire outside Europe. It was no mere abject reverence for British power. It was, above all, admiration for the culture of consent which British political institutions had created. Even in the twentieth century the Westminster model continued to be held up as something for other countries to emulate, if they could.

Would it not be reasonable to expect Britain to take the lead in any further development of representative government in Europe? Should not Britain, with its remarkable constitutional history, take the principal part in creating a federal Europe? But that has not been the case.

Rather the contrary. Successive British governments and many of the British political class have been sceptical, if not downright hostile, to the idea of creating new representative institutions for Europe. Britain sometimes seems to have taken over the viewpoint once championed by General de Gaulle: that the only acceptable Europe is a Europe of nation-states and not a federal Europe.

What has caused such a dramatic loss of idealism? Has Britain reneged on its own child? And to what extent should British doubts about ambitious political construction in Europe give pause to European federalists? After all, such doubts on the part of the people who have the longest experience of representative government in Europe ought not to be dismissed lightly.

I think that we can begin to answer these questions only by considering the peculiar nature of the British state. That is the second reason for discussing Britain at this point. For the nature of the British state explains why Britain finds it so difficult today to make a constructive contribution to the creation of Europe. The truth is, that it cannot. It has lost its voice. The contrast with the eighteenth and nineteenth centuries, when a patrician British voice gave hope to liberals throughout Europe, is truly painful. But not only that. It is also instructive. What can be called the crisis of British liberalism, rooted in the peculiar nature of the British state, reveals an important truth about representative government.

Far the most interesting question about Britain today is why, after two centuries during which it defended liberal values in Europe and the world at large, it has fallen silent. Instead of being the champion of representative government, civil liberty and social improvement, Britain is seen – not least by its European partners – as lacking enthusiasm for larger causes or ideals. Foreign observers even perceive signs that civil liberties are ill-secured by the British political system and, apparently, are of little interest to the public at large.

Why has British liberalism proved so fragile? The root cause is simpler than many accounts suggest. It has to do with ideas or beliefs. Pondering the fate of liberalism in Britain brings one straight up against the question of 'ideology' – a term which has so often, and often so rightly, been the subject of abuse. Nevertheless, I doubt whether it is possible to understand the *malaise* of late twentieth-century British liberalism unless the role of ideology is taken seriously. The traditional embarrassment of the British when faced with general ideas – that embarrassment which has contributed so much to comical writing – itself provides a clue to what has 'gone wrong'.

Every stable society rests on a shared view of the world – a way of looking at things which makes it possible to have settled expectations and which provides channels for both co-operation and peaceful conflict. Without such shared beliefs, no intelligible model of ambition is provided for the members of a society. They are thrown into the world merely with fragments of identity. Lacking a viewpoint or *core* of identity, they find it difficult to pursue any consistent course in life.

Has British society latterly provided its members with such a viewpoint? I think not. Whereas other European societies have in the last two centuries formally adhered to liberal principles, set out in written constitutions, British society has continued to seek unity in manners rather than ideas. It has discouraged discussion of ideology, preferring to rely on civility as the cement of society. 'Decency' and 'common sense' have been its watchwords. British society has prided itself on being 'broad church' – that is, eclectic and accommodating. Yet this pragmatic approach associated with the early achievement of representative government in Britain has taken a heavy toll. Britain has sought consensus in a mode of proceeding, in parliamentary sovereignty. But it is a mode of proceeding which is *not* formally constrained by liberal principles.

The early home of liberalism in Europe has thus become only equivocally liberal. Just how did this happen? It is possible to identify four crucial episodes. The first was the peculiarly English version of the Reformation. Whatever else might be said about the Church of England, there can be no doubt that it represented a form of Christianity which devalued ideas – preferring to accommodate different opinions and factions within a national Church, rather than take up a conspicuous doctrinal position. In that way it differed from both the post-Reformation Church of Rome and the Reformed Churches of the continent. As a result the Church of England has failed to make any contribution to the socializing process comparable to that made by Churches which emphasize doctrine (something that may help to explain the reputation of Presbyterian Scots in England as being more self-directed and austere). In England, 'sensible' conduct rather than correct belief has been held up. Doubtless the practical consequence for a long time was that people sought to live by the standards appropriate to their social station rather than finding motives in general ideas about man, his rights and duties. The genteel church of Jane Austen's novels, hardly distinguishable from the hierarchy of local society, was the result.

The second episode should be located in the later eighteenth and the early nineteenth century. Because civil equality, parliamentary institutions and a relatively open aristocracy provided a degree of mobility, the English middle classes did not have to develop the 'fighting' viewpoint which struggles against a more rigid caste system developed among the bourgeoisie of continental nations, notably that of France. But the tacit compromise reached between the English upper and middle classes once again had the effect of devaluing ideas. For that compromise was based on common interests and a manner which could be acquired, rather than on shared ideas. The lordly style of Whiggish politics nationally, and the squirearchical style locally, flourished on placating other interests rather than on developing a set of public beliefs or doctrine. It worked on 'intuitions' about what changes were needed rather than a systematic programme of reform or democratization. Any such 'radical' programme would have been unsettling to the 'polite' conversations of Jane Austen's drawing rooms.

The third episode followed at the end of the nineteenth century. As the British middle classes had not been obliged to develop a radically combative point of view, they had little or nothing to offer those lower on the social ladder and seeking to rise. Instead, what became a great irritant were the quasi-aristocratic attitudes of at least the upper reaches of the British middle classes. Their alliance with the older landed class had, with the help of the public schools and the need to govern an empire, created in them some of the attitudes of a caste. Their manners and accents set them apart from the rest of society, and contributed to their developing a point of view which could not become general because it implied the permanent subordination of another section of society.

Thus, in contrast to the American and French middle classes, the British middle classes had no conception of society to offer which did not *in principle* exclude some. A subordinate class was implied by their very style of being and speaking. That impression made it impossible for the English middle classes to act as unambiguous 'carriers' of an individualist model of society. The resulting perpetuation of class identities undoubtedly contributed to the eclipse of the Liberal Party by a new, class-conscious Labour Party early in the twentieth century.

The fourth episode is the most recent one. Frustrated by years of quasi-corporatist politics after the Second World War, and by what they saw as creeping socialism, the lower reaches of the British middle classes began to react against the patrician style which had for so long dominated the civil service as well as the parties. The habit of appeasing interest groups had (since the advent of universal suffrage and the Welfare State) led to what seemed the indefinite growth of the state sector. And the victims of the trend were especially the lower reaches of the middle classes, who did not find themselves reaping benefits in the same way as the organized working class or the upper reaches of society. The self-employed, skilled workers and small businesses felt increasingly threatened, and fell back on the economic kernel of liberalism – on the doctrine of a free market and its benefits, divorced from any broader social liberalism. For such liberalism was, in their eyes, associated with the accommodating, but unprincipled, paternalist style of politics which had led to statism and their own decline. That reaction was to provide the foundation for Mrs Thatcher's pivotal role in the 1980s.

In one sense Thatcherism saw the return of doctrine to English public life after a prolonged absence. That was its heartening aspect. But it was an incomplete doctrine, a liberalism shorn of much that makes liberalism humane and elevating, notably its emphasis on equal liberty and social justice. Instead of concerning itself with access to the marketplace and greater opportunity, the Thatcher Government placed almost exclusive emphasis on rationalization and efficiency, on fiscal and monetary policy joined to widespread privatization. All of this was justified in the name of a truncated version of liberalism which was almost a parody of nineteenth-century notions of *laissez-faire*.

Yet access to the marketplace is crucial to the creation of a dynamic and competitive society. And it is first and foremost a subjective matter. Before 'real' mobility comes imaginative mobility – the wish to occupy a different social position and the confidence that there is a reasonable chance of doing so. It was in this area that continental Europe made enormous strides after the end of the Second World War, approaching the American model of society. By the 1970s one sign of that change was how 'old-fashioned' and 'class-bound' English society seemed to visiting youth from the continent – a sharp contrast to the impression of eighteenth- and early nineteenth-century European visitors to England.

What had happened? The very success of English society in the early modern period had distorted British liberalism. For what continental visitors in the eighteenth century called the 'genius' of British institutions lay in the subtle mechanisms it had created for making possible and sanctioning a *limited* amount of social mobility. That small amount of mobility set Britain apart from the residually caste societies of Europe. Yet those mechanisms, which became more elaborate in the nineteenth century by way of the public schools and the professions, involved taking on a style, an accent and manners which set a section of the English middle classes increasingly apart from the rest of society.

Two unintended consequences followed. First, such a conspicuous élite, or 'Establishment', influenced the nature of personal ambitions, creating a strong attraction to status rather than power or wealth. 'Being someone' rather than 'doing something' became uppermost, with sad results for innovation and competition in Britain. But if that was the sad consequence for those who continued to aspire, the even sadder result was that many able people from working-class and lower middle-class backgrounds came to feel intrinsically unable to aspire – excluded from full competition because they were not 'the right sort'. Thus, the very mechanisms which had originally permitted limited mobility became obstacles to wider social mobility.

Now, the only way out of such an impasse is to create a society in which the full range of liberal ideas operates, what is called a 'rights-minded' society. A liberal constitution, with entrenched rights, brings to the surface the deep connection between representative government and social mobility. It encourages mobility by giving a formal sanction to personal ambition. By contrast, the obstacle to ambition in Britain was that liberalism had come to be associated with a paternalist style of government, with condescension and deference. That meant, in effect, that the terms of ambition were being set not by liberal doctrine but by a superior social class. The unwritten constitution itself testified to the paramount role accorded to manners rather than to liberal ideas in Britain. At this junction, therefore, it could not play the role that written constitutions might do in fostering self-respect and shaping a more robust citizenry.

That is why the legacy of Thatcherism is so mixed. Mrs Thatcher's policies in the 1980s were directed at accelerating economic change and stimulating competition rather than at political reform. Inadvertently, however, they not only revealed the inadequacy of the British Constitution, but also jeopardized its survival. For the Thatcher Government's policies rapidly undermined the independence of a range of inherited institutions, the informal means by which constitutional norms had been transmitted and enforced in Britain. These policies thus gave a new urgency to constitutional reform.

Unfortunately, Thatcherism resembled Marxism in the way it grossly underestimated the importance of political institutions. Thatcher presented herself as an *economic* radical, unafraid of change and determined to make British society more competitive. Yet on the constitutional front she turned her face against change. It was a very serious misjudgement on her part. For the type of society she sought to build required a more formal liberal foundation than the old, unwritten constitution could provide.

Thatcherism had been born of the malaise of the 1960s and 1970s in Britain. Industrial unrest, corporatist habits and symptoms of economic decline were rife. But the malaise was, under the surface, not merely economic. It was also political. The unwritten constitution could not provide the focus for liberal identity needed as British society shed its aristocratic form. By failing to provide an adequate focus of liberal identity, the unwritten constitution helped to demoralize Britain. Little wonder that by the 1980s disenchantment with the British political system became widespread. It sprang not only from academics enamoured of an American-style Bill of Rights or from centrist politicians worried about the justice of the 'winner takes all' electoral system. It had deeper social sources, sources which give rise to a less articulate, but for that reason a more dangerous cynicism about British political institutions.

The 'British liberty' so widely admired in the eighteenth and nineteenth centuries had been closely bound up with an aristocratic form of society. It relied on deference and a social hierarchy to limit the growth of state power. The Whiggish norms which had shaped intentions and constrained actions for 200 years – making it, for example, 'unthinkable' for a London government to jeopardize the autonomy of local government – had been 'carried' by a relatively coherent governing class. Recruits to that class imbibed those norms along with their claret and port. Always changing, and enforced in ways that struck foreigners as curious, such Whiggish norms had survived as an effective constraint even in the face of two world wars and the post-war Labour Government.

For long it was simply assumed that parliament would be dominated by a propertied, leisured class, which would disperse power by resisting encroachments of the executive and by keeping local affairs firmly in their own hands. That such a class would guarantee a range of individual rights, particularly property rights, was also taken for granted. Thus, the part of the constitution which provided a balance between legislative and executive power, protected local autonomy, and, to an important extent, individual liberties, was informal. It was the interface between social structure and political institutions in Britain.

But that made the British constitution particularly vulnerable to social change. And that is where Mrs Thatcher enters. Her government suddenly accelerated social change. She worked to widen and strengthen the middle sector of society, to propagate commercial values and to introduce a more populist politics at the expense of an older governing class. In that way, Thatcher completed the destruction of the informal supports which an aristocratic society had provided for British liberty. What the Thatcher Government accomplished was a basic change in social structure. More than any other government in the twentieth century, it was responsible for completing the middle-class or bourgeois revolution in Britain. Indeed, Thatcher made herself the embodiment of that revolution. She acted as the hammer of aristocratic attitudes and practices in Britain. Her policies were directed at completing the move to a more mobile and dynamic, a money-orientated rather than a status-oriented, society.

We can now see that such social changes had profound constitutional implications. As the protection previously provided by an aristocratic

71

social structure disappeared, what guarantee did the British constitution give to liberal constitutional values? Virtually none. In itself, parliamentary sovereignty provided no guarantee against the growth of executive power, the eclipse of local autonomy or even the erosion of individual liberty. Parliamentary sovereignty, while compatible with British liberal traditions, by no means guaranteed them.

If the great British success of the nineteenth century was to integrate the middle classes into the parliamentary system, the failure of the twentieth century was the incomplete translation of liberalism into a more democratic culture. And, as so often in history, the earlier success provides an important part of the explanation of the later failure. For in adapting to an informal, aristocratic liberalism, leaders of the British middle classes had come to underestimate the importance of constitutional norms. The contribution which a written constitution can make to the socializing process in a democratic polity was not readily understood by new members of the political class who had been assimilated into an aristocratic political culture. They learned to scorn the 'inflated' political rhetoric of republican nations and to bask in the glory of the 'understated' British constitution.

Yet the rhetoric of natural or inalienable rights – easy enough to ridicule in the French and American constitutions – has a contribution to make to any robust, rights-minded polity. In Britain, there was instead a kind of ideological vacuum. For the voice of the constitution remained an essentially upper-class voice, ironic and private rather than assertive and public. At its most philosophical, it was the voice of utility rather than of rights-based liberalism. It did not profess to provide individuals with a framework of identity. It took preferences or wants as given. Consequently, as older class identities were eroded, there was nothing to take their place. In that sense, the unwritten constitution contributed to a void – leaving advice about any deeper commitments, in Harold Macmillan's words, as 'a matter for the bishops'.

After 1960, the consequences of that normative void became increasingly noticeable. Many examples come to mind. But one is especially vivid and recent – the sudden, if only temporary, canonization of Diana, Princess of Wales. It was especially among younger people that the normative void resulting from an unwritten constitution took a heavy toll. It left them without any public profession of belief and, consequently, without any deep attachment to some of the major public institutions of Britain. It jeopardized increasingly the legitimacy of the monarchy, the House of Lords, perhaps even the House of Commons. All came to be associated by the young with the British *ancien régime*, with a stratified society that no longer carried conviction. In that way the British state was divested of idealism – leaving younger people searching for something or someone to admire. That 'unhinged' emotion settled briefly on Princess Diana at the moment of her death. Princess Diana's confusion about her own role, her subversive attitude towards established institutions, made her the focus of a nation looking for uplift but no longer able to respond to traditional symbols and rites. What the younger generation in Britain celebrated in Diana was, above all, her confusion. For her confusion was also theirs. They no longer had any 'constitutional faith'. They needed and sought a substitute.

That dangerous normative void in Britain has been beautifully captured by a recent definition of the constitution. It has been said, with only slightly more malice than truth, that the British constitution can be defined as 'what happens'. The almost primitive aspect of the constitution has been its minimal normative content, with emotional cohesion and uplift being provided by the pageantry of an aristocratic society. The British constitution itself has rested simply on the sovereignty of the Crown in parliament and the rule of law. Otherwise, the framework of British life has been defined by parliamentary legislation and court decisions. Procedures for constitutional change have not differed from the ordinary legislative process. Nor have any fundamental rights, with their role in sanctioning personal ambition, been entrenched.

Of course, that minimal normative content draws attention, in turn, to the crucial role which an unwritten constitution accords to custom and opinion. The role which the British constitution accords to custom and opinion is its sophisticated feature. For there is much to be said for the view that the informal part of any constitution is its most important part, and that custom and opinion are the final guarantees of any political system. That is why so many have resisted the call for constitutional change in the United Kingdom. What they admire in the British constitution is its flexibility, a flexibility which might be jeopardized by an elaborate written charter. Yet such a view, after the social revolution engineered by Mrs Thatcher, is now dangerously complacent. For those who dismiss the need for constitutional reform rely, whether consciously or not, on unstated, aristocratic assumptions about the nature of British society. But those assumptions no longer conform to reality.

So a terrible dilemma for British liberals has emerged. If they continue to defend the unwritten constitution and parliamentary sovereignty against demands for reform, they have to fall back on the assumption that British society possesses a special virtue which neutralizes threats observable in other societies – threats such as the centralization of power. But it is that assumption which long ago introduced complacency – the dangerous and misguided attitude that constitutional forms are not 'bread and butter' issues – and impoverished constitutional argument in Britain. It has acted as a sedative, drawing attention away from the challenges which social changes have posed for the political system. Fortunately, the assumption itself became more and more implausible in the course of the 1980s, as the Thatcher Government undermined the autonomy of local government and centralized power.

Mrs Thatcher's strategy was to create a far larger property-owning class, a class which could be relied upon to resist socialism more effectively than its patrician predecessor, a class less hindered by guilt about social privilege and so less sympathetic to paternalist policies. But while engineering a social revolution, Thatcher did not recognize the need to give this larger and potentially more powerful propertied class a political education. Nor did she recognize that the larger scale of this class made a public and didactic form of political education indispensable. Having struggled against aristocratic values, Thatcher seemed to have little awareness of the weaknesses of a democratic or bourgeois society. Yet some features of the new society – the need to make money, the commercial ethic and the inclination to leave public affairs to others – do not augur well for the political system or democratic liberty.

Mrs Thatcher did not seem to be aware that the movement towards a more democratic, less deferential society had created, in contrast with her deregulatory policy outside government, strong centralizing pressures in the British political system. Yet, beginning in the nineteenth century with administrative centralization in the interest of social reform, continuing (after extensions of the suffrage) with the emergence of the disciplined party system and Cabinet control of the legislature, and concluding, it is often alleged, with prime ministerial control of the Cabinet, British Government has yielded to these pressures. Most recently, the crisis over Kosovo suggests that Prime Ministers can even make war with little constraint.

The absence of formal constitutional norms designed to disperse authority and power has proved a major drawback in opposing the centralization of power in Britain. For example, when the Thatcher Government decided to bring local authorities (often dominated by the Labour Party) to heel, all that opponents could appeal to were instincts and memories rather than constitutional principles. Serious public debate did not result. And the legal profession, when it has in turn felt threatened by recent Lord Chancellors' proposals for reform, has had some difficulty identifying a constitutional principle sufficiently determinate to make clear just what was endangered by the proposals. The cumulative fusion of powers in the British political system has left local authorities and the judiciary with little formal protection. Some argue that press freedom and individual rights are hardly any better off, citing, for example, new police powers of arrest and detention on suspicion, or the proposal to restrict the right of trial by jury.

Just why was Mrs Thatcher not more alert to the constitutional implications of her economic and social policies? To cite the temptations of power is not enough. There is another reason. Thatcherism did not only contribute to an emerging constitutional crisis, but was itself a product of that crisis – reflecting in its ideology the complacency engendered by an unwritten constitution. For it is no accident that Thatcherite ideology was a narrowly economic form of liberalism. Thatcherism developed as a reaction against what it perceived as the moral vacuum in Britain. Yet, hampered by constitutional complacency, Thatcher and her supporters sought to fill that vacuum with a narrowly economic liberalism, a liberalism stripped of its political dimension.

The rootlessness and fecklessness which marked Britain in the 1960s and 70s – exasperating soon-to-be Thatcherites and leading to charges of 'nihilism' – had been the result of a serious erosion of the identities previously provided by a class system, when no new and generalized identity, the identity of citizenship, was on offer to British subjects. The sovereignty of the Crown in parliament stipulated equal subjection, but little else. Without a clear framework of citizenship being provided by the political system, British life had become a strange mixture of aristocratic insouciance joined with working-class vulgarity. A tawdry elegance suffused the country, with commercial values eclipsed by theatrical display and whimsy, interrupted only by bouts of anxiety about steady economic decline.

It was that moral vacuum which Thatcher and others reacted against in the late 1970s. It created their opportunity. Into it they introduced increasingly large amounts of economic liberalism, of market ideology with a Hayekian gloss. And they found a receptive audience. For it is seriously to underestimate Thatcherism to suppose that it made its way simply by fear – by creating unemployment on such a scale that panic emasculated the power of unions and a Welfare State complacency which had pushed capitalist profit margins down to a level undermining economic growth in the United Kingdom. Above all, it was moral uncertainty – strongly felt by the younger brothers and sisters of the protesters and romantics who had sought to go beyond good and evil in a Nietzschean way – which created Thatcher's opportunity. What the younger generation sought was a framework for belief and action in a world which looked so unstable. To be sure, they wanted not to be poor. But they also relished clear, definite beliefs in a way unknown to the 1960s generation of Swinging London.

Thatcher's simple but clear view of the marketplace, and of the qualities success in the market required, provided a framework of action which had been missing. For that, it can be seen in retrospect, was the Achilles' heel of the 'middle way' of Keynesian demand management which had dominated British public policy in the early post-war decades. The techniques which Keynesianism relied upon at the macro-level did not yield a consistent model for action at the individual level. Spending and saving, effort as well as gratification, were entailed by Keynesian policies. But their place in a coherent individual life-plan was far from clear.

By contrast, Thatcherism provided an easily readable map for steering through life: a liberalism stripped of its political and moral dimensions. It emphasized the rewards open to those operating in a market, rather than the variety of life-styles made possible by affirming equal basic rights or the concern for others implied by the rights of citizenship. Those features of liberalism which offset or mitigate its economic disciplines were absent from the Thatcherite message. In particular, new duties of citizenship which public-spiritedness might identify, played little part in it. Instead, civil society – with its work and profit, accumulation and leisure – was Thatcher's preferred rhetorical domain. In that way, Thatcherism stripped British liberalism of its idealism.

Both the nihilism which Thatcher associated with the 1960s and 70s and her narrow economic response to it would have been offset by a formally liberal, rights-based political system, a system providing a framework of personal identity as well as a focus for at least partly disinterested ambition. The more recent upsurge of interest in constitutional reform in Britain and the overdue beginnings of reform under the present Labour Government of Mr Blair – with the abolition of the right of hereditary peers to sit in the upper chamber, legislative devolution to Scotland and Wales, as well as the introduction of entrenched rights into the British judicial process – are thus by no means accidental. They are the results of a long accumulation of discontent with a political system which privileged custom or manners over principle.

A liberal constitution – in which authority is formally dispersed and in which a strong principle of justice is introduced through rights entrenched against executive or legislative fiat – plays a necessary part in the socializing process when custom has ceased to be an adequate vehicle of personal identity. It encourages individuals to take their own claims seriously, while at the same time providing them with criteria for judging the legitimacy of such claims. By giving a range of basic claims undoubted legitimacy, such constitutions help to confer self-respect and create a citizenry less embarrassed by the prospect of self-assertion – citizens who 'know their place', not in the old deferential way, but in a new more egalitarian way. Thus, it is clear that one of the central functions of a liberal constitution is to underwrite and encourage social mobility – in effect, to hold out hope.

For much of the twentieth century in Britain, the survival of aristocratic attitudes in the upper reaches of the middle class and resentments in the working class combined to prevent the development of a more democratic form of liberalism. Mrs Thatcher declared herself against both of these things, identifying them as obstacles to the proper working of a free-market society. She crushed aristocratic values, while trying to create a larger property-owning class which would act as a permanent buffer against socialism. She hailed the end of sterile class-conscious politics in favour of a party system contained by general acceptance of the capitalist or free-market system.

Yet her means to these ends were crudely economic rather than political. She evidently did not understand the connection between a liberal constitutional system, market motivation and social mobility. In that respect, Thatcher looks, in retrospect, not so much like a radical, as the last major figure of the British *ancien régime*. Altogether, the Thatcherite episode reveals that if political liberalism without economic liberalism is impotent, economic liberalism without political liberalism is blind.

Today the condition of Britain offers a twofold message to Europe. The first is a sad one. Britain is ill-placed at the moment to give a constitutional lead to Europe, since it is itself caught up in a major constitutional crisis. While older members of the British political class preserve attitudes shaped by local autonomy and a decentralized form of the state, younger members have been shaped by a far more centralized form of the state – in some respects the most centralized in Europe. The informal means of passing on older constitutional norms have thus been uprooted, and the way in which parliamentary sovereignty poses no formal barrier to an indefinite centralization of power has been starkly exposed. The danger is that a pattern previously associated with some continental states – ruthless use of central power interspersed with occasional violent reactions from the periphery – might begin to develop in Britain, at just the moment when movement towards European union is putting constitutional issues at the top of the agenda in Europe, giving the question of relations between the centre and periphery a new urgency.

So, alas, at the moment when Europe as a whole needs constitutional inspiration, the voice of the old British constitution can scarcely be heard, nor has a new constitutional voice as yet taken its place. The voice of the old constitution was essentially a patrician voice. It provided only informal guidance about the relationship between the centre and periphery – guidance encapsulated in terms such as 'common sense' and 'decency'. While such terms may have been powerful enough and effective within a traditional political culture, they scarcely provide intelligible or coherent constitutional guidance for a new Europe.

Ironically, in view of Britain's past role in creating representative government in Europe, the British are now the least constitutionally literate people in Europe. That emerges in the frequent attacks by members of the British political class on the Maastricht and Amsterdam Treaties and proposals for European federalism. Often British critics equate 'federalism' and 'centralization'. Thus, the political tradition which once inspired Montesquieu and the American federalists today produces spokesmen who seem not to understand that federalism seeks to disperse authority and power between the centre and periphery, creating a political system which protects local autonomy in the absence of aristocracy.

The attitudes and habits which led the British to create a representative form of government were so closely tied to an aristocratic structure of society, that the weakening of that structure has put those *moeurs* at risk. Sadly for Europe, the country with the longest experience of self-government has lost its voice – or if it has a voice, it is a rather primitive one, a voice unable to translate its instincts about the importance of self-government and a climate of consent into anything like constructive constitutional proposals. In the 1960s, the former American Secretary of State Dean Acheson said that Britain had lost an empire and not yet found a new world role. The deeper tragedy today is that the loss of aristocracy has left Britain unable to speak constructively.

Yet, even in its present plight, the British political tradition implicitly continues to offer one important message to Europe. For the unwritten constitution embodies an important truth about all political systems. It is that, at least in the short run, habits and attitudes or *moeurs* are more powerful than positive laws. The unwritten British constitution created a form of the state which respected custom and opinion to a remarkable extent, a form of the state which (until it was required to provide the formal framework for a new or democratic type of society) readily responded to changing social conditions. Now it is that role which provides one of the most important justifications for representative government. Representative institutions make it possible for a society to react on itself, to identify changed circumstances or new needs and begin to address them.

The old unwritten constitution made it clear that social habits and attitudes are the bedrock of law. When positive laws depart too far from or run against such habits and attitudes, they are unlikely to prevail. That is the truth which the British recognize instinctively. And that truth informs their criticisms of over-rapid European political integration. For the British notice the way in which a culture of consent, which is the legacy of self-government in Britain, leads to the conscientious observance of regulations emanating from Brussels, while the same regulations are often ignored or circumvented in Greece, Spain or even France – in countries where the roots of a culture of consent, like self-government itself, are more recent and fragile.

The confidence in the law which is the primary attribute of a culture of consent cannot be created overnight. And it is far easier to lose than to gain. That is the plausible heart of the British case against over-rapid construction of a federal Europe, a sudden move away from the political cultures of nation-states. The danger is that such a move will not really extend a culture of consent throughout Europe, but rather jeopardize it where it already exists. For only a fool can believe that the nations of Western Europe exhibit, with respect to the rule of law, anything like the same culture of consent.

5

Why Constitutions
are Important

Few societies are good at identifying the things they take for granted.
These are the things that structure their vision of the world, providing
them with categories which shape their experience of fact and underpin
their judgements of what is valuable. The result is that, when trying
to understand ourselves, we often miss the obvious.

This observation applies to Europe especially, I think, in the sphere
of government. We have ceased to understand what is distinctive about
the type of government invented in Europe since the later Middle Ages,
the state. Our lack of self-consciousness is betrayed by the way we use
language. For we have come to use the term 'government' as if it were
synonymous with 'state'. Yet that is far from being the case. Most
human societies have had governments radically different in character
from the European state.

The state is one type of government – a government in which
'sovereign' authority is attributed by a constitution, written or unwritten. The state was invented only relatively recently and in one part of
the world. There is nothing inevitable about it. It is not inherent in the
idea of society or a stable social order. Yet because the state as a
type of government spread so rapidly in the nineteenth and twentieth
centuries, becoming almost a universal form, it is now difficult for us
to recall what is distinctive about it. When we put on our spectacles,
we see it everywhere. And the more we see it, the less we understand
it.

Yet only if we understand what is distinctive about the state, can
we really understand the nature of the society which the state helps to
constitute, our kind of society. For that society is just as distinctive as
the state itself.

At times these things are perceived more clearly by non-Western observers. For there has been a powerful, if inchoate, reaction to the state as a political form in many non-Western societies. In such societies, creating a 'state' is perceived to be part of the process of Westernization. Non-Western peoples therefore sense that the state is a threat to their traditional cultures, to inherited moral beliefs and social practices. Nor are they wrong.

Why do non-Western societies feel uncomfortable with the state, even while adopting it? There is a good reason. The state is not a morally neutral mechanism, a mere machine. The idea of the state carries within it a 'deep' value which has not been shared by all human societies – far from it. The state carries within it a value which developed in the West and became the fulcrum of that modernity which the West has exported to other parts of the world. That value is equality, belief in the equal moral worth of humans. The state's connection with the value of equality may not be obvious at first glance. None the less, that connection is what makes the state distinctive as a form of government. It is that connection which also accounts for the kind of society constituted by the state, what we in Europe have come to call a 'civil society'.

Understanding the connection between the state and the value of equality is important not just for non-Western societies in the process of creating new states. It is also important for those reforming existing Western states or trying to create a new federal state in Europe. So our task in assessing the possible advantages and disadvantages of creating a federal Europe is threefold. First, we have to be clear about how the state differs from other forms of government. Secondly, we have to understand how the state carries in its wake a particular model of society, an egalitarian model. And, thirdly, we have to identify what advantages, if any, a federal constitution might have for civil society in Europe – as compared to a Europe of nation-states. Is federalism likely to serve the cause of justice, human liberty and dignity more successfully than a Europe of nation-states? At the end of the day, that is what matters.

Undoubtedly, the value of equality is not promoted to the same extent by all forms of the state. That is why the constitutions of states are so important. They can organize public power either so as to maximize the impact of the value of equality 'carried' by the state or to minimize its impact.

First, then, we must understand how the state is connected to the value of equality. The crucial attribute of the state has traditionally been expressed in terms of its 'sovereignty'. The concept of sovereignty developed as the state emerged in Europe at the beginning of the modern era, from the fifteenth century to the seventeenth century. Just what was being claimed, when it was asserted that states and their rulers possessed a sovereign authority? It was being claimed that all members of society were *equally* subject to the sovereign's authority. The legal supremacy of the sovereign ruler or agency meant that there were no customs or historical claims which could legitimately limit the sovereign's right to make new law. Law simply was the sovereign's command, and that command touched, at least potentially, *everyone*. Thus, the sovereign did not need to ask parents' consent to govern their children, in contrast to societies where rulers governed families through the paterfamilias. Nor did the sovereign have to regard the long-established privileges of corporations or estates of the realm – even of the Church – as beyond correction.

So the very idea of the state involves equal subjection to a supreme law-making authority or power – the sovereign. To speak of a 'state' is to assume an underlying equality of status for its subjects, an equality of status antecedent to the definition of specific, enforceable rights and duties. For that reason the concept of state sovereignty, when it develops in any society, introduces a kind of blank sheet. For once there is a sovereign agency or state, inherited practices and claims no longer have the status of law unless they are sanctioned by the sovereign – something which privileged bodies in Europe such as the French *parlements* long contested. There is no logical limit, therefore, to the degree of innovation in a society with a state (though there may be severe practical limits), provided only that it does not contradict the criterion of equal sub-mission which defines the sovereign's relations with subjects.

Today that implicit connection between the concept of the state and the idea of equality is important in understanding the reactions against modernism in many non-Western societies. Arguably, the concept of the state is now by far the most potent means of transmitting individual-ist values outside the West. For what is involved in building a 'state'?

The mere taking-over of 'the state' as a political form carries with it values which traditionalists in other countries may sense (even if they cannot articulate their misgivings) are deeply subversive of their customary social order and religion. But the problem facing them is how to express their objections without falling back on the very terms or concepts which are, in fact, carriers of the values they seek to oppose.

Thus, it might be argued that terms like 'Islamic state' or 'Islamic democracy' are essentially confused in so far as they mix incompatible ideas. On the one hand, 'Islamic' may stand for a rejection of the distinction between law and custom, and an appeal for a return to a customary society, in other words a rejection of the state as such. On the other hand, by relying on terms like 'state' or 'democracy', traditionalists carry into their own rhetoric egalitarian or individualist values which they ostensibly deplore, and probably do in fact deplore as Western or Christian. Thus, the dilemma facing such traditionalists is that they themselves can no longer conceive of government on any model other than the state. Yet that model carries with it the very individualist values which they wish to oppose. The state becomes a sort of Trojan Horse, bringing with it egalitarian or individualist implications which need not be explicit in the policy it pursues.

The most extraordinary example of that development in the last half century has been India since it gained independence – a society which has combined an ancient caste system, founded on the assumption of radical inequality, with a modern state proclaiming equality before the law. The impact of such utterly contradictory moral messages on a caste such as the Untouchables cannot fail to have been profoundly disturbing. To the extent that caste labels have continued to be the crucial sources of personal identity in India, Indian society may be said to have been suffering from a kind of collective schizophrenia.

Evidently the state's sovereignty has a remarkable moral consequence. No subject of the state has an intrinsic obligation to obey another subject as such. The right to command or duty to obey is no longer written into separate hereditary or customary roles. Particular social roles are henceforth circumscribed by the unlimited legal right of the state, by equal subjection to the sovereign. In that way the notion of sovereignty becomes the fulcrum of individual identity. So we fool ourselves when we regard the state as something completely external to ourselves, as something 'out there'. The norms of the state are within us, whenever we understand ourselves as enjoying an equal civil standing or status. That gives the state a basic role in the socializing process – indeed, the basis for the social role of the individual is provided by the state through the doctrine of its sovereignty. That has been the 'genius' of the European state, its distinctive historical achievement.

The emergence of the doctrine of state sovereignty introduced a new model of society in Europe, carrying with it something we now take for granted, an egalitarian model of society – society understood as a collection of individuals. The state's sovereignty over individuals involved the emergence of what can be called a primary role shared equally by all, while other social roles – whether that of father, government official or hairdresser – become secondary in relation to that primary role. To this primary role an indefinite number of other social roles may or may not be added, as the attributes of a subject. But they do not define the subject. Thus, being a father, a Roman Catholic, a doctor or a debtor may be added to (or subtracted from) an individual's identity, but the individual remains. *In a society without a state that is not true.* Then there is no primary or meta-role conferred by a sovereign agency, and so the descriptions conferred by particular roles are not mediated by a status or role shared equally by all.

Even the identity conferred by a common language or tribal bond is different from that conferred by equal subjection to a sovereign. A language or tribal bond enables social agents to distinguish themselves from *outsiders*, but it does not necessarily confer any fundamental or underlying equality of status *within* the group – so that being a Hausa or speaking Hindi does not entail that an agent is an individual, whereas (in the twenty-first-century world of nation-states) being a Nigerian or an Indian does. It is this separation of a primary role or status from secondary roles which the idea of state sovereignty brings about. For that reason personal identity under nation-states, shaped by the distinction between primary and secondary roles, is a more complicated matter than it was in tribal, clannish or feudal societies, where the unequal identities assigned at birth meant that there was no social description which all shared equally.

This rather abstract point can be illustrated from history. It is commonplace to assign the flowering of European individualism to the end of the Middle Ages. We feel we can readily understand Erasmus, Luther and Montaigne, entering into their thoughts and feelings, in a way that we cannot really understand St Louis, Richard the Lionheart or St Francis. But the connection between that sudden flowering of European individualism and the development of the sovereign state is not usually recognized. It needs to be, however. For the presence or absence of the sovereign state makes a crucial difference to the sources of personal identity. In the absence of the state, the sources of identity can be bewilderingly various. But they need not introduce any underlying equality of status, whereas the sovereign state does just that. Thus, it is probably no accident that the humanity of Shakespeare's writings – writings which probe a common nature lurking under different social roles – became possible just as the state was consolidating its claim to sovereignty.

To be even clearer about this, we might perform a thought-experiment. Let us imagine a room filled with a variety of historical types – say, an ancient Egyptian slave, an Untouchable from India, an Ashanti tribesman, a medieval European serf and a nineteenth-century Frenchman. Just who are they in their own eyes? What terms do they fall back upon, when pressed, to identify the bedrock of their identities? In the cases of the slave, the Untouchable and the tribesman, all that each can say finally is that he is a slave, an Untouchable or an Ashanti. The question of justifying that social status does not arise. Their social descriptions are, so to speak, self-justifying. At first glance that also seems true of the medieval European serf. But only at first glance. For the serf might also describe himself as having a soul, that is, as being a child of God. Here an appeal to an underlying equality of status makes its appearance. Yet the equality conferred applies only to the soul, to the 'other world' rather than this world. At best what we meet here is the individual as a moral status or role. It is not yet a social status or role because there is no institution like the state available to create and protect the rights which sustain the role of the individual. With the nineteenth-century Frenchman, however, that institution has appeared. He can claim to be a French citizen, with a formally equal social standing guaranteed by the state.

So the individual becomes the organizing or primary role in any society constituted by a state. Or, to put it another way, built into the very idea of the state is a criterion which limits the range of social structure. That is how the state carries in its wake an egalitarian or individualist model of society. It is important to notice this if we are to use the terms 'state' and 'individual' with any real understanding. Only then can we appreciate that the terms are strictly interdependent. It is that interdependence which underlay the flourishing of European individualism at the end of the Middle Ages.

This also helps to explain something which has long puzzled political philosophers. It helps to explain why individuals feel a kind of prima-facie or instinctive obligation to a state they live under, even when the constitution of that state is less than democratic – indeed, even if that state has not yet converted the equal subjection instituted by sovereignty into its first legitimate offspring, the principle of equality before the law.

Why should you or I acknowledge any obligation to obey the state? The classic responses to that question have derived the obligation to obey the state either from its role in creating and protecting a range of basic human rights or from its role in promoting utility or welfare, in maximizing the satisfaction of wants. But such arguments never quite seem to get to the bottom of the matter. They fail to identify the role of the state in founding the identity of individuals and hence do not seize what might be called the state's a priori claim to authority over the individual – a claim which has a presumptive plausibility that goes even deeper than the philosopher Hobbes's identification of the state's role in protecting us, in creating peace and order, as the basis of its claim on our obedience.

Of course this deep connection between the individual as a social role and the state as a form of government does not mean that individuals are obligated to obey positive or state-made laws, whatever their content. Nor should it be understood as preventing individuals from forming their own judgements about the validity of different forms of the state, the advantages and disadvantages of various constitutional arrangements.

The best illustration of my point is South Africa, when the apartheid regime was still in place. The difficulty of then assessing the South African state's legitimacy derived from the fact that its claim to sovereignty – the claim, in other words, to equal subjection – was not matched by the stipulation of equality before the law. That pairing is so usual in the modern world that it was bewildering to see the two separated in the case of South Africa. And it led, not surprisingly, to quasi-semantic disputes about whether South Africa *really* was a state and whether any of its laws or acts had a claim on the alleged subjects' obligation.

Something analogous can be seen in an earlier example, that of pre-Revolutionary France. During the last century of the *ancien régime* the French nobility no longer contested the sovereign right of the Crown – in principle, the King was acknowledged as the source of all positive rights and duties. But, at the same time the nobility still clung to an older notion of their own privileges as indefeasible or prescriptive. That notion, after all, helped to constitute them as a caste. They could hardly abandon it without ceasing to exist as such. But the incompatibility between prescription and the new notion of rights as generally applicable was felt even when it was not acknowledged. The result was an ideological erosion during which the nobility began to see their traditional rights as mere privileges, happy accidents rather than something justified by Natural Law or limiting the King's sovereign right. That ideological incoherence – which resulted from the individualist presuppositions of the idea of the state being increasingly felt – almost certainly contributed to the collapse of the *ancien régime* and the final disappearance of a caste society in France.

So the state cannot be combined with just any social structure. Rather, state sovereignty introduces an egalitarian or individualist model of society. Its presuppositions foster the idea of what we have come to call a 'civil society'. For what is fundamental to the idea of a civil society? It is that the equality of status attributed by states to their subjects creates, at least potentially, a sphere of individual liberty or choice, a private sphere of action. The reason should now be obvious. Because no one is born any longer with an intrinsic obligation to obey another, any society constituted by a state has a liberty potential. The beliefs and practices associated with the state provide the foundation for separating a public sphere from a private sphere, with the latter defined as a sphere in which choice both can and should govern action.

Yet there is another way in which the state sustains the social role of the individual. That is by means of a distinction between types of social rules, which follows necessarily from the emergence of a sovereign power. When sovereignty is attributed to some agency in society, it follows that there is a difference between positive laws – the commands or rules laid down by the sovereign – and other social rules or customs. Those rules which issue from the sovereign and are enforced by its agents (e.g., the killing of swans is prohibited) are obligatory in a way that other social rules or customs (e.g., men should stand when a woman enters the room) are not. In consequence, it is no longer true that all social rules have the same status. Some are enforced by public power, while others are not (although public opinion or religious belief may commend the latter).

If the law is silent, there can be no legal obligation on anyone to do something. For many Muslims in Europe, wearing a veil in public may still seem the only 'decent' thing for women to do. But in the absence of statute or positive law, such a custom cannot be legitimately enforced or claim legal status in a society with a state. Hence, outside positive law there is an important class of social rules and practices to which the state is, at least formally, indifferent. That contrast is the ultimate source of the distinction between public and private spheres. The notion that there is a private sphere, a sphere in which personal choice, whim or conscience have their play, would have been inconceivable and would have had no function in a society without a state, where all rules were customary – where all had the same status and were backed by the same kind of sanction. In societies without a state, there can be no formal separation between public and private spheres, no gap between the state and civil society. In such societies there can only be one sphere, because there is no basis in institutions or ideas for distinguishing between publicly enforced rules and rules which are, from the standpoint of the state, discretionary. Consequently, the self in such societies is not divided in a way that it is in any society with a state.

Nor is that the only consequence for human identity. The possibility of endless legal innovation in a society, introduced by the postulate of sovereignty, helps to create and sustain, in turn, the idea of individual autonomy, the idea that the individual can free himself or herself from the past and, within limits, start afresh. Again, Hobbes's blank sheet or *tabula rasa* – that break with inherited rules and roles (even if only a logical break), in order to confer unlimited legal right on a sovereign agency – can be seen as the institutional correlative of a change in the self's relationship with its own roles. For the right to legislate for everyone entails and helps to create a society in which the self sees itself in a newly abstract way, as distinct from any particular social roles it may in fact assume.

Even Descartes' famous formula – 'I think, therefore I am' – could be seen as symptomatic of the impact of the state on personal identity. That change in the self's relationship with its own roles marks the birth of the will in a peculiarly modern sense – the sense in which the potentialities of the self can never be exhausted in the actual, leaving an abstract 'I' over and above social structure. Here the analogy with the sovereign is very striking. In modern moral philosophy the individual is often deemed to be 'sovereign' in moral authority. Though not strictly entailed by the idea of state sovereignty, the idea of individual freedom draws plausibility from it.

Other historical evidence bears that out. In Europe, 'freedom' ceased to describe a particular social rank or status and became a moral principle during the period which saw the emergence of the state. And that is not surprising. Freedom would have had little role as a general principle in a society in which status was assigned at birth, a society in which no fundamental equality of status (or human nature) was acknowledged – except perhaps by the Church, custodian of the interests of the other world. It is possible to draw a further distinction, with respect to the state and social roles, between early modern society in Europe and society during the last two centuries. In the earlier period, the number of social roles was still very confined. Limited division of labour and the survival of feudal status differences, carried forward into the post-feudal period by property and education, at first restricted the impact of 'equal submission'. Even if people no longer had a legally fixed social status, they none the less occupied, *de facto*, clearly defined positions in a social hierarchy. The range of shared ('human') attributes was still minimal – though the appearance of Protestantism, which relied upon a principle of equality through its emphasis on the rights of conscience or private judgement, suggests how important and subversive even that minimal range could be.

In any case, since the nineteenth century the rapid multiplication of social roles has greatly reinforced the sense of an underlying equality of status. The increasing social division of labour, itself made possible by the structure of individual rights created by the state, has meant that people take on an ever larger number of roles. That, in turn, encourages and indeed requires the individual to see himself or herself as essentially a role-bearer – that is, in a newly abstract way – rather than merely as *being* one specialized role. The ability to take on and shed roles grows apace. Thus, the individual as a type of social role has developed from its merely formal basis in 'equal subjection' and become the outstanding social fact in Europe.

Clearly, the emergence of the state dramatically alters social agents' relationships with their own roles. It introduces a point outside themselves by which to judge the particular sets of rights and duties which define their various roles. In a society without a state – a society in which privileges and duties are assigned by custom, by the inherited ways of the group or culture – no such external point of reference exists. In such a society there are no individuals in the strict sense of the word. That is because there is no institutional framework which social agents can invoke in order to claim or defend an equal status.

Thus, the individualizing of society and the growth of the state are necessarily connected. They are two aspects of the same process of change. The equal subjection to a sovereign power which enables individuals to identify themselves *as such* is logically prior to, and historically preceded, the elaboration of basic civil liberties, the structure of fundamental rights which confirms and extends the 'individual' as a social role. But it is that structure of fundamental rights which turns the proto-liberalism introduced by the state into a real or substantial liberalism. In the history of early modern European political thought, that is the transition from Hobbes's *Leviathan* (1651) to Locke's *Two Treatises on Government* (1690).

Of course the laws of the state can ratify or create forms of inequality – say, unequal treatment of races or sexes – which may seem to run against any connection (even implicit) between the state and the idea of equal liberty. But that break is more apparent than real. For the mere existence of a centralized agency to which *all* are understood as *equally* subject sustains an awareness in subjects that there is at least one level at which they share an attribute, even if it is only equal subjection to the same authority. That shared attribute, and the sense of a common identity as individuals which it sustains, can then become the basis for insisting on extending the range of shared attributes, in a way that would be inconceivable in a society in which social roles and rights had their only source in custom. Historically, indeed, that has been the chief role of the European state. It has made possible what might be called 'the progress of equality'.

The deep connection between the state as a political form and the individual as an organizing social role also throws light on the phenomenon of nationalism. As we saw in an earlier chapter, Montesquieu supposed that the nation-states of Western Europe could only remain 'moderate' regimes and avoid tyranny if they fostered the 'honour' attached to unequal ranks in an aristocratic social organization. He supposed that the equality and 'virtue' of citizenship associated with the ancient city-state was not an option for modern Europe, while the equality of 'fear' which governed empires subject to despotic government was wholly undesirable. What Montesquieu did not understand was that the nation-state, through the equal status it introduces by way of state sovereignty, clears the ground for a new form of honour, what can be called democratic honour. Democratic honour is the morally acceptable content of nationalism. It asserts the moral importance of equal status in a society and interprets that equality as requiring a form of the state which allows individuals to feel equally respected and empowered.

The desire to affirm one's equal standing as the citizen of a nation-state – to be a citizen *without* being the member of a privileged caste, in the fashion of ancient citizens – creates a new form of honour, a form of honour which Montesquieu, clinging to the prejudices of aristocracy, did not recognize. Yet this form of honour is extraordinarily important today in understanding the aspirations of some regional and ethnic groups lacking statehood – a wish to tie together more closely their group identity and state sovereignty. For when clannish or feudal classifications have weakened, a formal sanction for equality of status is needed if ethnic and linguistic solidarities are not to become destructive. It is that formal sanction which the state as an institution can alone provide. Britain's Mrs Thatcher is famous for having insisted that 'there is no such thing as society', there are only individuals. But, in truth, there is no such thing as the individual – understood as a *public and enforceable* social status or role – without a state.

It should never be forgotten how difficult the creation of states can be. The creation of states is not something which can be decided upon at a moment's notice and enacted with confidence that it will take root. The difficulty which post-colonial African 'states' have experienced in overcoming tribalism and creating national identities by way of the claim of state sovereignty provides a vivid illustration. Even now being a Kenyan, for example, seems to mean little when compared to being a Kikuyu. Tribalism differs from nationalism because it does not presuppose anything like equal status within the group. As we have seen, tribal identities provide a means of exclusion and identifying others – of separating us from them. Tribal identities provide an identity, but not necessarily an equal status for their members. Modern nationalism, by contrast, is parasitic on the idea of the state, on the equality of status which the state introduces. Regions and ethnic groups become embittered if they feel that their members are not equally respected and empowered. Thus, offending national pride also involves offending an individual's dignity or self-respect.

The difficulty which, historically, some European nation-states have encountered in trying to integrate regional and ethnic identities under the umbrella of a common 'sovereignty' should provide a salutary warning against underestimating the potential of regional and ethnic resentments. In particular, the survival of feelings of inferiority and humiliation towards a group or region which is perceived as benefiting more from the process of state formation has no doubt long contributed to the strength of separatist sentiment in Catalonia, Corsica and Scotland. Separatist sentiment develops when it is felt that the equality of status deriving from membership of a state is more formal than real.

If the management of democratic honour has proved so difficult for some of the oldest and most successful nation-states in Europe, how much more powerful could that motive become if the creation of a federal state in Europe were to be accompanied by a new sense of victimization in any existing nationalities. For then the claim of legitimacy founded on the state's role in underpinning individual identity might begin to come apart – that is, the legal structure which formally guarantees civil equality would be perceived instead to be an instrument of inequality, because it was interpreted as serving the interests of a 'privileged' region or ethnic group.

That risk is real enough in smaller federal states, as the example of Belgium suggests. But it would greatly increase if Europe as a whole develops into a federal state. It would be very unwise of those making the case for European federalism to deny or even minimize that risk. Rather, they must seek to avert it. That is another reason why constitutional forms become so important.

What does this brief excursion into the history of nationalism suggest? It suggests that a written constitution can and ought to make a crucial contribution to self-awareness in any society with a state. A written constitution can bring to the surface and formalize the state's role in creating a society of individuals, drawing attention to the way the state fosters a value in all who are subject to it, the value of a fundamental or 'moral' equality. It is only if we understand what the state does for us in providing a practical foundation for the role of the individual, that we can move on to explore what else the state ought to do for us. That is what evaluating different constitutional forms involves.

How does federalism fit into this larger picture? At first glance federalism might seem the most obvious and 'natural' form of the state, in so far as its defining characteristic is the resolve to leave to each locality and region enough authority and power to manage its own affairs, while carrying to the centre only enough authority and power to deal with matters of general interest. In fact, the federal form – which looks so natural – is the most complex and demanding form of government. It requires considerable moral and intellectual development in a people attempting to govern itself in such a way. Why is that? It is because federalism seeks to minimize the need for coercive power and to maximize a willing obedience to laws, which are perceived as protecting local and regional as well as national interests.

The point was made over 170 years ago by the French historian and political thinker, François Guizot. Guizot argued that federalism requires an unusually well-educated and moral population, if it is to succeed. For the different spheres of authority created by a federal system place exacting demands on ideas and habits. Indeed, the complexity of such a system can only be sustained if it is matched by a new complexity of personal identity. Just as a society with a state introduces a primary role in relation to which all other social roles become secondary, so a federal system sub-divides this primary role. The citizen's role acquires local and regional as well as national dimensions, different sets of public rights and duties. That complexity is further increased if the whole system is constrained by constitutionally entrenched rights. Evidently, under federalism, conflicts of jurisdiction are an ever-present possibility.

It follows that public loyalties are less simple in a federal than in a unitary state. There are different claims on deliberation and action which have constantly to be balanced and adjusted. The disadvantage is that there may sometimes be temporary and partial inconsistencies in legal obligation, resulting from the different spheres of authority created by federalism and the slowness of integrating outcomes into a single legal order. It is for that reason that some form of judicial review is inescapable in a federal system, given the permanent threat of conflicts of jurisdiction opened up by such a system.

Even if such conflicts are considered a drawback of federal systems, federalism has an advantage which can more than outweigh it. That is its effect on the citizens' sense of justice or equity. For federal systems can, at best, foster a more complex and adequate sense of justice. That was another of Tocqueville's important discoveries in America. He found that one of the benefits of formally recognizing and protecting regional and local autonomy within a federal system was to encourage the emergence of a new theory of interests.

In Europe, when Tocqueville wrote, there were two competing theories of interests – one, dominated by utilitarianism, saw the public interest as simply an aggregation of individual interests, while the other, associated with the writings of Rousseau, postulated an objective public interest, knowable apart from the preferences of individuals. Each of these theories fed on the other. Both ignored the range of interests which were intermediate between the individual and the association of all, the state. By contrast, Tocqueville used his account of American federalism to suggest the need for a theory of concentric interests, interests which fanned out from the individual but did not ignore groups and areas less inclusive than the whole or the state. Such a theory of concentric interests remedied a weakness of the individualist or proto-liberal model of society which had emerged in seventeenth-century Europe.

The advantage of conceiving interests as a series of concentric circles – on the model of the American township, county and states – was that it helped to create a threshold sense of justice in a population, a sense of justice which worked against theories appealing only to aggregated individual claims or the reified claims of all. It provided citizens with a list of important interests, a kind of check-list, which ought to be considered in matters of public policy. It was remarkable proof of the way a political system can help to educate and moralize its members, making them sensitive to the claims of justice. Taken together, the constitutional arrangements embodied in American federalism encouraged a conception of interests which has since been called pluralist. Thus, by influencing the way in which we conceive of our own interests, and by providing a kind of chart or road map which organizes a particular social landscape, constitutions enter into our very souls. They help us to frame intentions and to act.

The more our conception of justice mirrors and is mirrored by the form of the state, the more that state acquires a legitimacy in our eyes. Then the basic procedures of the state are able to sustain a consent in us which can withstand the sometimes fierce strains on our loyalty when public policies adopted damage our interests or violate our sense of equity. Paradoxically, giving a constitutional basis to regional identities and interests, in the fashion of federalism, strengthens a sense of justice by making it easier for citizens to distinguish between the justice of a range of public decision-making procedures and particular policy outcomes. That confidence in the justice of public procedures is, in turn, probably the single greatest guarantee of the durability of free institutions, of the ability of a people to govern itself.

In making these claims for the importance of a written constitution, I do not think I am being naïve. Certainly I do not suppose that citizens often consult such documents or have more than a vague awareness of most features of the constitutions they are subject to. But that is not necessary for my argument. As we have seen, there are some respects in which liberal constitutions have a fundamental impact on citizens' lives and mark out borders on the maps of their personal identity. Constitutions have this potential of creating provinces in the mind.

There are three ways especially in which a constitution, whether unitary or federal, creates such provinces in the mind – through the formal separation of executive, legislative and judicial powers, through the relations it lays down between the centre and periphery of society, and, finally, by defining and seeking to protect a range of fundamental rights.

The separation of powers is important not just because it clarifies different functions of government – separating the making of rules from their application or administration, for example – but also because it affirms the importance of putting different powers into different hands. Above all, it works against the view of government as something monolithic, a single structure of power. It makes clear that legal uniformity does not require the fusion of powers. No doubt the separation of powers can create problems for a political system. Critics have argued, for example, that it leads to almost permanent confrontation between the American presidency and the Congress. Yet the impression of legitimate conflict, conflict authorized by the political system itself, may be no bad thing to leave in the minds of a people. By contrast, one of the serious weaknesses of the British political system as it has developed since the eighteenth century (when, ironically, it inspired Montesquieu's theory of the separation of powers) is that its cumulative fusion of powers does not serve to educate the public in constitutional proprieties. Indeed, by giving the executive control of the legislature (assuming a parliamentary majority), it often reduces interest in the process of government itself, making outcomes seem foregone conclusions.

By contrast, the relationship between centre and periphery laid down by a constitution can be designed to introduce delays and uncertainty into a political system. Even in a unitary system, popular election of the officers of local and regional government, responsible before the courts and to their electors, works against the idea that these officers are mere agents of central government and obliged to carry out its dictates. Degrees of local and regional autonomy deriving from popular election introduce at least short-term limits on the ability of a central government to impose its will everywhere and at once.

A federal system introduces far more formidable constraints on a central government. Federalism gives provinces or states their own portion of sovereignty, a sphere of authority which cannot be abrogated or altered unilaterally by central government. For the authority of both centre and periphery have a constitutional foundation – that is, sovereignty is divided between them. A 'fundamental law' divides law-making and law-enforcing rights between the centre and the periphery. Thus, in a federal system the obstacles to central government acting in certain spheres may be almost permanent, provided that public opinion is not so aroused and powerful that an amending procedure opens the way to constitutional modifications. Federalism greatly strengthens an awareness of the possibilities of legitimate conflict within a political system.

This advantage of a federal over a unitary system can be illustrated by recent British history. The British Government has faced no serious legal obstacles when it chose to make radical changes in the structure of local government. In the 1970s and 1980s successive British Governments not only reconstructed the boundaries of local government out of recognition, but also virtually deprived local government of its own sources of revenue – reducing its autonomy to a bare minimum. This high-handed treatment of local government illustrates the way a unitary system, resting on parliamentary sovereignty, imposes no formal limit on a government's ability to innovate, even if it means suddenly uprooting long-standing local loyalties and regional identities. The blank sheet introduced by the idea of sovereignty, if unconstrained by a written constitution which formally disperses legal authority, presents local and regional agencies of government as things at the disposal of central power, almost as playthings.

Yet, of the three ways in which a constitutional order can significantly impinge on everyday life, none is so potent as the definition and protection of fundamental rights. Judicial review gives the courts a role which can put them at odds with popularly elected assemblies and executives. At first glance such a role for the courts seems profoundly undemocratic, giving a role in the formulation of public policy to unelected judges. But that first glance should be distrusted. Judicial review, as Tocqueville noticed in the 1830s, is the most powerful weapon available in the defence of liberal democracy against a populist form of democracy, the unadulterated majority principle.

The operation of judicial review in the United States has created mixed feelings in Europe. The inflation of rights language, which I have argued should be seen chiefly as a result of the influence of economics and utilitarian philosophy, has sometimes been interpreted as the inevitable result of giving judges an inappropriate kind of power, a power which, so to speak, removes their inhibitions. But I think that is far from being the case. To a surprising extent, American judges have been reluctant entrants into policy-making, but have been forced by some other characteristics of the US political system – in particular, by the reluctance of the elected branches of government to settle particularly controversial public issues such as abortion.

Two things should be noticed about American-style judicial review. One is its larger influence on the political culture of the country. That culture is often described as rights-based. But what does that mean? It does not mean simply that rights entrenched by the constitution can be used by judges to overturn legislative or executive acts. It means that the American constitution succeeds in dramatizing its own role in the socializing process. Its contribution to the socializing process is raised to the level of self-consciousness. At times this may seem to have a disturbingly libertarian potential – as in the still widespread opposition to gun control legislation, even after massacres carried out by armed teenagers. But the other side of the coin is more important. For this is a culture which can, at best, give the disadvantaged and impoverished a sense of their own worth, and the confidence to demand justice. The sight of a semi-literate citizen of Alabama insisting on his or her constitutional rights may have its ridiculous side, but it is also a noble prospect.

It is not only noble but *prudent* for a liberal constitutional order to create such attitudes. Too often those who write about political systems seem to defend one value above all others – the value of social order or stability. But to construct a political system with only social stability in mind is to fall into a dangerous trap. Just as important as providing legitimate and peaceful means of resolving social conflicts, is the goal of providing people with the means and the incentive to express their discontents, particularly any deep sense of injustice they may feel. The semi-literate citizen of Alabama, invoking his or her constitutional rights, is surely expressing the attitude towards public authority that we ought to foster.

We want obstreperous citizens rather than submissive subjects. And we want obstreperous citizens not just because our self-respect requires it, but also because, in the long run, such citizens are far better guarantees of public order than their submissive counterparts.

An example that springs to mind is Northern Ireland. There judicial review and a rights-based political culture might have prevented the spiralling violence and long-term confrontation between Catholic and Protestant communities. How might it have made such a difference? The chief difference judicial review makes to a political system is that it distances the judicial branch from the other branches of government – from the exercise of legislative and executive power. In the public mind that distance suggests the possibility of appealing to the courts against the other branches of government, in the hope of remedying grievances which those branches – more directly influenced by majority opinion – have been unwilling or unable to remedy. Thus, if the opportunity of judicial review had been open decades ago to Northern Irish Catholics, who felt they were discriminated against in employment, housing and so forth, they might have been reconciled to the British state. In that way judicial review can have a crucial legitimating role, weakening the temptation to resort to direct action.

If entrenched rights and judicial review are to play this legitimating role, however, one informal pre-condition must first be satisfied. To understand why, we have only to look at the traditional British hostility to giving judges so much influence, a hostility noticeable especially on the left of British politics. Did that hostility spring from a deep moral objection to entrenched rights? I think not. Rather, it sprang from a strong and probably justified suspicion that the British legal class, from which nearly all judges were drawn, itself rested on too narrow and privileged a social base. It was the suspicion that entrenched rights could become a lever of social privilege that discredited any such proposal in the eyes of the British left, at least until recently.

The legal class in a democratic society must be open and be seen to be open. It must become the badge of social mobility in a society, if its role is not to nourish suspicions of anti-democratic prejudice. For, as Tocqueville observed about the American legal class, its role in the political system is quasi-aristocratic. Judicial review provides a powerful weapon constraining the operation of the majority principle, combating a crude or populist form of democracy. Judicial review can only maximize its potential, however, if legal education is easily available and entry into the legal class is perceived to be unproblematic. That is how American lawyers have continued to dominate the political system. Nothing has contributed more to the sense of opportunity in the United States than the relative ease of access to the legal profession, while becoming a lawyer is, in turn, perceived to be the means of entering many other careers. Thus, a kind of mystical fusion between the idea of fundamental rights and the prospect of social mobility has served to give American democracy its distinctively liberal form.

What are the usual complaints thrown up by social and economic change in Europe today? They are complaints about individuals being released from traditional social ties, about a new 'inhuman' scale of social organization and the unfeeling nature of market rationality, about the disastrous effects of competition and mobility on the traditional sources of social cohesion – notably, their effects on religion, the family and locality. But what, after all, did religion, the family and locality provide? They provided a framework for right conduct and comforting support for the actions deemed to be legitimate. Curiously, a rights-based liberal constitution does something strikingly analogous to that. The form it takes is of course less intimate and palpable than that of the family. Rather, it has more in common with the religious framework which so long acted as a source of identity and right conduct in the West. So once again we come upon liberal constitutionalism as a surrogate for religion, as the latest frontier of European Christianity.

6

Three Forms of the State

Since its formal inception, with the Treaty of Rome in 1957, a 'new' Europe has been constructed largely by means of an economic agenda. The language of economics has displaced the language of politics, with the construction of a single market and economic growth figuring in public discussion far more often than democratic accountability or the dispersal of power. Recently, the wish to accelerate integration has led, first to the Maastricht and Amsterdam Treaties, and more recently to the creation of a single currency and a European Central Bank, moves which – if joined by others to create a wide range of common European policies – should, at last, bring constitutional issues back into the centre of debate.

There is a great risk in the mentality such an additive process can foster. For a series of successful steps previously taken can lead participants into a kind of delusion – a delusion that the next step, whatever its nature, can also succeed. Even a step which has constitutional and cultural implications of the magnitude conjured up by a single currency and central bank 'must' succeed because the previous steps have done so. Yet that, of course, does not follow. Adding one more 'achievement' to a string of successes could simply bring the whole house down.

It is here that some of the limitations of economic thinking emerge and become dangerous. For all of its remarkable achievements, economic theory is not always alert to the institutional prerequisites of the policies it endorses or sensitive to its own cultural presuppositions. Yet it is just such underlying questions of institutions and culture which liberal constitutional thought was, at its best, devoted to exploring.

Different forms of the state are related – and necessarily so – to differ-

THREE FORMS OF THE STATE

ent types of political culture and political élites. That is, the latter have their roots in forms of the state which have created habits and attitudes that cannot be changed suddenly. Indeed, such habits and attitudes can be changed only very slowly and, if the object is to direct the course of that change, with great difficulty. Prudence, restraint and cunning are needed in any such enterprise. For it may be the case that the best course is not one that leads directly to the desired outcome, but one which leads there only indirectly. Such is the nature of human affairs.

Let us take just one example, the mobility of labour. It is a standard factor in economic argument, being cited both as a condition of greater economic integration and a single market and as a benefit of such developments. Yet does anyone seriously suppose that the mobility of labour in Western Europe will in the foreseeable future approach that of American labour? The linguistic and cultural obstacles to any such convergence on the point of labour mobility are simply too great to make such a supposition plausible. Here economic arguments can easily degenerate into mere economic rhetoric, becoming a fig-leaf which conceals what is happening or is likely to happen.

This has an important bearing on the creation of a common currency, the euro. For the creation of a common currency entails not only uniform interest rates across nations sharing the currency, but also more central control over national fiscal policies – something which was certainly not emphasized in the run-up to the introduction of the euro, but which has already led to Italy having to seek permission to relax its fiscal policy. Can Europe sustain a common currency, with uniform interest rates, when economic circumstances vary so radically between nations – between, for example, a depressed Italian economy and a booming Ireland threatened with inflation? In the United States, a common currency and uniform interest rates have been combined successfully with different regional economic circumstances for two reasons. Firstly, the mobility of American labour, made possible not least by a shared language, introduces considerable market flexibility. And, secondly, the federal government is able to use its tax and fiscal policies to redress the balance between more and less prosperous regions. Clearly, neither of these conditions obtains in Europe today – which is why at least some of the economic rhetoric associated with the creation of the euro is in danger of becoming a fig-leaf.

For the Stability Pact which preceded the creation of the euro – and is meant to govern its operation – is by no means transparent. There are, after all, only three ways in which a currency union with uniform interest rates can adjust significant regional economic differences: labour must be prepared to move in short order to other regions; labour must be prepared for real wages to rise and (especially) fall when economic circumstances warrant; or, finally, more centralized control of fiscal policy becomes unavoidable. It is the last of these three options which lurks behind the Stability Pact. For that Pact in effect points to the need for what might be called 'fiscal centralization' – a significant transfer of fiscal power from nation-states to a new central authority. Alas, the constitutional issues raised by such a transfer of power – issues concerning the *distribution* of power – are not openly addressed.

Much the same can be said about the political pieties which have accompanied the creation of a European Central Bank. For what are we told? We are told – especially by the French – that a 'stronger' central agency is needed to counterbalance the new Bank, to ensure political control and democratic accountability. The French also urge the adoption of uniform European policies in other spheres, including foreign policy, defence, taxation, policing and immigration. But exactly what institutional changes would the achievement of such uniform policies require? When placed against the background of sophisticated constitutional thought, such calls for political control and uniformity of policy ('harmonization') are at best simplistic, at worst misleading. Here it is political rhetoric that is in danger of becoming a fig-leaf which conceals what is really happening.

This is the plight of Europe today. Behind the fig-leaf provided by the rhetoric of economic and political integration is to be found a major development, the rapid accumulation of power in Brussels. Throughout the European Community, two symptoms of the growing power of Brussels are apparent. First, the major departments of government in European states are spending increasing amounts of time dealing with Brussels regulations, either real or anticipated. Second, leading European and international companies – and, to a lesser extent, trades unions – are spending increasing amounts of money to maintain a presence in Brussels, both observers and legal representatives. The reason is clear enough. These organizations recognize that in ever wider areas of public policy Brussels is prevailing. Thus, the fact that public debate has sunk into constitutional primitivism should not be allowed to obscure the fact that an important constitutional competition has been taking place in Europe, a competition between different models of the state. And the *de facto* accumulation of power in Brussels is evidence that one model is winning that competition.

We must not deceive ourselves. What is taking place in Europe at the moment is a competition between three models of the state to become the model for the European Community as a whole. These models are the French, the German and the British.

The French model is essentially a bureaucratic one, despite moves towards decentralization in France in the last decade or so. The power of the French executive has no real counterpart in other European countries, so that it was often said during the early years of the Fifth Republic that the Elysée governed through the upper echelons of the civil service, at times virtually ignoring the Prime Minister and the Cabinet, not to mention the legislature. Yet even when, during recent periods of cohabitation, executive power is shared between the President and the Prime Minister, the Constitution of the Fifth Republic gives a decisive advantage to the two-headed executive over the legislature and its committees. It is hardly too much to say that the French legislature has been neutered since 1958.

In such a centralized system there is inevitably a large arbitrary element in decision-making, an element that encourages a scramble to shape decisions at the top by interests and groups that are well-placed. Formal checks and balances and publicity play relatively little part. Thus, the crucial thing about the French model of the state is that it can be exported relatively easily – for it amounts to little more than the formalization of a centralized decision-making process, with a minimum of constraints. Power is the name of the game.

The German model of the state is at the other pole from the French. Partly inspired by American federalism, as well as by the diversity of Germany before its unification under Prussia in 1870, the German Constitution takes enormous trouble to create different spheres of authority and to protect each from the others – minimizing the risk of encroachments from the federal government, not least by means of a powerful constitutional court. For the Germans, therefore, talk of a 'federal' future means a future with strict constraints on the growth of central power and adherence to the goal of a *Rechtsstaat*, the rule of law. Authority is the name of the game.

The British model of the state differs from both of these. Apart from not being federal, and vesting sovereignty in 'the monarch in parliament', its hallmark is its informality, its reliance on precedent and custom – its common-law character, so to speak. In effect, the British model relies upon the existence of a distinct political class which implicitly agrees about the methods, if not the goals, of government. Until recent decades, it was also associated with considerable decentralization of political power – although that was always *de facto* rather than *de jure*, and, as we have seen, has proved vulnerable to centralizing pressures during the Thatcher years. But what has survived even the dangerous centralization of recent years, the virtual demise of local autonomy, is a model of government which is essentially consensual – putting a premium on mutual agreement, governed not so much by formal principles (as in the *Rechtsstaat*) but by 'common sense', that term so often used and abused in British political discourse.

In spite of its absurdities, that appeal to common sense does reveal something about the consensual character of this idiosyncratic political system, a form of the state in which custom is the name of the game. However, today that idiosyncratic form of the British state has become the problem. For it is a form of the state that cannot be exported. It is too embedded in a particular social context to make export possible. It relies on instincts, intimations and social pressures which cannot be created *ex nihilo*.

Yet the government of the United Kingdom and the British political class have not really faced up to this problem in their dealings with Europe. In their public statements, they go on relying on that British model as if it could be exported – and in doing so they are creating a danger that the least morally acceptable form of the state is the form that will prevail in the European Community.

The model that the British government has been holding up to Europe for emulation – with its emphasis on *ad hoc* development – suffers from a serious lack of clarity. But that is a key to the fact that it is a model inspired by the British state in its traditional form, a form which does not inspire clear constitutional ideas. The recent appeal to the principle of 'subsidiarity' to combat the centralizing of power in Europe perfectly illustrates this. Warmly welcomed by the British Government as a weapon against the pretensions of the Brussels Commission, the appeal to subsidiarity resembles nothing so much as the informal decentralization which long accompanied parliamentary sovereignty in Britain – an alliance of central authority and local autonomy which was dependent on manners or habits for the allocation of responsibilities between the centre and the periphery.

But 'consent' in that traditional British form cannot now provide any adequate guidance for the construction of the European Union. All that can be said about it is that as a model for emulation, it requires more than mere economic association but less than federalism. Apart from that, it remains guesswork. But for Britain to offer guesswork at this stage in the construction of Europe is extremely dangerous, for it is often accompanied by strong British attacks on the goal of a federal Europe, the goal which has long inspired democrats in Germany and smaller countries such as The Netherlands. In that sense, the reliance on the radically unclear British model of the state has been joined to rejection of the German federal model of the state for European construction.

What, then, remains? It is the French model, with its in-built predilection for power rather than authority. And that, of course, is precisely what lies behind the Maastricht and Amsterdam Treaties and recent pressures to move ahead rapidly along their lines towards political integration. These developments amount to projecting something like the French state on to the rest of Europe.

Let me say at once that I do not intend to suggest a conspiracy by the French. Rather, it is a matter of habit and attitude induced by the powerful administrative machine at the disposal of the French élite. When the French executive has decided that it wants something, it gets its way more often and more easily than is the case with the executives in most European states. Examples of this are legion – some are matters of great moment, others perhaps hardly more than matters of vanity. In the latter category should probably fall the extraordinarily ambitious projects which successive Presidents have adopted under the Fifth Republic to commemorate their own terms of office – projects such as the Pompidou Centre, the Louvre Pyramid, and most recently, Mitterrand's grandiose National Library. When the French executive has decided upon such a project, costs, planning permission and private rights suddenly seem hardly to matter. Such obstacles are rapidly overridden, and the project is carried through in a time-scale which must be the envy of other governments – or at least of their executive branches!

A far more serious example of French executive power is the way France moved ahead to provide itself with nuclear power after the first oil crisis of 1973. No environmental lobby or scientific doubt was allowed seriously to interrupt or delay the process. Within a relatively few years France was deriving most of its power supply from such nuclear power stations. The contrast with the serious obstacles placed by constitutional arrangements, courts' decisions, public protests and interest group manoeuvrings in countries such as Britain or the United States could hardly be greater. For example, when the British Government considered creating a new airport for London in the county of Buckingham, the opposition proved in the end too much. The project was abandoned. Delays in building new British nuclear power stations, owing to public protests and official inquiries, also turned the completion of these projects from being a matter of years into a matter of decades.

Germany's federal system can result in similar delays and abandonments. For the German states or *Länder* retain important powers and areas of competence, and the Federal Constitutional Court can intervene with decisive effect against any layer or branch of German government. Perhaps the *locus classicus* of the kinds of delay and resistance which a constitutional system can throw up against an executive project is the story of the opposition to granting landing rights in New York to the supersonic airliner, Concorde. Those groups opposing landing rights for Concorde on environmental grounds were able to take advantage of the fact that the New York Port Authority involved two states, New York and New Jersey – so they were able to act in different states' court systems, to play off the state against city authorities, before having resort to Congress or the Federal Courts. In the end their opposition was at least partially successful.

There is, of course, a price that has to be paid for such dispersals of power. The multiplication of jurisdictions, which creates the possibility of playing one off against another, inhibits and sometimes even makes impossible coherent, rapid action by a central government. The kind of concerted economic and social planning which the French state has gone in for since the Second World War, with government bringing together industry, trades unions and capital to pursue agreed targets, becomes far more difficult when public power is more dispersed than it is in France – and, in particular, when the courts can be used to constrain executive action. Anything like the French strategy for making Paris the transportation centre of Europe, constructing a TGV network with a view not just to internal transport needs but with international interests in mind, would be scarcely possible in, say, the United Kingdom. The delays and muddle associated with the British rail-link to the Channel Tunnel provide a tragicomical contrast.

So we must now ask whether it matters that something like the French model of the state may be projected on to Western Europe by way of Brussels? And the answer must be yes, it does matter.

The French model of the state is the one least likely to foster a culture of consent in Europe. The ability of a central agency to impose its will quickly, and despite widespread misgivings or against important local interests, is calculated instead to foster a culture of suspicion and cynicism – to generate a view that power is always in the hands of others (les autres), who exercise it not in the fashion of a conscientious justice of the peace trying to balance claims and carry public opinion, but rather in the fashion of a military chief who expects his orders to be obeyed. It is that bureaucratic model which has for 300 years shaped French attitudes towards the state and the exercise of public power. The popular perception has been that public power is there to be abused. Is that perception wrong? Until recently, the French state has even restricted parents' choice of first names for their children to a very short list. But, then, the forms of the tutorship (la tutelle) of the state have been legion.

One sure sign of the resulting political culture of suspicion is the way the operation of the French state has since the early nineteenth century generated a counter-tradition in France – a counter-tradition almost obsessed with the defects of a bureaucratic form of the state and insisting on the virtues of devolution. Thus, it is no accident that the threat of bureaucracy was first signalled to the modern world by French liberals, who coined the term 'centralization' because they were the first to have encountered the threat in its distinctively modern form. Nor is it an accident that nineteenth-century French liberals such as Tocqueville began to take an interest in American federalism, while their British contemporaries remained utterly confident of the superiority of their ancient constitutional order.

What Tocqueville and other decentralizers in France quickly realized was that the revolutionary tradition in France – that antithesis of representative government, properly so-called – was parasitic on a bureaucratic state. It fed off that form because the greater the ability of a remote central agency to ignore local opinion and impose its will in the short run, the greater the likelihood that accumulated discontent will boil over in the middle term. And that, of course, has been an important part of the history of France since the Revolution – with regime-threatening crises punctuating republican history, the most recent such crisis being that of 1968.

But even when a crisis is not regime-threatening, the political culture of French has been such that it has been marked by groups taking, from time to time, what they call 'direct action'. That means that when such groups have decided that the state machine is unresponsive to their claims, they feel free to ignore the law, indulging in intimidation or even violence in pursuit of their goals. On such occasions, the way the French police sometimes stand aside from, and do little to prevent, illegal action amounts almost to a ritualized recognition by the state that periodic violence is a condition of its survival in such a centralized form.

Now it is true that since 1981 there have been significant moves in the direction of decentralization in France. For more than a century republican politicians had paid lip-service to that goal, but once in office they found the levers of power too attractive to be relinquished. Since the election of Mitterrand and a Socialist majority in 1981, the first major steps towards dismantling the Napoleonic state machine have been taken, steps which have not only altered the balance in departments between the prefects, who are agents of the state, and popularly elected councils, but also given regional and local authorities greater power to tax and borrow. These reforms represent the beginnings of an institutional move away from the fabled tutorship of the state, which had once reached the idiotic point that, at least in theory, no assembly of local people could gather without first gaining permission from agents of the state.

One of the avowed aims of the decentralizers in France has been to create a new, more widely based political class in order, in turn, to foster a culture of consent and reduce the habitual, if intermittent, reliance on violence in French public life. I have no doubt that the experience of greater local and regional autonomy will, if genuinely pursued, eventually have that consequence. It has already made a very noticeable difference to the civic life of villages, cities and departments in France. Anyone observing the intense interest generated in villages by meetings of the local council or following the competition (in urban planning, architecture and other spheres) between cities such as Montpellier and Nîmes will be impressed by that difference.

But such changes in habits and attitudes take time. In the meantime, the French élite remains an essentially bureaucratic one, dominated by graduates of ENA (the National School of Administration) and self-consciously formed to be the nation's guardians. They have, as I have said, had extraordinary success in the post-war period in rebuilding the fortunes of their country – domestically, through the series of Plans, and on a European scale, through the Common Market and the European Union. For the new Europe is essentially a French design, designed at first to prevent the resurgence of German power, but becoming by and large, especially after de Gaulle's veto (in 1963) excluded Britain from membership for many years, a sphere of French hegemony. Recently, the *fait accompli* of German reunification has made the French élite both more anxious about and more determined to preserve that hegemony.

The extent to which the French state creates and sustains administrative power, at the expense of liberal constitutional arrangements designed to disperse power, can hardly be exaggerated. Recently this has been emphasized by Pierre Secret, the president of the Union of Administrators and Inspectors General of INSEE, who wrote in *Le Figaro* (18 June 1999) drawing attention to the implications of a series of scandals which have hit the public service in France.

We [civil servants] control all the wheels of the state from the Presidency of the Republic to the National Assembly, where we are in a majority, passing through a Cabinet composed for the most part of civil servants. We control also the judicial, financial, trades union and even economic powers: civil servants are at the head of public enterprises and the largest private enterprises as well.

This all-powerful position conferred upon us can only be justified by an exceptional probity in our activities, by pre-eminent human and moral qualities – those very qualities which resist selection through competitive examination – and by a constant concern to put the public service at the service of the public. Recent events and many others of lesser importance . . . reveal on the contrary that our all-powerful position has created in us feelings of impunity (for we are judged by other civil servants . . . anxious above all to protect the state and its institutions), irresponsibility, and a confusion of public and private interests.

In ever larger numbers higher civil servants wish to see the introduction of effective responsibility into their careers and their status. Many seek the advent of a 'new civil servant' who would be personally responsible, judged by his or her effective results in working for the public, and whose ambition would be to remain in public service rather than seeking as quickly as possible well-paid positions in the semi-public or private sector.

In contrast to the recent Elf scandal, discovered by chance, how many others have taken place protected by the opacity peculiar to a society dominated by civil servants? France must not remain the only country in Europe where the absolutism of the administrative state continues to reign supreme, the only one which can be considered underdeveloped with respect to democratic norms.

What is striking and worrying about the above avowal is that, instead of seeking adequate constitutional remedies, the writer hopes to overcome the defects of the French form of the state by postulating an *Ideal Civil Servant*.

So the question of what form of the state is to be imprinted on Brussels really matters. If it is the traditional French bureaucratic form, then the cause of self-government in Europe will have received a serious setback. For the form of the French state is the one which more than any other in Europe still bears the impress of seventeenth-century continental monarchy. Royal power, only precariously offset by the rule of law and secondary authorities, is still successfully reproduced by the French executive and the powerful bureaucratic machine under its control. The ethos of the republican tradition in France is itself perhaps the best testimony to the survival of a quasi-royal concentration of power. For until Charles de Gaulle managed to reconsecrate presidential power in 1958 and afterwards, distrust of executive power had been virtually the defining attribute of the French republican tradition. The French republicans' almost compulsive determination to bolster legislative power against executive power fed on memories such as Louis Napoleon's overturning the Second Republic in 1851 – though, arguably, what the history of the Third and Fourth Republics established was that, in the absence of political control provided by a strong executive, power devolved chiefly to the French bureaucratic machine, to the civil service rather than to any range of popularly elected authorities.

The natural inclination or warp of the French state is towards administrative power, whether it is subject to firm political control or not. In that way the French state is still the shadow of the French *ancien régime*, the old monarchy and its centralizing penchants. It may even be that the programme of decentralization introduced since 1981 has, whether consciously or not, led the French political élite to reassert at a supra-national level the habits and attitudes which are just beginning to be challenged in France itself by an incipient culture of decentralization.

In any case, there is little doubt that Brussels has in some respects become an appendage of Paris and of the French political élite. That is true both of policy-making and recruitment. In part, French hegemony is a result of the coincidence that the construction of Europe has taken place at the same time as the renewal of France under the Fifth Republic. The determination, born of defeat in 1940, to rebuild France and restore its 'proper' place in Europe – a determination which had already generated a series of five-year economic and social plans under the Fourth Republic – was given a new impetus after 1958. De Gaulle pursued French interests in an intransigent fashion during the 1960s, shaping the core policies of the Common Market and even imposing acceptance of a *de facto* national veto (on matters declared to be of national interest) against the rules which formally allowed for majority decisions.

The French were thus not only chiefly responsible for creating the Common Agricultural Policy (CAP), which has given France significant long-term financial advantages. They have also been extremely successful at preventing any major reform of the CAP. When early in 1999 the new Schröder Government in Germany decided to seek reform of the CAP, an atmosphere of crisis developed suddenly in Paris and the message went out to Brussels and to Bonn that the CAP was a French national interest. It was not long before the Germans, in effect, desisted. A similar story could be told about the Brussels Commission's monopolies and mergers policy. The traditional Colbertian or corporatist character of the French state – with state control of a wide range of industries and nearly fifty-five per cent of GDP passing through the hands of the state – has survived remarkably despite the neo-liberal commitments of the Brussels Commission. The French have proved highly resistant, moreover, to any international take-overs of major French banks or companies, invoking the national interest in a fashion quite foreign to, say, the British or the Dutch.

Not surprisingly, the French have also come to attach great importance to securing the most important European posts for French or French-sympathetic candidates. This emerged again recently when France sought the first presidency of the European Bank for a Frenchman, against the wishes of virtually the whole of the Community – desisting only when it was able to claim that the Dutch candidate, Wim Duisenberg, would make way in the middle of his formal term of office for the French candidate. In this matter, France's lack of compunction in asserting itself testifies to a *situation acquise* in Europe.

However, it is the history of the European Commission during the presidency of Jacques Delors, a former French civil servant, that best reveals the extent to which a French conception of Europe's interests and agenda, pursued in a style which conjured up the French state machine, led to the Maastricht and Amsterdam Treaties, to the establishment of a single currency and European Central Bank and, most recently, to pressures for further political integration – that is, the creation of uniform European positions in foreign policy, military affairs, immigration, policing and even taxation. These rapid, essentially French-inspired moves during the 1990s are testimony to the French reaction to the unnerving event of German reunification. The acceleration of European political integration is the French response to that event.

The concentration of power at the centre of Europe now proposed clearly reflects the instincts of a political élite shaped by the French form of the state. Their recent conversion to a federalist goal for Europe – something which is more than mere rhetoric for the Germans and the Dutch – does not really conceal the statist habits and attitudes of the French political class. By using Brussels and the post-Maastricht process to gain an important say in the government of Germany, the French political class has the opportunity to prolong French dominance by way of projecting the French model of the state, a bureaucratic model, on to the whole of Europe. As I have said, this is not so much a conspiracy as the natural consequence of decades of dominance in Europe. None the less, it is hardly too much to say that, in important respects, the French have been taking over Europe.

The French, after all, have an enormous advantage. They know what they want. The European Union is a French creation. The major initiatives – from Schuman's plan for a Coal and Steel Community, through the Common Agricultural Policy, to the single currency – have been French and have served French interests.

Of course, the French political élite would not, indeed perhaps *could not* acknowledge their project in the terms which I have relied upon. For one thing, to do so would create such a widespread opposition in other member states that the project would almost certainly fail. But that is not the only reason. Because French hegemony dates from the earliest years of the Common Market, the French have not had to distinguish sharply between the French national interest and the European interest. Nor is that identification of interests merely cynical. The desire to re-create France and Europe which has moved the French political class since 1945 – a desire born of bearing the brunt of three German invasions in less than a century – combines prudence and idealism in equal parts. But the upshot is that the ideas of French and European interests have become categorically fused.

The circumstantial evidence for that fusion of ideas is considerable. Apart from persistent failure to reform the Common Agricultural Policy and France's willingness to fight 'tooth and nail' to reserve major European appointments for its own nationals, perhaps the most striking evidence is to be found in France's lack of enthusiasm for enlargement of the European Union. Significant enlargement would almost certainly put paid to the degree of political integration France has been promoting latterly. The French do not admit openly to this lack of enthusiasm. But it is a fact noticed by many observers – diplomats, civil servants and journalists.

Finally, there is still another sort of evidence available – the repercussions of the French project within France itself. As we have seen, the original Gaullist conception of Europe was that of a *Europe des nations*, a Europe of nation-states joined in what would be, at best, a confederation. It was the almost traumatic experience of German reunification which led to a revision of the original Gaullist project – and to the French coming to advocate a so-called 'federalist' outcome for Europe, an outcome which none the less conjured up the unitary French state through its emphasis on centralized power and uniform policy. That revision of the French project for Europe was carried out under the Socialist presidency of Mitterrand. The election of a Gaullist President, Jacques Chirac, in 1995, at first called into question whether the new project would survive. Would France revert to championing the earlier Gaullist model for Europe? After some hesitation Chirac and his right-wing government endorsed the new project, continuing along the path that had been cleared by Mitterrand and Delors.

By no means all Gaullists are reconciled to this development, however. What we may now witness in France is a deepening fissure within the Gaullist party – a fissure which could even destroy Gaullism as it has existed since the foundation of the Fifth Republic. That would be the unintended consequence of a political culture shaped by and still closely tied to a bureaucratic model of the state. For when centralist habits and attitudes are projected on to the European stage they prove to be incompatible with a *Europe des nations* and, ultimately, with French national sovereignty. In that way, the very success of the new French project for Europe could gradually undermine support for it within France itself. The recent resurgence of nationalist opposition to the European project within sections of the Gaullist party provides important evidence that the French project is federalist in name but not in content – i.e., that the content is centralization.

Unfortunately, this French project is facilitated by a more general development in Western government – by a trend which affects all forms of the European state and which, if it is allowed to continue unchecked, threatens to subvert the whole tradition of liberal constitutional government as it has developed since the eighteenth century in the West. That trend is the undermining of the long-established distinction between foreign and domestic affairs, an undermining which is closely tied to growing economic interdependence and the dominance of economic categories in discussions of public policy.

But why does this matter? The long-established distinction between foreign and domestic affairs matters because it helps to underwrite the doctrine of the separation of powers, a doctrine which is pivotal to liberal constitutionalism. At least two powerful influences are at work undermining that distinction. One is institutional, the other intellectual. Though distinct, each has an important reinforcing effect on the other. Taken together, they give reason for concern about the future of liberal democratic government in Europe.

What I have called the 'institutional' influence has already been operating at the national level for more than half a century. The increasing involvement of government in the economy and the creation of the Welfare State have had a marked effect on the structure of European governments. The need for detailed regulation and the complexity of the measures required have thrown power away from legislatures into the hands of the executive branch of government. For civil servants or bureaucrats are better placed to acquire the information and draft measures required than are elected representatives, who can at best define legislative general principles and exercise a general oversight. Even the latter becomes extraordinarily difficult when so much legislation delegates to the bureaucracy the details of social and economic regulation, allowing civil servants to fill in an almost blank page of 'law'. Clearly, such delegated legislation, which promotes a fusion rather than the separation of powers, is a serious threat to the traditional norms of constitutional government.

Some of this erosion can be traced back to the First and Second World Wars. War is always a threat to constitutional government – that is, to the separation of powers and public scrutiny – because of the imperative need to centralize decision-making and simplify the lines of control, in order to draw rapidly on the resources of the whole nation. That effect of war is well understood. But what has not received enough public attention is the steady erosion of legislative power which has resulted from the far more complex role of government in the later twentieth century. Even the American Congress, which has struggled more successfully than most legislatures against the erosion of its power, has found its role reduced. In Britain and France, it is hardly an exaggeration to say that for the most part it is now the executive which legislates.

So much is familiar to students of government, if not to the public at large. But what is much less well understood is a development which has begun to exaggerate this trend, to exaggerate it in a way that threatens the very notion of the separation of powers. That development is the growth of a world market, the increasing interdependence of nations economically. For such interdependence has introduced a way of dealing between nations which poses a threat to constitutional government as traditionally understood.

A hundred years ago economic regulation, the regulation of the marketplace, was deemed to be essentially a national matter, the province of national or domestic legislation. As such it belonged, according to the canons of liberal constitutional thought, to a sphere which ought to be subject to the constraints of the separation of powers, checks and balances, and public scrutiny. This domestic sphere stood in contrast to the sphere of foreign and military affairs, which was recognized as largely and almost necessarily the prerogative of the executive branch of government. Liberal constitutional thought acknowledged that the need for speed and coherence in decision-making over foreign and military affairs justified granting an unusual degree of independent action or power to the executive, freeing it from the constraints otherwise imposed by constitutional safeguards and publicity. This relative independence and secrecy of executive action in foreign and military affairs was allowed in the name of the national interest.

But our conception of the national interest has changed. It has had to change. For as the global market and economic interdependence have developed, the distinction between foreign and domestic policy-making has been undermined. Matters which were once supposed to be the province of domestic policy-making are now matters which necessarily involve dealings with foreign governments. Domestic voices are no longer the only ones which need to be heard. Domestic interests are no longer the only ones consulted. And if this is already true in matters of trade, it is likely to be even more true as environmental issues come to the fore. The result is that foreign and domestic policy are increasingly hard to separate. They tend to be fused.

How, then, are these fused matters to be settled? That is the rub. For the intrusion of foreign into domestic policy has created a strong temptation to settle such matters in the fashion of foreign and military policy rather than domestic policy – that is, by falling back on executive prerogative and dispensing with the constitutional safeguards which were traditionally designed to constrain domestic legislation. The relative latitude and secrecy permitted to the executive when dealing with foreign and military affairs have insinuated themselves into what had previously been considered the domain of domestic policy-making.

The result is that democratic controls have suffered. A democratic deficit has grown. And if that is true of governments generally with respect to trade negotiations – not least in connection with GATT and its successor, the WTO – it is even more true of European governments in the process of constructing a single market. Not only have the legislatures of member states been forced to take a back seat. There has also often been a dreadful paucity of information about the background of decisions taken by the Council of Ministers and carried out by the European Commission. Anyone who has ever tried to get sensitive information from Brussels – for example, information about the *net* contributions of member states to the budget of the European Union – will recognize the problem.

These institutional developments have been reinforced by the intellectual changes already discussed, what I have called 'economism'. As the spheres of domestic and foreign policy have become intertwined, the language or idiom for discussing public policy has changed. Increasingly the language of the marketplace has driven out traditional political and constitutional language. The idiom of the economist has replaced the idiom of the statesman. The object of concern is no longer the citizen, but the consumer.

During the nineteenth century liberal constitutional thought was directed to understanding and offsetting the political consequences of a fundamental change in the structure of European society – that is, the destruction of its aristocratic or corporate character, with the growth of civil equality and social mobility. The means adopted were to disperse power by creating both formal and informal substitutes for aristocracy – substitutes such as separate powers, entrenched rights, local autonomy and voluntary associations. In this way liberal constitutionalism sought to avert the danger of an excessive concentration of power in central government resulting from the 'atomizing' or levelling of society.

Just as these older constitutional devices were designed to be 'artificial' counterweights to the centralizing of power, so it must now be the task of liberal constitutionalism to devise new means of protecting the distinction between domestic and foreign policy in order to reinforce democratic accountability in the face of economic interdependence and a global market. It will not be easy. Yet it is indispensable. For unless ways can be found to preserve and protect some such distinction, democratic liberty will be disastrously eroded by bureaucratic discretion.

At the European level, signs of that erosion are already only too clear. For four years running the Court of Auditors refused to endorse the accounts of the European Commission. But this had disturbingly little effect on the operations of the Commission. Indeed, when the Santer Commission was finally censured and brought to account in 1999, it was due more to the 'accidental' disclosures of a Dutch civil servant (risking the displeasure of his masters) than to regular formal procedures. This is not the way to create a constitutional order.

These recent institutional and intellectual trends amount to a formidable challenge to all those concerned with constitutional government, with the dispersal of power and democratic accountability. If democrats are even to begin to respond to the challenge, they must be prepared to explore at least two possible avenues of reform. One avenue should lead to a requirement that national legislatures, and especially their committees, be involved at a very early stage in the details of any proposed changes to European social and economic regulation, so that they can contribute to and learn from the negotiating process. After all, there is no need for either national executives or the European

Commission to invoke 'secrecy' in economic and social matters, as if they were matters that needed to be protected from public scrutiny in the fashion of military or national security decisions. A second avenue of reform should lead to the establishing of higher standards for public access to information about decision-making, not only within but also between national governments, especially in relation to the proceedings of the Council of Ministers and the European Commission. Such freedom of information will be required not only to protect the public from the growth of bureaucratic discretion, but also to empower legislators in their dealings with administrators, whether at home or in Brussels.

These suggestions are a mere beginning. But it is important to begin.

7

Creating an Open
Political Class

The direct election of Euro MPs is itself hardly more than a fig-leaf which fails to conceal the over-sized member of the European body – the power of the European Commission and a bureaucracy imperfectly controlled by the Council of Ministers. I am not saying that Europe has already become a super-state. But the increasingly important relations between Brussels and member states *have* worked to the advantage of bureaucratic power on both sides. As a result, democratic account-ability in Europe is in danger of becoming perfunctory. In many states the election of Euro MPs has meant simply another election added to an already over-full calendar of elections, often with abysmal turnouts. The names and personalities of Euro MPs are for the most part unknown, as are the extent of their privileges and tax-free allowances. The latter, if more widely understood, would probably contribute to just that attitude of being governed by *les autres* which a democratic political class exists to minimize.

There is, of course, no alternative to a political class or élite if any nation-state or, more obviously still, a federal Europe is to enjoy the reality of self-government. Such an élite or political class, provided that it remains open, can and should be the expression of a healthy civil society – a society in which private associations or pressure groups flourish, and in which therefore the habit of association acts as a powerful brake on state power. It is when the habit of association is weak that bureaucratic government prospers, civil servants and the state machine becoming if not the exclusive, at least the preponderant, nexus of power. Thus, when closely inspected, the modern idea of 'self-government' requires a private sector which breeds self-reliance and the habit of association – rather than dependence on state initiatives and state control.

Until the fall of communism, the regimes of Eastern Europe illustrated in an extreme way the hypertrophy of the state (alias the party) and the atrophy of private association. The only officially acknowledged élite was the party. But, in Western Europe, France under the Third and Fourth Republics represented a much less extreme form of the same pattern. When intermediate associations are weak and the state machine so powerful, private interests are always tempted to establish clientele relations with the state. They seek favours in the dark, so to speak, rather than demanding justice in the light of day.

The keystone in the arch of any vigorous civil society must be a political class or élite which has emerged in a morally acceptable way – representing the claims of talent, education and wealth as well as ambition. In the early nineteenth century French liberals began to call such an élite a 'natural' aristocracy as opposed to an aristocracy founded on birth. The notion of a natural aristocracy entails not only equality before the law but reasonable equality of opportunity – a widespread perception that it is possible to join the class which gives a lead to society. Thus, it is a mistake to suppose that a democratic society rejects élites as such. But the élites which emerge are more open and diverse, while the political class, in turn, is a compound of them. It is no longer the case that nearly all advantages are concentrated in one social class, that monopoly of advantage characteristic of aristocratic societies. In a democratic society a kind of pluralism and even fragmentation becomes the norm, a fragmentation which can, from the vantage point of earlier élitist cultures, look like mere vulgarity and normlessness.

Nor is this more open and porous pattern of élites the same as a 'bourgeois' élite. Of all European countries it was France which, in the nineteenth and twentieth centuries, was most successful in creating a bourgeois élite, an élite which resembled, in its homogeneity and self-consciousness, the aristocratic class which it succeeded. Probably that resemblance is no accident. As Tocqueville once observed, it is rather like children who, in reacting against their parents, come to resemble them closely. Formally, that bourgeois élite in France based its claims on competitive examination and merit rather than on the privilege of birth. But, in fact, the French élite drew its members largely from the upper reaches of the bourgeoisie. In its sense of cultural superiority, it resembled nothing so much as the French aristocracy of the seventeenth and eighteenth centuries – and, like its predecessor, it often gave the impression of treating the rest of society like children incapable of growing up, children who needed to be tutored for ever.

Such an impression is fatal, however, to the self-respect of any democratic society. It also brings into disrepute the role of leadership. Unfortunately, one of the ways in which liberal thinking has been coarsened by the infiltration of economic language and economic models emerges in recent discussions of leadership – or, rather, in the recent lack of careful consideration of the nature and conditions of leadership in a democratic society.

On what conditions can leaders be identified and formed – leaders who can be said to have a democratic mandate because they have reached their positions through fair competition? Such leaders ought to possess at least three virtues – viz., sensitivity to existing wants and preferences, the strength of mind to identify morally and socially desirable avenues of change, and the ability to mobilize consent through educating public opinion. These are stiff tests for democratic leadership. Evidently they turn not just on the details of electoral systems or recruitment procedures which secure something like equality of opportunity. They also turn on the quality of public conversation in a society, on the rhetorical skills of those called upon to give a lead, and on their ability to change the terms of public discourse. President Franklin Roosevelt offers perhaps the best twentieth-century example of a democratic leader who embodied these virtues – helping the American people to realize that 'fear itself' was the obstacle to combating the Great Depression of the 1930s, and that a free market system did not preclude government ('Keynesian') management of demand. Roosevelt's evident willingness to experiment, both economically and socially, helped to prevent American public opinion turning against the democratic system itself.

Whenever these virtues are in short supply, however, it is increasingly clear that the media will call the shots in advanced Western societies. But today who educates the media or brings the media to account? Doubtless the extraordinary development of the communications industry has provided society with a larger and more accurate mirror of itself, of its rapidly changing needs and wants – a mirror which can easily make the procedures of representative government seem cumbersome, perhaps even archaic and redundant. All too often, however, the chief result of media developments has been a kind of political voyeurism – an awareness of problems and discontents so various, that, far from shaping the human will or intentions, it creates instead a kind of weary bewilderment and passivity. The will sags, so to speak, after such saturation.

Yet it is precisely the object of the democratic political process to shape the will, to change personal wants and intentions in view of a wider range of public needs. That ought to be the first responsibility of any democratic political class or élite.

It is here that the limitations of the economists' view of democracy again become obvious. In fact, economic models have driven recent liberal thinking about democratic leadership into a *cul de sac*. Led by Joseph Schumpeter, a Central European economist who had experienced the upheavals caused by fascist movements in the inter-war period, some liberals have argued that a 'realistic' account of modern democracy must acknowledge that parties are the political equivalents of companies offering products – that is, of companies competing for consumer preferences. Parties are élites which can be described as democratic chiefly in the sense that they seek to win the competition for votes through the products they promote. If they promote unpopular products, they will be 'thrown out' in general elections held at regular intervals.

On Schumpeter's account the citizen and elector, now cast in the role of a consumer, has relatively little to do with the political process between elections. Between elections, serious debate and decision-making are portrayed as a domain reserved for experts. The less popular or mass participation the better, for, in the eyes of Schumpeter and his disciples, mass politics is perceived as a recipe for political extremism, for populism of the left or right. The implication of that view is, of course, to invest existing patterns of wants or preferences with a special legitimacy. Wants created through advertising are, tacitly, given a legitimacy that is denied to new wants which might be created through widespread political participation. This helps to 'cover' the process by which economic cycles are manipulated by parties or élites in the interest of their own re-election. What could be more natural in a democratic polity?

The above views are only a slightly caricatured account of the market-dominated model of democracy shaped by economists. Evidence that the caricature contains a large element of truth can be found, curiously, in the pattern of reaction against an economic interpretation of democracy which has developed recently. For this pattern is just as partial and one-sided as the view it is reacting against.

Drawing on a tradition of citizenship which goes back into early modern political thought and is associated especially with the writings of Rousseau, some have argued that the élitist model of democracy which presents political parties as companies competing for consumer preferences misses the point of democracy entirely. Democracy, they argue, is about education and civic virtue. The point of participating in the political process is to transform oneself from a consumer into a hero – from a preoccupation with private desires into a public actor, intoning a script about the common good or public weal. Now when citizens are heroes there may be no need for a distinct political class. Leadership ceases to be a virtue when all become leaders or are, at least potentially, leaders. For the expansion or improvement of the self which engagement in the political process yields should result in a reformation of the will – the formulating of intentions which can pass the only test that matters, the test of whether a policy or law serves the public weal or common good. The creation of citizens in that sense is the final goal of a democratic politics, of widespread political participation. That is why I have called this the politics of heroes in contrast to the politics of consumers.

Now this is a false and dangerous dilemma. Yet it represents the dilemma into which recent liberal thinking about democracy has fallen. If the latter account of citizens as heroes is utopian, the former account of them as mere consumers is anti-utopian. The truth is, of course, that political thinking cannot do without both utopian and anti-utopian components. Without a utopian component, political thought and discourse ceases really to make any claim on the will or on intentions – ceasing to act on the assumption of at least partial human free-will. On the other hand, political thinking which gives itself up entirely to the consideration of what ought to be the case, is always in danger of blurring the distinction between ought and is – of investing some institution or process with an inherent legitimacy which no human institution or process should ever be accorded.

We have already seen one respect in which liberal thought in the post-war period has been hamstrung by economics – resulting in an apparently unbridgeable gap between theories based on 'rights' and theories based on 'wants' or preferences, at the expense of a liberal constitutionalism which, through the dispersal of power and the fostering of citizenship, seeks at a practical level to overcome that dilemma. But we can now see that this is not the only way in which the influence of economic models has impaled liberalism on the horns of a dilemma. This has also happened latterly when liberals have taken an interest in the role of élites. Yet, just as the first dilemma does not look so intractable when approached from a practical constitutional perspective, so the second dilemma proves to be illusory when it is considered carefully.

On what conditions is it possible to have a truly democratic élite? How should democrats address the problem of leadership, the undoubted need for leaders?

Given the scale of modern social and political organization – given a market economy, an advanced division of labour and nation-states – the model of citizens as heroes, which has roots in the ancient world of small city-states, is always at risk of being hijacked by populism. A popular movement with a 'charismatic' leader is intrinsically more likely to come up with the emotive, over-simplified appeal which can be claimed to represent public virtue or the general will. Indeed, reliance on the term charismatic – which *means* gaining a hold over people through emotion rather than reasoning – has helped to discredit leadership by associating it with the darker part of the human psyche, with the development of 'irrational' mass movements. It was that prospect, as well as the habits bred by their profession, which led Schumpeter and other economists to prefer the account of the citizen as consumer to that of the citizen as hero. It is as if, to adopt a musical analogy, the only alternative available in the repertoire to the 'dangerous' operas of Richard Wagner were the comic operas of Gilbert and Sullivan.

For the scenario which casts the citizen merely as consumer *does* turn the habits of modern Western societies into music-hall simplifications. It treats people simply as role-players, and can lead to a political outcome which, if not as nauseating as fascism, takes an equally high toll of free-will and the human capacity for self-improvement. In fact, the scenario which treats citizens as consumers updates an old vision, the vision of an administered society. This is a society in which power is assumed to belong rightfully to scientists, bankers and industrialists because of their expertise and contribution to production, a society which takes its humane aspect from the goal of maximizing production in order to improve the distribution of goods and, *a fortiori*, happiness. But notice something here. The rights of the weakest – of, say, non-producers – become a matter of benevolence rather than justice. That technocratic and condescending vision of society, with roots in utilitarianism, has surfaced at regular intervals in Europe since the writings of Saint-Simon early in the nineteenth century. The danger today is that the European Union may give it a new lease of life.

It is no accident that since Saint-Simon's time this technocratic vision has been associated with the assumption that, when society is properly organized, serious political conflict can be superseded. Then, in his famous form of words, 'the government of people will give way to the administration of things'. Externality does indeed here provide the key. People, whose wants are taken as given, are treated like objects moving in space. The goal of public policy is to prevent collisions. But the trouble is that such a view neglects the shaping of human intentions – of precisely those features of human experience which are the proper stuff of political life, the subject matter for those who seek to lead and for those who have to decide whom to follow. In fact, such an enterprise puts government 'for the people' in the place of government 'by the people'.

So here we find the terrible drawback of thinking about democratic leadership in a way which either reduces it to consumers choosing between competitive élites or one which elevates it to a citizenship involving irreproachable moral conduct. The first is demeaning, while the second runs the risk of self-intoxication.

The reason why the form of the state matters, and why the state should be organized to maximize participation by citizens, is not only that such participation can change citizens' wants and intentions – lifting them from mere consumerism on to the foothills of heroism. No, there is another reason. And it is utterly down-to-earth. It is that experience of the political process beyond merely voting in elections, the experience of helping to define and make choices of public policy or applying rules of law to particular cases (in the case of jury duty), brings people into closer contact with each other and makes them more 'knowing' – better judges of the claims of those who seek to lead. Up to a point, it could be argued that radio and television have had this effect, by exposing political figures to close questioning before enormous audiences. But it is only leading politicians who are usually so exposed, politicians who have already emerged as leaders. Television, at least in its present form, does not help much in the earlier stages of selecting a political class. It does not provide the kind of filter required to sift potential leaders. Nor does it create the active citizenry able to evaluate the qualities of those who seek to lead as well as being in a position to encourage those who *ought* to give a lead.

Active citizens are not just consumers of leadership in the way that television audiences consume programmes. Active citizens develop a sense of being part of a public process with goals – goals which include not just the content of public policy but the quality of the democratic process itself, the nature of the relations between leaders and led. In some respects, the process of decentralization initiated in France since 1981 testifies to what the French have long considered a weakness of their own bureaucratic and *dirigiste* form of politics. It has been a conscious attempt to create a wider political class and thereby give French public institutions a deeper anchor in local opinion and local interests – in fact, to promote the kind of intermediate associations that would work against the disjuncture of élite opinion and popular opinion which has, at frequent intervals since 1789, led to revolutionary upheaval in France. To that extent, the recent decentralization programme in France represents a *mea culpa* on the part of the French élite, a reflection on the drawbacks of the kind of political class created by a bureaucratic form of state.

By contrast, a truly democratic political class is one which minimizes the temptation for ordinary citizens to think of the political élite as *les autres*, as a privileged and remote group able to manipulate the machinery of state for their own advantage. That is why, in the long run, active citizenry encouraged by a devolved form of the state is the only satisfactory filter for a democratic political class.

These are not merely academic issues. The prospect of European political integration makes them acute and unavoidable. For European integration raises the question of whether it is possible to create a democratic political class or élite across Europe. If not, the future looks bleak. In the absence of such an élite or political class, democracy in Europe will become a mere façade for bureaucratic rule from the centre or, worse still, for a plebiscitary and potentially demagogic form of politics. For let us be honest with ourselves. European federalism *could* lead to ugly reactions within member states, perhaps even to new forms of Caesarism.

So we must now look closely at the project of creating a democratic political class across Europe – and, in particular, at the obstacles facing it.

It might be alleged by Danish or British Eurosceptics that creating a political class on a European scale is simply impossible. After all, there is no European people, no European language, no European public opinion, no shared standard of public accountability in Europe. In the eyes of Eurosceptics, the cultural and linguistic differences between the United States and Western Europe are far too great for any lessons to be drawn from the American experience. Yet European history provides at least one interesting counter-example to such blanket scepticism. For there is no doubt that for a number of centuries Europe did have what might be called its own trans-national élite, with roots in a shared culture. That élite consisted of the clergy in a Christian Church as yet undivided by the Reformation.

Of course, it might be countered that clergy were a kind of aristocracy in medieval Europe and therefore not a helpful example. But that depends upon what is meant by aristocracy. Indeed, the most striking thing about the medieval Church is that, embedded in feudalism and a caste society, it remained relatively open. It recruited clergy from all the ranks of society. That openness was one of the things which gave the medieval clergy a prodigious moral influence in Europe.

The clergy of the medieval Church provided an acknowledged means of social mobility in a society otherwise founded on the privileges (and liabilities) of birth. In that sense the clergy formed a profoundly democratic institution, an élite which was to an important extent meritocratic – although not publicly accountable in any modern sense. Yet the medieval clergy had still another democratic attribute. Because of the requirement of celibacy the clergy could not degenerate into a caste. In contrast to the *nomenklatura* which emerged in Eastern Europe after the Second World War, the Church had constantly to renew itself by recruiting from other ranks of society.

If we use the medieval clergy and its recruitment as a model, we can perhaps draw a few conclusions about the problems facing any attempt to create a democratic élite or political class across Europe. The first test which must be applied is that of belief. For the medieval clergy was unified (at least in theory) by a shared creed, a creed which had generated an elaborate and sophisticated theology. What can Europe today offer in the way of shared beliefs? Obviously the European Union's commitment to 'democracy' is the crux. That commitment involves at least three things: self-government, in the sense of represent-ative government; the rule of law; and the recognition of a range of human rights as 'basic' or 'fundamental'. But of course the European Court has not yet created a jurisprudence which can match the subtlety or sophistication of Catholic Canon Law. Nor has there been time to create anything like the rights-based political culture of the United States – that almost instinctive appeal to the idea of fundamental rights which animates American public life.

A second test which the example of the medieval clergy suggests is cosmopolitanism. But here the growth of nation-states and national political traditions in the intervening centuries has created a formidable difficulty. To some extent the growing importance of national identity, if not nationalism, was offset as late as the nineteenth century by the survival of the aristocracy of Europe – by the affinities, contacts and even intermarriages of a trans-national social class set apart by its memories, habits and manners, even if it was no longer always the richest or most powerful social class. But the two wars of the twentieth century – the European 'civil war' – have taken a dreadful toll of those informal aristocratic ties between nations.

Paradoxically, despite the new rhetoric of Europeanism, Europe has perhaps never been more divided by national cultures than at present. The partial fusion of political élites in Europe resulting from the necessities of the early post-war period has largely disappeared, along with the leading personalities themselves. The Monnets, Adenauers and De Gasperis have not really reproduced themselves. Nor – with the possible exception of Germany and The Netherlands – has their Christian Democratic vision of the European future, a peculiar mixture of idealism and *realpolitik*, survived the collapse of communism and prodigious economic growth in Western Europe. Increasingly, the pursuit of a European strategy as a facet of national self-interest has replaced it.

Instead of the partial post-war fusion of national élites, the media and mass tourism have now become the most conspicuous supports of European cosmopolitanism. But will they be powerful enough supports? It seems unlikely. The media and frequent foreign travel cannot even begin to generate a coherent political class for Europe. But they do highlight another serious problem, the way in which language barriers still limit the depth of social relations in Europe.

For the third test suggested by the model of the medieval European clergy is a shared language. In the case of the clergy, of course, that shared language was Latin. From the seventeenth to the nineteenth century French to some extent replaced Latin as a lingua franca for Europe, especially in polite society and the world of diplomacy. French, however, began its irremediable decline as an international linguistic currency during the last century. So what remains as a basis for communication in Europe? Only, I think, English. English has emerged not just as Europe's, but virtually the world's, shared second language. Certainly it comes closest to being for the middle classes today what Latin was for the educated section of medieval European society.

Yet there is a problem with English, when compared to Latin. English is also the language of one state and a national tradition in Europe. So it arouses hostility, if not envy, in a way that Latin did not in medieval Europe. If we consider the problems that competing languages can cause within a nation-state – for example, in Belgium or Canada – then the importance of linguistic frontiers and linguistic competition raises serious questions about European political integration. The example of Switzerland might be cited on the other side. But how telling an example is it? As I argued earlier, the smallness of Switzerland, joined to the fact that it was surrounded by larger, powerful states, traditionally did more than anything else to ensure Swiss national unity, despite linguistic divisions. Switzerland also enjoyed a relatively homogenous society in a distinctive physical setting. It contained nothing like the social or geographical diversity of the European Union – nothing to compare with the differences in circumstances, beliefs and practices of, say, the Swedes and the Sicilians or the Greeks.

In fact, far from being an awkward example for my argument, Switzerland provides powerful support for it. For on the question of language, the attitudes of the Swiss today suggest what has happened over much of Western Europe in recent decades. Opinion polls reveal that all three major language groups in Switzerland – German, French and Italian – would now prefer to study English as a second language than another of the languages spoken *within* Switzerland!

At least 60 per cent of German-speaking Swiss would prefer to be taught English at school before French, and 57 per cent of French-speaking Swiss would prefer to learn English before studying German [according to the Swiss weekly *Facts* as reported in *The Times* of 17 November 1997]. The survey was published as education chiefs sought to defend the teaching of French, German, or Italian as a second language throughout Switzerland. Regional authorities in Zurich are examining a project that would break away from national practice by introducing English early in primary schools . . .

Clearly, popular attitudes which could provide Europe with a lingua franca have already developed. It is the élites of Europe which have not caught up with popular attitudes.

For the fact is that continental élites at times seek to arrest this process and prevent Europe developing a lingua franca, if that lingua franca is to be English. The most conspicuous such élite is that of France. Its policy of protecting French against incursions by English – by attacking and even applying legal penalties to the use of *franglais* – is almost certainly doomed, but it is none the less revealing. It betrays the limits which the French political class imposes on its willingness to integrate, the implicit conditions which have to be satisfied before French co-operation can be assured.

The contrast with the attitudes of the Dutch political class could hardly be greater – a contrast which illustrates two very different modes of cosmopolitanism in Europe. For the Dutch are so used to and so comfortable with the international role of English that the nation has become virtually bilingual. Not long ago, for example, there was a serious debate in Dutch universities about whether English should become the official language of instruction throughout the system. In the end the proposal did not gain the day. But it was a close thing, and the debate did not really foster xenophobia. Dutch identity was not felt to be at risk.

So here again we come up against deeply rooted habits and attitudes, what the French call *les moeurs*. If differences in *moeurs* are not only reinforced by linguistic differences but artificially 'protected' by national policies, then both the importance of creating a European political class and the great difficulty of doing so become apparent. It is the recognition of that difficulty which accounts for the likely American reaction to any idea of extending the common-market between Mexico and the United States into some sort of North American political union. Most Americans would consider such an idea utopian and dangerous – dangerous because it neglects the deep cultural and linguistic differences between the two countries. Creating, in the foreseeable future, a political class which spans those differences would be dismissed as a fantasy.

So where does that leave the project of creating a European political class or élite? In Europe, the enforced co-operation of the early post-war period has been succeeded by the habits of co-ordination associated with the creation of a Single Market and the European Union. And beyond these new institutions, the practice of regular consultation between the major partners – especially between the French and the Germans – has also grown up. So we are not talking of a situation in which laws or rules have to create something out of nothing. There are some elements of a political class in Europe. But what exactly do they amount to? And, in particular, how democratic are they?

Here we must be very careful. It is important to be hard-headed without being cynical, to see things for what they are without falling victim to a conspiracy theory.

What can we see? Different patterns of state formation in Europe have, inevitably, left distinctive marks on the habits and attitudes of national political classes. Yet only one such political class has left *its* distinctive mark on Brussels and the European Union. Nor is that surprising. For if we ask about élites within European states today, one thing is clear. Easily the most formidable, the best educated and most determined political class in Europe is that of France. Shaped crucially by the older, unreformed model of the French state, the French political class has, in recent decades, exhibited a fixedness of purpose and ruthlessness of will which reflects the traditional bias of the French system – the predominance of administrative power. Although utilitarianism in its classic form was a product of British moral philosophy, the French state system has incorporated its values far more clearly than either the British or German systems. Impatient of opposition once it has settled on a course of action as 'rational', the French political class prizes outcomes more than conciliation, coherence more than consent, ends more than means.

The record of the French political class in transforming the fortunes of its country since the outset of the Fourth Republic is undoubtedly impressive. Beginning with the successive (Monnet-inspired) plans for economic development and the Coal and Steel Community, the French political class has transformed a nation of peasant small-holders, shopkeepers and artisans into an urbanized, industrialized, high-tech society with world-class clout both as a trading and military nation. The traditional centralization of the French state, the power of its administrative machine, has helped to make this remarkable achievement possible. It has helped the French élite to construct a system of planning into which both labour and capital, the *Patronat* (the employers' organization) and the syndicates, were drawn. The informal aspects of the French planning system have been at least as important as the formal aspects. For the French state has made it possible for its administrative 'high-fliers' to move with relative ease between the state bureaucracy, an active role in party politics and jobs in the commanding heights of industry.

And success bred further success. Recruitment into the higher reaches of the French civil service, by way of the *Grandes Écoles*, became increasingly meritocratic with the foundation of the *École Nationale d'Administration* (ENA) under the Fourth Republic. The ENA was intended originally as a reformist measure to broaden the social basis of recruitment into the French élite. But the upper bourgeoisie, especially of the Paris area, has proved more than able to rise to the challenge. Since the advent of the Fifth Republic, the French élite, for whom political and administrative careers are increasingly bound up together, has become an ever more coherent, self-conscious and relatively small group, well known to each other and presiding over the destinies of France. In fact, the composition of the French political class has changed under the Fifth Republic. *Fonctionnaires* or civil servants have come to dominate the political class – so that whereas under the Third and Fourth Republics it was sometimes said that France was administered rather than governed, it might now be said that France is governed by administrators.

It is this French political class dominated by administrators which has, to an extent not always understood, shaped the destinies of the European Union so far. For, benefiting, in the 1960s, from the weakness of German political will and the absence of Britain from the Common Market, the French political class was able to construct in Brussels a European edifice which reflected the French vision of Europe, French habits and French interests. In effect, the French political class became used to presiding over Europe. Enjoying a new-found confidence under the Fifth Republic, the French political class has set about re-establishing France's traditional role as the heartland of Europe – trying to defend a European identity against facile Americanization by insisting that the state should intervene in the marketplace, and in some respects shape it, rather than capitulate to 'Anglo-American' neo-liberalism.

This vision has helped to give the French political class a clarity of intention and strength of will which, up to a point, justifies their domination over European affairs. One happy consequence for France, as we have seen, has been the development of European policies such as the Common Agricultural Policy (CAP) which corresponds closely with her interests. Yet, as is the way in human affairs, the French soon came to take their domination for granted. In particular, they took for granted having considerable political influence over German economic might. Can it be mere accident that France, one of the wealthiest European nations, pays so little into European coffers or that the French occupy so many key positions within the European Union?

Only recently indeed have figures about the net contributions by member states become available – and that because Germany is at last showing signs of discontent with the status quo. Here are the figures released by the German Government, together with those subsequently released by the Brussels Commission (given in brackets). It could be that the former are closer to the mark than the latter, given the pressures on the Commission to minimize discontent among some of the net contributor nations.

Net Contributors			Net Beneficiaries		
Germany	10.0	(10.94)	Spain	6.1	(5.93)
Netherlands	2.4	(2.27)	Greece	4.1	(4.37)
UK	2.3	(1.79)	Portugal	2.8	(2.72)
Italy	1.3	(0.06)	Ireland	2.3	(2.67)
Sweden	0.7	(1.12)	Belgium	1.8	(1.07)
France	0.4	(0.78)	Luxembourg	0.8	(0.72)
Austria	0.2	(0.72)	Denmark	0.2	(0.06)
			Finland	0.1	(0.05)

(in billions of ecus)

Just how extraordinary these figures are, emerges if one remembers that France now has a markedly higher per capita GNP than Germany and one notices that The Netherlands, with a population only a quarter of that of France, pays at least three and perhaps six times as much to the European Union as France!

As late as 1980, the French combined this *de facto* dominance with belief in a *Europe des patries*, a Europe of nation-states. That had been General de Gaulle's model for post-war Europe, and remained the rallying cry for Gaullist governments from the outset of the Fifth Republic, in 1958, until the victory of the left in 1981. In the mid-1980s, however, French rhetoric began to change. The Socialist Government under Mitterrand had as part of its inheritance a Jacobin tradition which placed great reliance on centralized state power and, noticing the resurgence not just of German economic might but also of German political will, began to call for tighter political integration in Europe – 'ever closer union'. Probably that seemed the only way France could preserve the hegemony to which it had become accustomed. Thus, the mid-1980s represented an important turning point in the French conception of Europe.

The new preference for tighter political integration might not, however, have marked a permanent change of direction for France.

For Gaullist doubts about a more centralized European Union remained alive and would probably, in time, have led to a reversal of socialist policy. What changed everything, I think, and made this new direction far more durable, overcoming some, if not all, Gaullist doubts, was one event – the sudden, unexpected reunification of Germany in 1989–90.

That event created a great fear (*grande peur*) among the French political class. It has even been suggested that a panicky President Mitterrand flew suddenly to Kiev in order to discuss with Gorbachev reconstructing the old Franco-Russian alliance! In any case the accrual of population, economic power and political self-confidence likely to result from the merging of the German Democratic Republic (GDR) with the *Bundesrepublik* obliged the French élite to rethink their strategy for Europe. Evidently they concluded that new institutional constraints on German power were desperately needed, and that France, if it were to be safe, must have a hand in the government of Germany. Aided by the concern of some Germans (not least, at times, Chancellor Kohl himself) about their accretion of power, the French developed an agenda which stipulated that the Single Market could only develop further if it were crowned with a single currency and a European Central Bank. What would be the effect of these new institutions? *They would enable the French to have a formal share in German policy-making and decisions.* So the French made it clear to German leaders that monetary union was a quid pro quo for French 'acceptance' of German reunification. At first the Germans may not have reacted favourably, with Chancellor Kohl allegedly asserting that a single currency was 'not in Germany's interests'. But the French persevered.

The new constraints on Germany were not intended to be merely financial or economic. They were to be political. Closer political integration now became the persistent French call, with the development of a shared defence policy and foreign policy being among the first objectives. That was the import of the Maastricht Treaty negotiations, which saw President Mitterrand and Jacques Delors – who, as President of the European Commission, provided the crucial link between the French political élite and the Brussels machine – persuading Chancellor Kohl to accept their new agenda for Europe.

Not surprisingly, the French soon made it clear they wanted greater political accountability of the new European bank – something which, as they put it, would ensure democratic control over central bankers. But here it is important to look closely at what they meant. The sense of 'democratic' that the French invoked – and which was eventually accepted by a reluctant Germany – was essentially Jacobin and centralizing. It had little to do with Germany's long-standing promotion of federal institutions for Europe, which would make careful provision for the formal separation and dispersal of powers. By contrast, it is clear that the French regarded the Stability Pact as a means of consolidating power and creating a Mediterranean bloc which could offset German and Dutch influence over European Central Bank policy. The subsequent watering down of the stern criteria which the Bundesbank had originally suggested as the condition of monetary union – criteria which would almost certainly have excluded Italy, Spain and Portugal – testifies to the skill of French diplomacy in Europe.

The story which I have just told is not the conventional one. For in the European media Germany is usually presented as the primary source of pressure for a more integrated Europe. In the British media especially, Germany's long-standing advocacy of a United States of Europe is taken as evidence that Germany is responsible for the recent acceleration of the European project. Germany thus becomes the villain of the conventional story. Indeed, parts of the British media have gone so far as to suggest that the European project is the latest form of German expansionism, a kind of recasting, in terms acceptable to contemporary opinion, of the Third Reich.

Even when this interpretation is stripped of its paranoid features, it misses the point about the source of the project for 'ever closer' political integration in Europe. Germany has not really been the motive force. At most Germany has co-operated or acquiesced in what is basically a French design, the design of a political class which has achieved remarkable things since 1945 and will not easily relinquish the dominant role in European affairs which it acquired in the early years of the Common Market – a role which reflected the moral limbo which post-Nazi Germany inhabited and the absence of Britain from the Common Market in the years following de Gaulle's veto of her application to join. De Gaulle himself once remarked, only half jokingly, that in the EEC Germany was the horse, while France was the coachman driving the carriage.

The truth is that French successes over several decades have re-created a pan-European and quasi-imperial outlook which had shaped French policy from Louis XIV to Napoleon, but had been undermined by class conflict and domestic instability from 1815 to the fall of France in 1940. That pan-European outlook has been thrown into sharper relief, moreover, by French suspicion of post-war American influence in Europe, not least through what the French perceive as the frequent American domination of British foreign policy, Britain's role as a virtual Trojan Horse in Europe.

Only two other political classes might have rivalled France in having a pan-European or quasi-imperial outlook – those of Germany and Britain. But after 1945 each of these political classes was bent on shedding rather than acquiring imperial responsibilities and the habits of mind attached to them. Indeed, occupying not much more than half her former territory, Germany had, for forty years, withdrawn into itself – preoccupied with creating the rule of law and a buoyant civil society within the framework of a federal system designed to limit the power of central government. During the same period Britain was in the process of extricating itself from world-wide imperial possessions, obliged to recognize its diminished resources on the one hand, while consoling itself with a shadowy, intermittent role in the new American hegemony on the other hand.

How have the German and British political classes reacted to *de facto* French domination of the European Union? The Germans have, by and large, turned a blind eye to this development – or, at moments of extreme irritation with the French, contented themselves with wink-ing to others about those 'impossible' French! The British, by contrast, have been more quarrelsome and difficult. But the British have been inept in the way they have identified the threat to Europe posed by the developing French project, portraying it for the most part merely as a threat to their own national sovereignty.

These divergent but equally ineffective reactions to French dom-ination reveal, I think, something important about the nature of the German and British political classes.

In Germany, federalism as well as the role of a powerful constitutional court mean that the habits and attitudes of the political class have been shaped by a system in which checks and balances constrain decision-making. In fact, the federal system is a formidable obstacle to the emergence of the kind of unified, self-conscious élite recently characteristic of France. The dispersal of authority and power under German federalism does not yield a tidy political class. Decisions are more openly the result of bargaining between the federal government and the *Länder*; they remain more tentative and often are less coherent than in France – which is not to say that an able Chancellor, backed by majorities in both houses of the federal legislature, cannot, especially if he has been in power for some time, acquire quasi-autocratic power.

Once a consensus, backed by such a Chancellor, has been established in Germany, the danger is that it becomes fixed and difficult to reform. There are two reasons for this. One is the quasi-corporatist character of German society – that network of national associations which lies behind the German political class and has roots which antedate the formation of the German state in the nineteenth century, creating a political culture which puts a premium on consensus, slowly formed and not easily recast. The other reason is the survival of a peculiarly German form of deference to authority, which can result in public opinion taking its lead from the political class rather than the political class taking its lead from public opinion. The deference of Germans to the policy of abandoning the Deutschmark in favour of a common European currency, when that policy excites deep misgivings in the country at large, is only the most recent example of this pattern. Here too we meet an important unintended consequence of German federalism. By dispersing the elements of a political class, federalism makes it easier – given traditional German respect for authority – for a skilful and determined Chancellor to impose himself, in the fashion of Adenauer and Kohl. So that, at the end of the day, it may not even be the German political class but the federal Chancellor who gives the lead to opinion.

In Britain the pattern of opinion-making is more complex – or, rather, there are two patterns, one on the decline, the other emergent. The older manners of the British political class reflected that informal decentralization which for so long co-existed happily with parliamentary sovereignty – extensive local autonomy and an important role for intermediate bodies such as the Church, the legal profession and the universities. The residually aristocratic character of British society and the composition of the parliamentary parties created informal checks and balances which contributed to the need for a consensual political culture. As long as these subtle, quasi-aristocratic mechanisms of consultation and consent survived, they helped to make British political culture distinctive in so far as it minimized the resort to force and maximized the role of opinion, of governing by consent. It is these older habits and attitudes of the political class that have made Britain a thorn in the side of the French project for Europe. In playing that role, the voice of the unwritten British constitution can still, just, be heard – a voice proud of an ancient tradition of self-government and deeply sceptical of a bureaucratic model for governing Europe. Unfortunately, as we have seen, British opposition has been formulated chiefly in terms of the defence of 'sovereignty', a formulation which gives British opposition a bleak and unconstructive quality.

The new manners of the British political class – especially that part of it shaped by centralization under Thatcher, the virtual eclipse of local autonomy – are less coherent than the old manners. On the one hand, the new manners reflect and exploit that centralizing of power, the weakening of traditional checks and balances. On the other hand, they betray a growing sense that constitutional reform is needed to create a political system more appropriate to a less stratified, less deferential society – a system which, through devolution, brings govern-ment closer to the people and encourages citizenship. This emergent political class can see that falling back on the assertion of parliamentary sovereignty is no longer an adequate response to events, either within the United Kingdom or in Europe as a whole. But as yet it lacks experience of – and, at times, even the taste for – formal constitutional checks and balances, experience required for it to pursue a coherent reformist policy in Europe. Instead, ashamed of the negative approach to Europe of the Thatcher and Major Governments, it is in danger of acquiescing in European arrangements of which it does not really approve.

So where are we? Only three of the political classes of Europe can be said to have 'imperial' pretensions and memories, memories and pretensions of giving Europe a lead and a style of government. They are those of France, Germany and Britain. Yet two of these three are now at a severe disadvantage when it comes to shaping a Europe-wide political system. The British are held back by the task of completing the destruction of the British *ancien régime* and renewing the British form of the state. The Germans are held back by residual guilt about Nazism, by a mandatory idealism which no longer corresponds entirely to their instincts and situation. By contrast, the French political class has the advantage of momentum – of having to all intents and purposes been in the driving seat of Europe for several decades now. Its resolution has been sharpened by the fears unleashed by German reunification. But not only that. The slow work of decentralization in France may already look like ominous writing on the wall to the French élite. How tempting, then, to turn Brussels and the European Union into a refuge for *dirigiste* habits and attitudes which may at last have had their day in France itself.

For I do not doubt that decentralization will gradually make French government a more truly democratic affair. But it is the nature of human affairs that changes in habits and attitudes take a long time. Just as the *moeurs* of a decentralized form of the state have survived in Britain, despite the centralization which has taken place in recent decades – a survival which gives hope that constitutional reform in Britain may arrive in time to 'save' its free *moeurs* – so the *moeurs* of the French political class remain those shaped by that administrative despotism which traditionally marked the French form of the state.

Now, as we have seen, those *moeurs* have provided the basis for an extraordinary accretion of French power in Europe. Despite British obstruction and reservations emerging in Germany, the French project for Europe is on the point of succeeding. The French have not only gained a crucial voice in the new European Central Bank. They are pursuing their goal of establishing uniform European policies across a wide range of issues. On the other hand, questions about the distribution of power and democratic accountability have been glossed over. Altogether, the French political class has for years displayed a will which has prevented them from falling victim to economism – to anything like that belief in 'iron laws' of the market which has infected other European élites. The drawback is that the French élite's notion of political will remains one shaped by a bureaucratic model of the state.

But the French political class now finds itself in a dilemma. For it cannot tell its own people that France is on the brink of carrying the day in Europe. Why not? *Because it might be overheard* by the other peoples of Europe, particularly the Germans and the British – releasing a far more powerful current of opposition to the French project for Europe, a current which has thus far been more or less successfully dammed. As a result, for example, the burdens which French policy imposed on its own people in order to keep the franc tied to the mark in the run-up to monetary union, with its consequences for unemployment in France, could not be eased by proclaiming the long-term gains to French prestige and power accruing from domination in Europe. Yet it may well be that the French have gained a long-term economic advantage by tying an over-valued mark to the franc through the new euro.

But, as I have said, the French dare not boast of these things. The result of this dilemma is that the most likely way in which French policy might still be undone is through domestic strife within France itself. For here we come once again upon the drawbacks of a *dirigiste* political culture. Here we come again upon the pattern which has haunted French history since the Revolution – a pattern in which the political class or élite loses touch with popular opinion, only finally to be called to account by widespread civil unrest, if not revolution.

If Europe is created on the model of the older, unreformed French model of the state – so that a 'federal' Europe becomes the façade for a political class and a political culture shaped by bureaucracy – then the danger for Europe is that its history will come to resemble that of France since 1815. The tutorship of a bureaucratic state will be rejected from time to time by Europeans angry at being treated like children, but unused to the disciplines of citizenship.

Tell-tale signs are already present, for those who care to read them. The débâcle of the European Commission under Jacques Santer has both confirmed and reinforced a widespread perception that an over-privileged and unaccountable élite has misused the growing power of Brussels – that mismanagement, nepotism and even fraud have been rife. That perception has, in turn, taken a dreadful toll of idealism about Europe. So the obvious drawback of the French project for Europe is that it does not address the problem of creating an open and accountable political class for Europe. Perhaps more than anything else, that failure betrays the bureaucratic inspiration of the French project. No care has been taken to educate the public or stimulate a debate about how a political class for Europe might be formed – about the prerequisites for a democratic political class operating on a continental scale and in the face of linguistic differences.

Another tell-tale sign is the direction taken by European opinion in the last decade. A really serious gap has opened up between the peoples of Europe and their élites – a gap between popular indifference or opposition to monetary union and the determination of national political classes, led by the French and abetted by the Germans, to push ahead with the project as rapidly as possible. Their ability to ignore public opinion, and the degree of insulation from popular pressures it reveals, is only too redolent of the pattern which long sustained the revolutionary tradition in France. Will it now be generalized through Europe?

The peril is real. If the idea of Europe becomes associated primarily with the arrogance of unaccountable élites, the prospects for Europe are bleaker than they have been since 1945. For then the idea of Europe will divide rather than unite. It will divide nations within themselves and may even set nations against each other.

Can anything be done? The first thing is to face the truth. In the short run, there is *no* way of creating a political class for Europe, at least not a class which is open and has emerged in a morally acceptable way. To suggest otherwise, is to be either naïve or deceitful. It is to neglect the difference between the time required for changing laws and the time required for changing *moeurs*, the difference in kind between imposing regulations by public authority and creating habits and attitudes which can alone provide an adequate foundation for self-government in Europe.

The price we have paid for allowing economic thinking to overwhelm political reflection in recent decades, is a tendency to move between economic events and political structures without considering the human beings who, so to speak, mediate between the two – their prejudices and traditions, their beliefs and practices. Legal obligation and economic advantage have become the organizing principles of our thinking. The social content of our lives, it is too often assumed, can and will mould itself to the requirement of the state and the market. But that view is false and dangerous. It is false because it neglects the habits and attitudes which are required to make laws enforceable. And it is dangerous because it neglects the different attitudes towards the state and public authority characteristic of the several national traditions in Europe – differences which make the social soil on which any European political construction will have to stand utterly different from the social soil on which American federalism rests.

In the middle to long term, of course, habits and attitudes *can* be remoulded. And that is where those who are truly serious about the construction of a democratic Europe ought now to direct their attention. There are a number of things which have to be done – two of them are indirect measures, the other two direct. The first indirect measure is to enhance the democratic character of national political classes in Europe through the reform of existing state structures, reforms which foster participation at local and regional levels and thus begin to change the composition of national political classes. Here recent events offer some encouragement. Movement towards a more devolved form of the state has been on the agenda of many nations latterly. In different ways the French, the Spanish and, most recently, the British forms of the state are being subjected to reform with a view to strengthening regional identities, protecting local autonomy and opening out recruitment to the national political class. Of course, the process is not without risks. But the risks of doing nothing are greater, even from a narrowly national perspective – as the extent of support for the separatist Northern League in parts of the Venice region reveals.

Another indirect measure which can be taken is just as important, if a truly European political class is to develop. It is the formal acknowledgement that English has an indispensable role to play as the second language of Europe. Why should its role *de facto* have to be converted into a role *de jure*? Because the shared standards of accountability, the attitudes needed to convert nominal democracy into real democracy, require a common political idiom if they are to develop and flourish. Without such an idiom or vocabulary, and the consciously shared standards of accountability it makes possible, disagreements within Europe are far more likely to result in the kind of permanent distrust which can, ultimately, foster sedition.

Cultural homogeneity, at least in the civic sphere, is necessary if European federalism is to succeed one day. Acknowledging the role of English in Europe would of course involve a sacrifice of French pride, a sacrifice which will not easily be made. But the French have something to gain as well as lose from such a sacrifice. If their distinctive contribution to the building of Europe has been an insistence that European interests can be identified apart from American interests and should at times be defended against them, then their opportunity is to put the case against American domination and neo-liberalism in the language of Anglo-Saxons. It is a case which would gain in power because it was divested of the paranoid element with which French defence of linguistic purity and attacks on *franglais* have surrounded French policy.

It is not at all obvious that a shared language paves the way for cultural domination by the United States. In many respects, English life has proved more resistant to American cultural influence than has French life. Indeed, it could be that the price the French élite has paid for its own ascendancy and its resistance to Americanization has been the increased attraction of American styles and habits for that large section of French society which feels itself to be the victim of *les autres*. If so, the extent of the Americanization of France may chiefly reveal the failure of the French political class to become more open and democratic. By accepting that English will be Europe's second language, the French political class could be in a better position both to argue the case against supine acceptance of American political hegemony and to resist American cultural influences.

Finally, there are two direct measures that can and should be taken. The first is especially important. For the institutions of the European Union are at present incomplete. *A European Senate is badly needed to complete them.* By creating an upper chamber in the European parliament, a new bridge could be built between national political classes, which retain democratic legitimacy, and the decision-making process in Brussels. Such a Senate should be recruited by indirect election from existing national parliaments. Indirectly elected Senators would retain their national parliamentary careers, while acquiring closer knowledge of European institutions and the habit of co-operating with each other. Such Senators ought to be leading national politicians,

politicians with an experience and stature not typical of European MPs today. To ensure that the role of Senator did not become merely honorific, a reward for geriatric politicians, the prerogatives of the Senate would have to be formidable and carefully defined – giving the Senate a right of initiative and veto-power over certain types of legislation, as well as the right 'to advise and consent' to senior Commission appointments. Invested with real power, the European Senate would play an important part in the careers of leading national politicians. Although their European role would be only part-time, Senators would, I suspect, quickly acquire an influence denied to full-time European MPs. For they could act as a filter between national political classes and the European élite, a point of contact which is at present missing.

Nor is that all. The jurisdiction of a European Senate could be used to promote two goals simultaneously – both of which are prerequisites for creating an open political class across Europe. The first, as I have already suggested, is to provide the nation-states of the European Union with more effective guarantees against centralization, against encroachments by a Brussels bureaucracy which threaten the dispersal of power and would make the Union less sensitive than it ought to be to the variety of attitudes and habits in Europe. The first duty of a European Senate must be to ensure that the authority of Brussels is used to impose only *minimal* standards across Europe – regulations which correspond to our basic intuitions of justice but do not go beyond them. Thus, discrimination against women or homosexuals would be suitable subjects for European norms, but the length of the working week or the contents of the sausage need not be. One of the pre-conditions of rallying support for Europe and recruiting members of a European political class is reassurance for national political classes that they are not in danger of extinction or even demotion.

The second goal to be promoted by a European Senate might, at first glance, seem to be at variance with the first. It is to encourage greater devolution of authority and power within nation-states, so that regional autonomy becomes the vehicle for improving the democratic credentials of national political classes and bringing national govern- ments closer to their peoples. In order to encourage reform of existing states with a view to increasing democratic accountability, as well as levels of popular participation, half the seats of a European Senate (say, 80 out of 160) might be given to representatives of national regions, provided that they satisfied certain standards of autonomy. Such regional Senators should be indirectly elected by regional assemblies. Significant devolution within member states could thus be made a condition of a nation's taking up half of its seats in the European Senate. This formal sanction for a devolved form of the state would not only help national political classes to become more democratic. It would also combat a powerful centralizing mechanism – that is, the resentments felt in many regions against national capitals and state bureaucracies still viewed as 'oppressors' or 'conquerors'. The danger of such resentments is that Brussels may be viewed by European regions as a weapon to be used *against* their own nation-state. It is that temptation, as well as the fear it excites among existing political classes of Europe, that must be removed. A European Senate, formally charged with both protecting national autonomy and with encouraging devolution with nation-states, could play an important part in creating the kind of political class that Europe desperately needs – one that is open, suspicious of bureaucracy and sensitive to the claims of social variety.

Nor would the fact that European Senators were only indirectly elected reduce their legitimacy or influence. After all, the United States Senate, perhaps the most powerful legislative body in the Western world, began as an indirectly elected chamber, its members being chosen by the legislatures of the American states. Not surprisingly, that helped to make Senators zealous in the protection of states-rights. A European Senate, equally concerned and formally charged to defend the prerogatives of national governments and made up of leading national politicians, could help to develop European law in such a way that the 'subsidiarity' principle acquired teeth – turning a vague presumption in favour of decisions being made at the lowest level possible into real habits and enforceable expectations. In that way something like a vigilant, rights-based political culture on the American model could begin to develop, providing the habits and attitudes needed to found federalism in Europe.

And that suggests the second, closely related change that will be needed, if Europe is to move towards a more rights-based political culture. Lawyers will have to play an increasingly important part in the political system. That is because some form of judicial review is inescapable in a federal system. The multiple jurisdictions created by federalism lead to conflicts of jurisdiction. Such conflicts, in turn, require something like a Supreme Court to adjudicate and decide. But that is a role which brings judges and lawyers directly into the political arena.

In America, an informal condition of lawyers playing such an important political role has always been the extraordinary openness of the legal class – the ease with which a legal education can be obtained and the way a law degree provides a spring-board into other areas of American corporate and professional life. That openness of the legal class has been crucial in sustaining the belief in social opportunity in America, a sense of mobility which is, as we have seen, one of the prerequisites of a democratic political class. It is their close association with the idea of social mobility which has made it possible for American lawyers to play a major political role without creating much protest about their role being undemocratic. By contrast, the long-standing opposition to courts and lawyers playing any such political role in the United Kingdom has been due chiefly to the more 'closed' character of the British legal class, its narrower social base. And, in that respect, the other nations of Europe probably resemble Britain more than they do the United States. Recruitment to the legal class thus assumes quite a new, perhaps even a decisive, importance.

So here the example of American federalism provides an important practical lesson for European democracy. Easier access to a law career and a proper civic education for lawyers amount to a necessary condition for the creation of an open political class and a rights-based political culture in Europe. So, too, is the creation of a powerful European Senate, an upper house which can begin the difficult task of fusing existing national political classes together. But the nature of these changes makes something else clear. Each of these conditions can be satisfied only slowly. For that reason, building democracy in Europe is a matter of decades rather than years – indeed, it is probably a matter of generations. To suppose that it can be done more rapidly is dangerous. For if Europe is built without an open political class, Europe will be ruled by civil servants.

8

Europe and the Global Market

I have emphasized how great a toll the language of economics has taken of political argument, and especially constitutional thought, in recent decades. But of course economic considerations both do and ought to take an enormous part in any serious consideration of European political integration, its advantages and drawbacks. So we must now turn to them.

The development of a world market has become one of the received truths of our time, a cliché. And like so many received truths or clichés it can get in the way of clear thinking. That is not so much because of what it perhaps exaggerates, as what it conceals. For what it conceals has an important bearing on the construction of Europe.

Two views about the construction of Europe have long been in competition. One view, associated with Britain, lays stress on the completion of a Single Market, with economic integration and interdependence yielding, in due course, a peaceful and prosperous Europe. The other view, associated with France and Germany, places far greater emphasis on political will, on the need to construct new public institutions which will safeguard human rights and promote social justice in Europe. The choice offered, then, is one between relying on market forces slowly and indirectly to create a European identity – what might be seen as traditional British gradualism, the expression of an unwritten constitution – and a more *dirigiste* attempt to create a new European order, comprising foreign policy, internal policing and military affairs, as well as economic relations.

Yet behind these opposed views about how Europe should be constructed, lurks a more fundamental question: just what is the relationship between a free-market system and liberal democracy? Does the development of a free market bring in its wake, almost irresistibly, liberal democratic institutions, so that we can simply rely on the removal of barriers to the spread of market relations to create the kind of society we want to live in?

Are liberal democratic institutions the mere corollary of a free market, bound to follow its development sooner or later? Or, are they something which has to be struggled for and carefully nurtured – something which not only does not follow automatically from a single market, but may even be a necessary condition for the full development of a free-market system?

Clearly, much follows for the construction of Europe from the answers given to these questions. But not only for Europe. The future of developing nations such as China, India and Indonesia is also hostage to the answers given to these questions. With only a touch of travesty, I think it is possible to identify two major competing answers. One I will call Capitalist Triumphalism, while the other might be called Capitalist Catastrophe Theory. Capitalist Triumphalism celebrates the collapse of Communism as the end of ideological competition ('the end of history'), the emergence of a universal liberal democratic culture alongside a global market, with economic integration and an ever-increasing social division of labour underpinning a new and more peaceful world order. Capitalist Triumphalism portrays the market as a benign force 'carrying' liberal democratic norms and gradually creating a world-wide consensus.

In contrast, Capitalist Catastrophe Theory portrays the market as, at least at times, a frightful and inhuman machine, a machine which shreds traditional social ties in the pursuit of efficiency and profit. Capitalism, with the constant rationalization it entails, destroys the solidarities of community and family, by enforcing self-interest as a motive at the expense of duty, affection or deference as traditionally understood. The chief hope held out by Catastrophe Theory is that the corrosive effects of the marketplace can be offset, to some extent, by the state intervening to constrain the profit motive and foster social solidarity.

Evidently these visions have radically different implications not only for the construction of Europe but also for Europe's relations with the rest of the world. For the Triumphalist, the expansion of world trade is far the best guarantee of a peaceful and liberal democratic world in the long run. For those persuaded by Catastrophe Theory, on the other hand, Europe must be prepared to become a fortress, a fortress designed to protect human rights and social standards which the rest of the world is unable or unwilling to protect. This school of thought is appalled by the potential social costs of Europe trying to compete openly with the low-wage economies of Asia.

Evidently, this is not just an argument about the future of the European Welfare State, with its high level of social protection and the consequent costs imposed on employers and taxpayers. It is also an argument about the strategy which Europe ought to adopt in future world trade negotiations, in particular whether Europe can or ought to use such negotiations to promote human rights and seek to improve the conditions of work in non-European nations – banning reliance on child labour, for example. Here again, the two sides reach very different conclusions. Thatcherite Britain, espousing to some extent the Triumphalist position, was inclined to rely simply on free-market disciplines, the elimination of barriers to trade, in order to maximize efficiency and profit. Continental Europe, on the other hand, has espoused at least elements of the Catastrophe Theory, and has been quite prepared to adopt protectionist measures for Europe, not least in the form of the Common Agricultural Policy.

There is something unconvincing about both of these alternatives. If we want to understand why, we have to look more deeply at the relationship between the state and the market. For the two positions I have described above polarize that relationship and thereby over-simplify it – implying that we have to choose between assuming that the market creates the state or that the state creates the market. Up to a point these alternative assumptions have deep historical roots in Europe, roots in different traditions of law. The English Common Law tradition tends to affirm the priority of social relations and the market to the state, while the continental tradition of Roman Law affirms the priority of the state to social relations and the marketplace.

Common Law and Roman Law traditions embody 'negative' and 'positive' views of the nature and role of the state. The negative view of the state implies that the state develops as exchange relations make it clear that a legal framework is needed to penalize fraud and, perhaps, remove privilege. Thus, the state develops primarily as the means of guaranteeing what has come to be called the 'transparency' of market relations. Its role is to enable economic agents to pursue their self-interest free of encumbrance, removing obstacles which might hinder exchanges. The positive view of the state, on the other hand, presents the law as the crucial means of social improvement and ethical life. Thus, the state becomes the defender of a kind of national community, limiting the claims of the marketplace not only when the latter cannot provide social goods, but also when it fails to promote social justice. Here we meet a far stronger suspicion of self-interest as a motive, a greater emphasis on the notion of the common good.

If we are obliged to choose between oversimplified alternatives, then, I think, the positive view of the nature and role of the state has more truth in it. For the negative view places too much faith in unintended consequences – that is, in the co-ordinating role of the market and the beneficial effects of the pursuit of self-interest. In that way what is now called neo-liberalism carries on what has been the central theme of capitalist argument since the publication of Adam Smith's *Wealth of Nations* in 1776. Since Smith's book became famous, Europeans have tended to understand economic development in his terms: the increasing social division of labour made possible by exchanges has held out the promise of greater prosperity for all concerned, European and non-European alike. The older mercantilist ideal of trade working largely to the advantage of one nation – allowing it to maximize its holding of gold or bullion – has long been discarded in favour of a liberal model which emphasizes the pursuit of individual self-interest curbed only by law.

Yet recently neo-liberalism has added, perhaps unwittingly, an almost Marxist emphasis on the priority of economic relations to the law, a subordination of the state to the market which was not really a part of Adam Smith's argument. Whatever else may be said about it, then, a positive view of the state does at least assert the creative role of law and the autonomy of politics against any such economic determinism.

In a crucial respect, however, both the negative and positive views of the state's relationship to the market suffer from the same weakness. They make an assumption about economic agency – about the character of the actor in the marketplace – which is in fact culture-bound. Yet neither makes this fact clear. To that extent, both the negative and positive views fail to capture the way particular moral intuitions underlie *both* the state *and* the market as understood in Europe. It is these moral intuitions which have, to a crucial extent, generated both institutions. So, in order to avoid being misled, we have to look more closely at the nature of the economic agent presupposed by modern economics and liberalism. When we do so, we find that our assumptions about economic agency ultimately derive from a set of moral beliefs.

In order to understand that moral foundation, it may be helpful to think in terms of liberal capitalism developing through three stages:

1 Formal liberalism. In the first stage the state introduces equal subjection (its 'sovereign' right), which, in turn, makes it possible to proclaim equality before the law. That equality before the law provides the legal framework for a market economy – the condition which, in effect, England achieved a century before continental Europe.

2 Early liberalism. In the second stage, a significant gap remains between the formal equality now guaranteed by law and *de facto* inequalities of status and opportunity surviving from a pre-capitalist order and perpetuated by property rights.

3 Mature liberalism. In the third stage, increased social mobility and a greater sense of opportunity significantly erode pre-capitalist status differences and reduce (although by no means eliminating) the advantages deriving from inherited wealth.

What I have called the third stage, mature liberalism, was first achieved in the United States, aided, no doubt, by the fact that America lacked a feudal past. But a comparable social mobility and sense of opportunity have developed in many areas of Western Europe since 1945, pushing those areas from the second to the third stage.

What this model makes clear is that attitudes towards the marketplace can take very different forms under liberal capitalism. In the third stage of mature liberalism, the market can plausibly be seen as something embracing everyone, something everyone has at least a tolerable chance of turning to his or her advantage. But, under early liberalism, the market is seen by many as something external and hostile, serving the interests of one well-defined section of society – a residually privileged section of society whose members, by contrast, see the market as something to be manipulated, something which exists to promote the interests of their own class or group.

The almost affectionate attitude towards the market which characterizes mature liberalism might be described as middle-class or bourgeois, the market perceived as a bedfellow. By contrast, the earlier stage of liberalism, which polarizes attitudes towards the market, induces in the majority what can only be described as a proletarian attitude, the market perceived as a devouring monster, while making it possible for some to adopt an essentially upper-class attitude, perceiving the market as a poodle. Thus, the defining characteristic of early liberalism is that two antagonistic attitudes towards the market predominate, while the middle-class attitude – regarding the market as a bedfellow – has simply not spread widely enough. The latter, bourgeois perception, which depends upon people imagining themselves into the marketplace without feeling radically disadvantaged or advantaged, has only really developed in Western Europe in the post-war period, putting an end to class conflict, at least in its most strident, class-conscious form.

Such deep, instinctive attitudes towards the market are shaped largely by the family and, perhaps, by early schooling. Identifying either with people who seem to be *in* a market, *above* it or *below* it, is the crucial experience – an experience compared with which mere learning about the workings of the market at a later age can hardly compare in motivating force. And if that is the case, then it follows that any truly progressive liberal capitalist government will always have to address itself to social arrangements which impede mobility, both social and geographical. It will have to ask difficult questions about the distribution of wealth, premature specialization in the schools and ease of entry into the professions, if it is to forestall the return of class-conscious politics. The creation of a single European market implies, therefore, co-ordinated state action to foster reasonable equality of opportunity.

Now when Europeans and Americans consider the development of a global market today, they tend to do so relying, I suggest, on something like the model I have just sketched. They suppose that countries which have adopted the state as a political form, and thus acquired the legal framework for a market, are more often than not in the second stage of development – that is, the stage in which pre-capitalist status differences and inherited wealth continue to constrain market relations. But they also suppose that the second stage will, in due course, give way to the third stage, liberating individuals as economic agents (their 'rationality') and creating a more transparent society.

Alas, in supposing these things, Europeans and Americans take far too much for granted. They project Western moral intuitions on to societies which often have very different religious and moral traditions, and therefore seriously underestimate the constraints on the market (as understood in the West) operating in such societies. Europeans and Americans project Western assumptions about economic agency on to societies where they do not hold. They fail to understand the extent to which the moral intuitions governing non-Western societies continue to identify and sustain the family as the effective economic agent rather than the individual.

It is relatively easy to create the formal legal framework for a market economy understood in the Western sense. Hence, the nearly universal adoption of the nation-state and the principle of equality before the law has made possible, at least in a superficial sense, the rapid development of a global market since the Second World War. But the question is, to what extent these new legal structures have been imposed on recalcitrant social soil, on habits and attitudes which limit the development of market relations in the Western sense. That is why ambiguity about economic agency in a society is so dangerous. Is the effective economic agent the individual or the family? If it is the family, then a society is likely to respond only to some of the cues of the capitalist market, while ignoring or circumventing other cues. A society in which the family, more or less extended, remains the economic agent is likely to generate clientele relationships, mafia-like groups, loyalties and behaviour which make anything like transparency impossible to attain.

This is no mere academic worry. It is central to the future of developing nations such as Indonesia, China and India, as well as a developed nation such as Japan. If clientele relationships break through formally separate spheres, the barriers set up by law between government ministries, the banking system and private companies, the result can be a manipulation of the market which makes the price mechanism almost meaningless. What has sometimes been called the Japanese model of 'managed' capitalism was long able to sustain the appearances of competition and a marketplace, when in fact officials in the Finance Ministry decided nearly everything important. The deep crisis which developed in Japan in the 1990s suggests that capitalism understood as a free-market system has not sent down roots deep enough to overcome social habits and attitudes which turned a formally capitalist system into almost a command economy. The crisis which has hit Indonesia provides an even more vivid illustration of the impotence of a formal legal system if it does not reflect the *moeurs* of a society.

These examples help to suggest why it is important to look again briefly at how European capitalism developed – how a particular set of moral intuitions gradually gave rise to the norms which have come to be embodied both in the market and in the state. For these moral intuitions are often simply taken for granted by defenders of capitalism, without their foundational role being made clear.

For a long time historians and sociologists have debated the relationship between capitalism and Protestantism, some insisting on the causal priority of Protestantism, while others have been inclined to see Protestantism as the expression of emergent capitalism. Yet I suspect that the crucial factor is Christianity itself, rather than merely its Protestant form. To understand why, it is necessary to look at the way that the medieval city differed from the ancient city.

The development of European capitalism cannot be understood unless the distinctive character of the medieval city is grasped first. For the early medieval city in western Europe came to differ significantly from the cities of antiquity. The most important figure in urban life during the transition from antiquity to the early Middle Ages was the local bishop. In the last century of the Western Roman Empire it was the bishops who became the *de facto* rulers of the cities, taking up many functions previously provided by the Imperial administration and supplanting the hereditary urban élite or *curialis*. Now the distinctive thing about these Christian bishops' urban role was that it was based on an appeal that was 'democratic' rather than 'aristocratic'.

Although bishops often came from the traditional privileged urban élite of the Empire, their authority was founded on a new faith shared with much of the urban population. The rhetoric which such bishops relied upon was inclusive rather than exclusive. It was a rhetoric which encouraged women, the urban poor and even slaves to feel a part of the city in a way that they had not previously been able to. This inclusive rhetoric had a physical counterpart as well. In contrast to the segregated spaces of the ancient city, the Christian population of the cities began to share the same spaces, hearing the bishop's *ex cathedra* words in the principal church, and taking part in the same rites – viz., baptism, the mass, marriage and funerals. In that way the equality of souls postulated by Christianity began to be seen and felt. The translation of a moral status into a social status was under way. The result, ultimately, was the destruction of the aristocratic or corporate character of the ancient city.

The ancient city had been founded on privileges of birth and the hereditary possession of urban offices by particular families. The ancient city had originated as an association of slave-owning families, each with its own cult. The paterfamilias was not only – in our terms – the chief magistrate of the family but also its high priest. Civic and religious functions were combined in the ancient family. What Christianity did, in effect, was to downgrade the religious function of the family, by making the clergy as a class the spokesmen of religion. It was that which – only many centuries later, to be sure – ensured that the medieval city ultimately generated the conception of society as an association of individuals rather than an association of families.

The nineteenth-century French historian Guizot argued that one of the first symptoms of this revolutionary change was to be found in Visigothic laws dating from the early sixth century AD, laws which introduced the notion of representation.

In the ancient Roman municipality the superior magistrates . . . exercised their jurisdiction as a personal right, not at all by way of delegation and as a representative of the *curia*; it was to themselves, not to the municipal body, that the power belonged. The principle of the municipal regime was more aristocratic than democratic. That had been the result of the ancient Roman *moeurs* and especially of the primitive amalgam of religious and political powers in the superior magistrates. In the *Breviarium* [Visigothic code], the aspect of the municipal regime changes; it is no longer in his own name, but in the name of and as a delegate of the *curia* that . . . [the magistrate] exercises his power. To the *curia* as a whole now belongs the jurisdiction. The principle of its organization has become democratic; and so is under way the transformation which will turn the Roman municipality into the medieval commune.

Guizot was quite right to draw attention to the importance of this change in the juridical basis of urban government, showing how the rejection of aristocratic social organization made the early medieval city the harbinger of a new democratic organization of society. Thus, it is no accident that the predominant principle of medieval urban government was that superiors were chosen by inferiors, magistrates by the people rather than superiors choosing their own successors. Election rather than birth became crucial, even if it was often hedged around.

The transfer of religious authority from the paterfamilias to a clerical class, the Christian clergy, initiated this subversion of the ancient family and, with it, the aristocratic composition of society. So the social class which the medieval city bequeathed to modern Europe – the bourgeoisie or 'middle' class – was made possible by the separation of religious from civil authority, the diminution of paternal authority (which remained considerable over property but much less over persons, with sons enjoying complete freedom on the attainment of their majority) and the absence of a large class of urban slaves (which meant that labour was rehabilitated, losing its servile connotations).

The medieval city developed, slowly but surely, as an association of individuals sharing a cult rather than a hierarchical association of slave-owning families, with each family having its own cult – that is, an 'ancestral' altar of the sort described by Fustel de Coulanges in his famous study, *The Ancient City*. Thus, when urban life began to revive extensively in Western Europe in the tenth and the eleventh century, the refugees from the countryside who settled in the boroughs and began to play a crucial role in the revival of trade, inherited a form of urban life which had already been shaped by the Christian Church. Moreover, when the boroughs sought to free themselves from formal ties of dependence on local feudal lords, the Church and its beliefs remained central to urban life. And despite the important place the Church had come to occupy in feudal society, a society founded on privilege, the moral beliefs of the Church remained deeply egalitarian.

Of course, the patriarchal family, the subordination of women and the organization of labour in only semi-voluntary guilds long remained important features of urban life in Europe. It is also true that class conflict within medieval cities, the conflict between oligarchical and democratic factions, was central to their life. None the less, the social class which the medieval city ultimately generated – the European bourgeoisie – became distinguished by its adherence to individualist moral norms. In that way, the influence of the Church, reinforced after the development of Protestantism, penetrated urban society and directed its development to an extent which is not usually appreciated. Yet, in part, that influence was not what the Church ever intended. For Christianity's egalitarian norms contributed to the growing importance of the marketplace, of market relations in which social status began to follow money rather than money following social status.

No doubt humans have exchanged things from the outset – it is almost a defining attribute of our species. But the terms of exchange have not always been the same. Far from it, in fact. Apart from societies where some humans, suffering under the condition of slavery, were not in any sense free agents or able to exchange, most other historical societies have restricted the terms of exchange by means of the family as a unit. The family, whether extended and clannish or restricted in size, became the basic economic agent in such societies. That is, the apportionment of tasks within the family imposed limits on the social division of labour – for these tasks were defined by the convenience of the family as a unit rather than by the advantage of individuals (in the modern sense of the word). Thus, not only were women usually assigned a status and role which restricted their activities, but so too were younger sons made subject to patriarchal authority and fixed tasks.

The convenience of the family as a unit rather than the advantage of individuals, as perceived by themselves, has provided the *modus operandi* in most historical societies. In that sense they were corporate societies, societies organized by assigned status and kinship, the advantages and liabilities of birth.

Western Europe came to differ from such societies quite early in its history. Perhaps the peculiar status of serfs – the ways in which serfdom differed from ancient slavery – was itself a symptom of the individualism (the 'equality of souls') which Christian beliefs about God and man generated and which began to impact on social arrangements. In any case, when refugees from the countryside gathered in what became the boroughs or towns of medieval Europe, the Church was the only body offering systematic beliefs in their midst. I do not for a moment suppose that the equality of souls postulated by the Church did more at first than sustain a certain kind of hope in the urban population – offering them the vision of 'another world' in which that equality might have real meaning. The Christian Church was by no means socially subversive. But that does not mean that the moral beliefs it proclaimed did not have long-term social consequences which it did not foresee.

The egalitarian potential of Christian moral beliefs emerged among townspeople chiefly as a hatred of feudal privilege – something analogous to the sentiments which had animated so many peasant rebellions during the Middle Ages. But whereas rural movements remained essentially movements of protest, contained by the dominance of feudal landlords, the urban movement – so successful at keeping haughty feudatories at bay that Guizot speaks of a general 'insurrection' of the boroughs by the twelfth century – began to create a new way of life. In the boroughs, as we have seen, Christian beliefs conveyed by common rites and in shared spaces replaced the unequal statuses and exclusive spaces of the ancient city. As the Church's rhetoric was inclusive rather than exclusive, the idea that urban government should represent all those living in the *urbs* (city) seemed increasingly self-evident. If everyone had a moral claim on the city, then anything like the aristocratic social organization of the ancient city, in which the government of the city was a form of private property, was ruled out.

The roots of European capitalism and of what ultimately became the Industrial Revolution are to be found in the individualism of the medieval city. For the medieval city began to foster the conception of society as an association of individuals rather than an association of families. In that way it laid the foundation for a new economic and social system, by removing – at first in principle rather than in fact – the barriers to a far more elaborate social division of labour, barriers which had traditionally been imposed by exchange relationships, restricted to and serving the family as an economic unit.

That removal of barriers could only have its full impact when the egalitarian moral norms of the Church came to be formalized in the legal structure created by the nation-states of Europe, by the principle of equality before the law which, in due course, they introduced and defended. In that way it is fair to say that the European nation-state grew up around and was moulded by a particular social structure. It formalized the norms of that social structure, of a society of individuals, and made possible its further development, dissolving the remains of feudalism in Europe. The nation-state and civil equality were thus not suddenly imposed – like some alien agency – on later medieval society. They grew out of the social conflicts characteristic of that society, and the moral intuitions which underlay the struggle between the new cities and the old feudal class. It is no accident that the commercial activity which became central to the medieval city gradually created a new 'middling' social class – a class intermediate, that is, between the noble and serf castes of feudal society. The identity of this new middle or bourgeois class was constituted by egalitarian norms and, as it expanded, it began to engulf social conditions founded on privilege rather than equality. Increasingly, status followed wealth.

We have already seen that the development of this new class and the development of the state were closely and necessarily connected. For it was the state as a new form of government in the later Middle Ages which began to create that structure of individual rights – limited at first to men, of course, but capable of extension beyond the gender barrier – that on the one hand ratified the market relations which had already developed, and on the other created the formal or legal basis for further expansion of market relations. The European nation-state as it developed in the early modern period became a living testament to the distinctive nature of the medieval city – for it perpetuated the egalitarian norms which had, *au fond*, animated that city and became the means of generalizing them throughout society.

As those egalitarian norms developed – as they became more elaborate and their implications better understood – they removed impediments to the division of labour which had affected previous historical societies. Thus, the disappearance of serfdom and the growth of civil equality meant that everyone found himself in a market condition, not only free to move about and sell his own labour, but *de facto* obliged to do so, unless possessed of enough property to make such labour unnecessary. Imposing on everyone, in that sense, a market condition is the most distinctive thing about the equality before the law which has accompanied the development of the middle or bourgeois class. That progress of equality continues dramatically in our own day, especially with the weakening of traditional barriers to the commercial activity of women. In doing so it simply adds another step to a process that reflects the egalitarian moral beliefs which have underpinned the growth of the market in the Western sense.

But we must never forget that there are other kinds of market. We must not assume that markets in the Western sense constitute themselves or that merely technical changes or even the invention of the state were sufficient to ensure the development of capitalism in the West.

For that is not true. It is the Christian-derived belief in the moral equality of humans, translated into the stipulation of equal basic rights, which created civil society in the European sense and provided the fulcrum for the development of market relations or capitalism. It is that structure of equal basic rights which results in the individual rather than the family becoming the effective economic agent. That is what has been the remarkable achievement of Western Europe and its colonial offshoots. Whereas in most human societies the family has been the crucial unit of economic activity, with burdens and rewards sorted according to roles within the family, civil society in Europe has turned the individual into the focus of burdens and benefits, the medium of exchange relationships. Thus, it is a moral transformation which underpinned the emergence of a historically unprecedented type of society in Europe – a society which, through individual exchange relationships, has achieved a scale and complexity previously unknown to history.

We ignore or underestimate the importance of moral and cultural considerations at our own peril. Yet a kind of economic determinism has come to shape Western thinking, giving Marxism a vengeful after-life. It emerges in that view about the relationship between the market and the state which I have called Capitalist Triumphalism. Thus, it is often assumed that the growth of market relations will bring in its wake the moral disciplines required by civil and political liberty. But that assumption turns on a certain notion of self-interest and self-respect, of incentives which lead *the individual* to recognize the claims of reciprocity. But if the effective economic agent is the family rather than the individual, then economic incentives no longer carry the same moral message. They neither underscore the equal fundamental status of humans nor the rights and duties which follow from moral equality. In that way, the potential of market relations for reinforcing the moralizing process – that process intrinsic to giving the rule of law a firm foundation in attitudes and habits – presupposes that the economic agent is the individual rather than the family.

But, as we have seen, whether or not that is the case is a matter of cultural tradition. It is not something which can be taken for granted or assumed to be 'natural', genetic rather than cultural in origin. The potential conflict of values can be described in terms of different conceptions of the family. The modern European conception assimil-ates the family, once the children have grown up, to a voluntary association, an association of equals, while traditional, non-Western conceptions of the family remain sternly hierarchical and patriarchal. That conflict of values also accounts for very different conceptions of property rights – witness the difficulty which Russia, traditionally lacking any conception of individual ownership of land, has encoun-tered in trying to develop a legal code appropriate to a market economy.

So merely proclaiming the rule of law and introducing the state as a form of government cannot turn the effective economic agent from being the family into the individual overnight. Introducing the state and the rule of law merely begins a drawn-out process by which the individual can be released from the ties of status and kinship to become the effective economic agent. It is a necessary but not a sufficient condition.

That is why in speaking of the global market or the triumph of capitalism we can easily mislead ourselves. For the fact that the nation-state as a political form has become almost universal, carrying with it formally the rule of law and the individual property rights which are a necessary condition for the development of the market, does not mean that the deeper habits and attitudes which sustain capitalism or a market economy have suddenly appeared everywhere. On the contrary, as we have already seen, there is plenty of evidence that clannishness and clientism continue to operate behind legal superstructures, giving to economic activity in such countries a character which defies modern Western categories – falling into a kind of no man's land between the legitimate sphere of what we understand as civil society and outrightly criminal activity. Of course, such a pattern is not wholly unknown in Europe. 'Tyrannical' family ties and clientism have survived in southern Italy to the present day, frustrating all attempts by the Italian state to give any reality to the legal framework which is supposed to underpin Italian life. It is that failure which, in large part, accounts for growing North Italian resentment against the South – a feeling that the inability of the South to create a civil society creates a gulf which neither can nor ought to be crossed. The appeal of the Northern League is thus a testament to the great difficulty of creating the attitudes and habits required for the proper – that is, *transparent* – operation of a civil society.

It could be argued that none of this matters. Different societies have no obligation to share the values of Europe or conform to Western ways. Yet the issue is more complicated than that – and more fraught too, for both sides. For in adopting the nation-state as a political form, in proclaiming the rule of law domestically and adhering to international agreements framed in terms of human rights and commercial transparency, non-Western nations have, up to a point, formally accepted Western values and ways. Moreover, such nations often seek Western investment, and accept aid and loans on terms which are ostensibly those applying in Europe or the Americas. Those terms presuppose institutions like banks, stock markets and free exchanges which determine prices, a legal framework which guarantees that exchanges are made at prices which have some meaning. I do not mean to suggest that it is hypocritical of these non-Western nations to proclaim their commitment to such values and institutions. But their formal commitment may be misleading not only for us, but also for them. At times such nations suffer from a condition which, in an individual, would be described as schizophrenia. They have the makings of two personalities. And, depending upon the circumstances, one or other of these personalities comes to the fore. In the one case, it is assumed that the economic agent is the individual. In the other, it is assumed that the family is the more legitimate agent, the agent whose claims ought to prevail.

To describe this tension simply as 'cronyism' – which many Western commentators have recently begun to do – misses the point entirely. For cronyism as a description implies the prior acceptance of individualist moral values. Otherwise the word would have no condemnatory force. Cronyism completely fails to identify the problem, which is that the habits and attitudes of a pre-individualist society distort the meaning of a 'market'. They create solidarities that operate behind and outside of the framework of individual transactions which legally constitute market operations. That transparency which is meant to tie together the operations of the marketplace and the rule of law is clouded over by habits and attitudes which, contrary to appearances, are decisive in market 'exchanges'. Thus, the market becomes a travesty of itself. For individual choice and the operation of companies are constrained by solidarities and forms of deference which make market outcomes opaque. It is just that opacity which legal regulation of the minimum standards of the workplace – rules about hours, health, and so forth – as well as anti-monopoly legislation are designed to prevent.

Pre-individualist solidarities make a mockery of the market as we understand it. The story of post-war Japan – what used to be described as the Japanese economic 'miracle' – can be understood against this background. To a crucial extent, the directors of banks and business corporations have, in decision-making, taken their lead from officials in the Ministry of Finance. In that way Japanese markets long remained 'orderly' and 'solid', less prone to the ups and downs which affected Western economics. Japan was indeed virtually immune to unemployment, so little was it affected by world trade cycles. Because of their cosy relationship with banks, Japanese firms were not so preoccupied with the profit motive, while workers could count on lifetime employment provided they accepted the norms of a managerial culture.

Habits of command and obedience which had characterized traditional Japanese society were used to redefine role-playing in a fashion suitable to an industrial society. But the model remained that of role-playing, rather than one of an individual taking 'rational' decisions in his or her own interest. Thus, capitalism in Japan was founded not on rationality or self-interest in our sense but rather on the kind of ritual behaviour associated with playing an assigned role in the family and corporation. Japanese 'managed' capitalism was able to dispense with the dispersed decision-making which both defines and justifies free markets, replacing it with centralized decision-making. It is for this reason that, behind the surface, problems accumulated in Japan which its authoritarian system could long conceal but not really deal with. The marketplace was not allowed to play its co-ordinating role. In its place decisions were made by civil servants and bankers in the interest of stability and prestige. That was the background to the crisis of Japan's managed capitalism in the 1990s. A poignant illustration of the continued power of traditional Japanese social attitudes was the increased incidence of 'family suicides' during those years. The family collectively felt obliged to share in the ruin of its head.

I am not saying that economic rationality did not make progress in Japan during the long post-war prosperity. Indeed, the crisis of the mid-1990s in Japan can be seen as the result of a kind of schizophrenia developing – with the Japanese consumer torn between traditional role-playing and market rationality, and so responding to traditional disciplines only up to a point and, in particular, preferring to save rather than consume in the face of serious doubts about the stability of the banks and the property market. This emergent rationality in Japan simply compounds the problems of managing its economy in the traditional fashion.

Hong Kong, after its return to China, illustrates this problem in reverse.

For the risk in Hong Kong is that the social structure of China – in which the family remains the primary economic agent rather than the individual – will impose itself upon and subvert the rule of law launched under British rule. Law, instead of grounding the marketplace and economic rationality, may become a façade manipulated by mafia-like families and clannish associations of families. That retreat from the rule of law and transparency would amount to the victory of traditional, pre-individualist habits and attitudes over economic rationality. The latter, with its European roots, undoubtedly made remarkable progress in Hong Kong under British rule. But it remains a fragile plant, and it is doubtful how long the social soil of China, when no longer tilled with a view to the rule of law, will allow it to survive.

That does not mean we have to despair of the future. There is an important sense in which the exercise of market freedoms and the formal rule of law give a glimpse of wider freedom, of the benefits of civil and political liberty, even to those whose moral intuitions remain more firmly rooted in family, tribe or caste than do those of modern Europeans. Historical evidence suggests that exposure to market relations *does* begin a process of change which it is difficult to reverse. But that is not the same as supposing that such exposure is enough to carry those changes through to the establishment of a liberal democratic order.

That is also why the gradualist and oblique approach recommended by the British – reliance on the marketplace to do the job of democratiz- ing – will not do. It is easy to see how the instincts of an unwritten constitution contribute to this British attitude, a distrust of grand political projects. But, in truth, a far more positive emphasis on human rights and the form of the state is needed if the growth of world trade and economic interdependence is to be crowned with liberal democratic institutions. To that extent, the instincts of the French are right. Political will remains crucial. And here the truly idealistic side of the policies pursued by the French élite emerges, their concern that Europe should have a clear identity and a will. The French are anxious that Europe should be able to chart a course independently of the United States, and not sink into the abject condition of a client. That is why, in the French view, Europe will sooner or later have to turn itself into a single state.

Unfortunately, the idealism in the French view often gives way to something less elevated – to the habit of dominating, of trying to shape Europe as a bloc which, when required, could indulge in an important degree of economic autarky. 'Political will' thus gets translated into a 'political control', supposedly needed to defend Europe against other blocs, whether North American or Asian. In that way, the *étatist* habits of the French political class reassert themselves.

Yet in many respects the determination to create a European political will need not involve any friction, let alone conflict, with the United States. Both the United States and France have demonstrated their concern that freer world trade should be accompanied by guarantees about minimum labour standards, so that the standards achieved in Western societies are not jeopardized. Clearly this is a delicate matter – for it often leads developing nations to argue that the West is trying to undermine their competitive position, denying to them advantages which Western capitalism had at an earlier stage of development.

Here a difficult balancing act is required – one which recognizes the importance of defending higher social standards, while recognizing that poorer countries cannot immediately match our own. But that is not the only issue. Do they really want to? Or, are their moral intuitions firmly on the side of the family, preferring that it remains the chief provider of social welfare, as well as the effective economic agent? In due course, they will have to decide.

It has been argued recently – no doubt in reaction to the complacency associated with what I have called Capitalist Triumphalism – that we seriously underestimate the importance of religions and their future divisive potential. Some are convinced that the end of ideological conflict, with the collapse of Communism, will lead *not* to a new liberal democratic world order, but rather to prolonged confrontation between the Christian and Islamic nations. They point to the upsurge of Islamic fundamentalism in countries like Algeria and Egypt, indeed throughout the Middle East, as a symptom of the struggle to come.

That is far too despairing a point of view, if by it is meant that religious differences will lead directly to conflicts between nations. But what *will* become increasingly important are the moral differences inadvertently revealed by new efforts to regulate the global market – by efforts to create a normative framework which can suppress clientism and guarantee transparency. Such efforts will, in fact, bring to the surface the conflicting moral intuitions underlying the operation of capitalism in countries with different religious traditions. It will throw into stark relief the difference between pre-individualist and individualist visions of society. So we must begin to prepare ourselves for moral conflicts being expressed increasingly in economic terms – something which turns the Marxist model for understanding social conflict upside-down!

9

Europe and the United States

At first glance one of the more surprising features of the post-World War Two climate of opinion has been the consistent support of US administrations and leading American politicians for the construction of a federal Europe – for something resembling a United States of Europe. I say surprising because it is easy to think of reasons why such a development might be deemed to run counter to American interests. It might be deemed to do so especially because the creation of a hegemonic power in Europe could offset and reduce the political and economic influence of the United States in the world. Is that really what Americans want?

It is clearly what the French want. French support for European arrangements and initiatives, whether economic, diplomatic or military, has always been accompanied by arguments and rhetoric designed to establish that only by organizing itself can Europe contain American influence. The French want Europe to be a 'major player' in the world, a player quite on a par with the United States. Suspicion of American influence, its nature and implications, runs very deep in France, especially among the political class or élite. They have indulged in what at times is something close to a conspiracy theory, seeing the self-interest of American capitalism at work behind nearly every post-war American initiative.

The French are well-placed to take that view. For the fact that both leading world powers since the displacement of France as the leading European power in the eighteenth century, first Britain and then the United States, have been English-speaking, arms the French against any naïvety about American intentions – a naïvety to which the British, who may experience vicarious satisfaction in the *pax Americana* through a shared language and political culture, are more prone. But, of course, things are more complicated than that. The deep suspicion of American influence which runs through the French political class also reflects a growing cultural insecurity in France – for, paradoxically, despite official suspicion and even hostility to the United States, popular culture in France is probably more open to American influence than that of any other European country. From jazz, through films, to male fashions, American models reign supreme in France, to the discomfiture of the French political and cultural élite. Is it an accident that France has taken the lead in attempts to restrict the import of American 'cultural products' into Europe?

If the French are right about the relentless pressure of American commercial self-interest, and if the creation of a federal state would put Europe in a better position to resist that pressure, then our original question returns even more emphatically. Why have American leaders so consistently favoured closer European Union?

It might just be stupidity – the survival, beyond its time, of a prejudice in favour of integration which understandably took possession of American policy in the early post-war years, when the fragile nations of Western Europe seemed to be at risk both from the military might of the Soviet Union and political subversion from domestic communist parties. But that seems an odd, unconvincing conclusion – especially if the French hypothesis about America's devious and relentless pursuit of self-interest is taken seriously.

What other explanations can there be? One might simply be con- venience, the advantage of dealing with a Europe that could speak, as American spokesmen have at times wistfully opined, with a 'single voice'. As Henry Kissinger remarked, when he was Secretary of State, 'When I want to speak to Europe, who do I call?' Another possible explanation is not so cynical or pragmatic – namely, that post-war American policy has from time to time, at least marginally, represented the triumph of belief over self-interest. We have seen that American nationalism has been shaped crucially by the experience of self- government, with that self-government conceived on a federalist model. The belief that such a form of government would be a natural and desirable development in a Europe long plagued by national rivalries, an escape from the old pattern of European *realpolitik* which cost the world so dear in the twentieth century, can be seen as a plausible extension of American confidence in the virtues of its own form of government.

The survival of this kind of teleology in the United States is not unimportant. Yet even this more high-minded motive may contain within it an element of self-interest, though self-interest of a non-economic kind. What I have in mind is this. One of the healthy by-products of a liberal democratic system of government should be and often is a kind of modesty, an awareness of the ambiguity of the results of any public decision-making process, the difficulty of identifying the public weal and wariness about populist pressures taking over the democratic process. Thus, a sense of the possibility of not living up to the professed standards of liberal democracy is an ever-present aspect of the experience of self-government.

Woodrow Wilson stormed the continent of Europe in 1919 with his call to 'make the world safe for democracy'. It was a call which the residually aristocratic societies of Europe found both naïve and unsettling. But it remains a constant theme in American foreign policy. Perhaps Europeans misinterpret it, however. Instead of interpreting it as aggressive and vulgar self-advertisement, Europeans might be wiser to interpret it as a call for help. For the very pride which leads Americans to consider their own form of government as 'blessed' – and the United States as 'God's country' – can contribute to a gnawing self-doubt, to doubt about whether the United States alone is an adequate or reliable champion of the 'good cause' of democracy in the world. Oddly, what looks like overweening American confidence, its political evangelism, can conceal an appeal for solidarity in working for the spread of liberal democracy. That is a better interpretation of the American wish for Europe to speak with a single voice.

To have in the world another major champion of liberal democratic values might be something of a relief, removing complete responsibility for the defence of such crucial – in their own idiom, 'God-given' – values from American shoulders. Something like that sense of a shared cause, and the relaxation that can come from having a friend, has played an important part in the United States' 'special relationship' with Britain. Its alleged weakening in recent years may have more to do with the failure of liberal idealism in Britain than with the decline of British economic and political power, usually cited as the cause.

Further evidence of the American search for solidarity emerges in the warmer relationship which has developed between the United States and Germany. Here instincts born of a shared federalism have come into play and have been more important than is generally realized. After all, the post-war German Constitution was not only inspired by American federalism but actually written at least partly by a Harvard professor, Karl Friedrich (a German-American, it should be noticed). German federalism does not, of course, have merely American origins. It has roots in the decentralized character of the German *ancien régime* – an *ancien régime* which survived into the second half of the nineteenth century and thus remains alive in the German mind and sentiments in a way that is not possible in a country like France, where the process of despotic centralization took place so much earlier.

Yet the closeness of today's federal Germany to its decentralized pre-Bismarckian past suggests one way in which American reliance on its own history may lead it into a serious misjudgement – into overlooking a problem that Europe will encounter, if it moves towards a federal organization. For the question of what ought to be the constituent parts of the American union, the states, has never been in doubt and has never been contested. But the same cannot really be said of Europe.

In Europe there are regions which retain memories of a political existence earlier than those of nation-states. There has, moreover, been a clear connection between the resurgence of such regional identities and loyalties and the growing power of Brussels in recent years. The lure of Brussels for resurgent regionalisms is that it provides a centre which can be played off against the traditional 'oppressors' – i.e., existing nation-states. Thus, Scottish, Corsican and Catalonian nationalists see an unrivalled opportunity to weaken the states to which they are currently subordinated, by using Brussels as a fulcrum against London, Paris or Madrid. In that way both the European 'centre' and regions have been gaining at the expense of the old nation-states recently.

This pattern might be called the revenge of the regions. For many of these regions look back to an earlier era of independence which was destroyed during the period of European state-making, which extended from the fifteenth century into the nineteenth century. Even if the 'nationalists' of these regions do not seriously expect them to become nation-states, they may nourish dreams of a Europe which more closely resembles the patchwork quilt of late feudal Europe. Nor are they short of arguments. Their claims can be framed either in terms of defending historic communities or on grounds of decentralization – that is, the creation of political units smaller than nation-states and closer to the people.

As I mentioned earlier, the mechanism which has recently been and may continue to be exploited by these regions has some analogy with the mechanism of early European state-building itself – for example, the way the French burghers or townspeople allied themselves with the French Crown to struggle against local feudal oppressors. It was that alliance which gradually destroyed feudal jurisdictions in France, creating in their place a sovereign agency or nation-state. But that historical precedent should amount to a serious warning to anyone tempted to imitate it, uncritically, on behalf of regional autonomy in Europe today. For the first and major result of that mechanism was to throw power to a more remote centre rather than retrieve power for locals. The result was to create a bureaucratic form of the state.

Yet even if the encouragement of regionalism could be managed without that result, there is another problem that is raised by the resurgence of older regional identities in Europe and the weakening of existing nation-states.

Few such regions have any civic tradition, any tradition of democracy or citizenship in working order. The experience of self-government, when it was last enjoyed by such regions, took place on very different social terms from those of modern Europe. That is, such regions may once have enjoyed autonomy and, in a sense, 'liberty' – but it was an aristocratic liberty founded on social ranks, on a corporate model of society. It was a form of liberty which threw authority and power into the hands of leading regional feudatories, the Church or civic corporations rather than into the hands of the people as a whole – the people conceived, that is, as a civil society founded on equality before the law. Something important follows from that. Regional identities and loyalties in Europe are not as closely tied to the rule of law or democratic principles as they ought to be, if such regions are now to become in any formal or juridical sense constituent parts of a federal Europe. European regions have yet to create democratic political cultures.

In that way, European regions differ radically from the original American states, which had been self-governing colonies for more than a century before there was any question of their association into a larger political unit (except, of course, under the British Crown). In American states, by the late eighteenth century, traditions of citizenship and a civic culture had resulted from prolonged experience of self-government. And even if the traditions were not completely democratic in the modern sense – and that was more true of the oligarchic South than of puritan New England – none the less, the tradition of citizenship was founded crucially on a sense of social equality (excluding slaves and, as yet, women) that distinguished the American colonies from European societies which had known permanent distinctions of rank.

The contrast I am making does not apply equally to all European regions. It applies less to Catalonia, for example, than to Corsica or perhaps even the north of Italy. But the danger in all cases is that, to a greater or lesser extent, the kind of democracy unleashed by any project for a Europe made up of regions rather than nation-states would be what I have called democracy *simpliciter* – a populist kind of democracy which is defined chiefly in terms of liberation from foreigners and which offers little guidance to the complex and hazardous business of self-government. The danger is that in throwing off the 'shackles' of the nation-state – rejecting national subordinations which are perceived to be oppressive – there will also be thrown away civic cultures which, even if imperfect from the standpoint of fostering citizenship and consent, none the less incorporate democratic norms which have, by contrast, played little or no part in shaping regional identities.

It is true that, with the help of the model of American federalism, Germany seems to have overcome this danger – conciliating to an important extent central power with respect for traditional regional identities, all constrained by a constitutional system which privileges human rights and throws considerable power away from executives and legislatures into the hands of the judiciary. But even Germany has to cope with the recent addition of a number of *Länder* which, previously parts of the German Democratic Republic, have as yet to develop civic traditions that can be relied upon. To be sure, it can be done. The Netherlands offers a precious example of how originally oligarchic provincial cultures can be adapted to a democratic national culture.

If the populist threat posed by regional 'independence' movements in Europe is to be contained yet not merely repressed – that is, reshaped in a democratic mould – new flexibility in arrangements for distributing power between the centre and periphery will have to be devised. Probably the most instructive example available today in Europe is the Spanish state, which has, in effect, been steadily reconstructing itself since the death of Franco. New arrangements between the centre and periphery, granting rather different degrees of autonomy to regions such as Catalonia and the Basque country, have enabled Spain to move a long way from the notoriously repressive, centralized state apparatus of the Franco era.

By contrast, the Italian state has been less successful at accommodating regional pressures, perhaps in part because the state itself has been so weak in some respects. In Italy, making concessions of power to the regions has seemed either redundant or out of the question. Lacking any formalized system of establishing a balance between the northern and southern regions, which have indeed no formal constitutional existence, has made it easier for Umberto Bossi and the Northern League to call for complete independence for the north, arguing that the economic and social differences between the north and the *mezzogiorno* are so great as to amount to two different 'productive systems'. That fusion of populist argument with economic reductionism testifies to the imperious need of giving subsidiarity a careful constitutional standing, by defining the areas and spheres which are deemed capable of generating legitimate claims on the state. For Italian unity and the Italian state seem at times to be in real danger of dissolution, illustrating some of the problems likely to arise if the development of European union were to involve the reversion of Europe to anything like the patchwork quilt of regions which preceded the development of the nation-state. And it is of course interesting that the Italian state, one of the last states in Europe to be created, is now perhaps the one most threatened with dissolution.

I do not want to be understood as wholly identifying regionalism with populism. Clearly, the legitimacy of many regional interests and identities must be acknowledged and catered for by any adequate political system. An encouraging example of that has been the development of regionalism within the framework of the unitary French state since 1981. For not only have recent decentralizing moves in France worked to the benefit of established authorities like the communes and departments, they have also involved the creation of new regional authorities, combinations of departments, responsible for economic and social planning and the co-ordination of resources.

Ironically, it could be argued that one of the weaknesses of the American federal structure is that it pays little attention to and provides no organizational focus for regional interests as opposed to state and local interests. Probably the state structure inherited from the colonial period seemed adequate to regional questions in the earliest decades of American history, at least until the issue of slavery came to dominate politics and strongly demarcate regions. But the rapid enlargement of the American Union after the Civil War, until it became a truly continental nation, has left the issue of larger regional identities and interests untouched by the American federal structure.

To that extent, in the United States too, there is an important potential connection between regionalism and populism – a danger that regionalism might, in the future, unleash democratic pressures of an undesirable kind. And it is here that we may have come upon the deepest motive for American support for a federal Europe. It is perhaps only a half-conscious motive. But the modesty which, as I argued above, often accompanies and certainly ought to accompany the process of self-government may have contributed to enthusiasm, especially among members of the American political class, for a federal or 'United States' of Europe for the following reasons.

Even more than European political thinkers, the subtlest American political minds, such as Hamilton, Madison and Jefferson, have recognized how fragile an enterprise self-government is – and how persistent is the danger that liberal democracy can give way to a much more dangerous and vulgar form of democracy, a plebiscitary or populist democracy. In the United States that danger of slippage towards populism has been contained by two things. The first has been the role of lawyers as a class in the political system and in the parties. The ubiquity of legal training and the way legal education provides a basis for careers, not just in law and politics, but also in commerce, industry and banking, have enormously strengthened constitutional norms and the practice of judicial review. Thus, the formal means by which the operation of the majority principle has been restrained in American federalism – especially, the Bill of Rights – have been reinforced by the dominant role of lawyers in the political and economic élites. That dominance has shaped the rights-based political culture of the United States.

The second, and closely related, condition which has operated in the same direction has been the great influence in the American political system of what its opponents describe as the 'Northeastern Establishment'. This influence originally reflected the greater wealth, population and education of the Northeastern states. But, to the surprise of many observers, it has long survived many social and economic changes in the United States, changes which led some observers to predict the eclipse of the Northeast more than a century ago. How did its domin-ance survive? Northeastern or 'Yankee' dominance survived mass immigration from southern and eastern Europe, the expansion of the Union to the west coast and the steady reduction of the 'Wasp' element of the population by one means especially. The universities and law schools of the Northeast remained pre-eminent, and provided the means of assimilating upwardly mobile individuals from other parts of the nation – endowing them with legal and constitutional attitudes which kept the United States as a whole 'safe' for liberal democracy.

It is therefore a matter of great moment that in recent decades the Northeastern Establishment has come under threat and has probably lost at least some of its traditional influence, if not its identity. The movement of population, industry and wealth to the South and West since the 1960s has put the traditional hegemony of the Northeast at risk. It has given Southern and Western states, not least through urbanization, prosperity and the development of a two-party system in the South, as well as much improved higher education, the self-confidence and means of exercising far more influence within the political system.

That shift of population, industry and wealth to the South and West has already had and will continue to have important consequences for the political culture of the United States. For these regions have always been far more populist in their political attitudes than the Northeast. Their political attitudes have been shaped by a fundamentalist brand of Protestantism (typified by the Southern Baptists), by distrust of Washington and of the political and economic élites known, no doubt over-simply, as the Northeastern Establishment. Hence political argument in these regions has been marked by anti-intellectualism, by 'states rights' rhetoric and a deeply moralizing approach to public policy, not least foreign policy, an approach which bears traits of religious dualism. In these regions 'good' and 'evil' are at times so sharply separated that the principle of equal liberty seems at risk.

In a peculiarly American way, Southern and Western populism is also mixed up with rampant commercialism. That combination is beautifully represented by the novelist Sinclair Lewis's character Elmer Gantry, a tub-thumping revivalist preacher who is also utterly commercial and indeed corrupt. To make Elmer Gantry the symbol of the dominant political culture in the South and West is, of course, unfair. The fundamentalist, 'born-again' religion, so powerful in these regions, shapes some powerful moral convictions – as movements opposing the legalizing of abortion, homosexual rights and attempts to control the sale of firearms reveal.

But even if the image of the corrupt revivalist preacher is a travesty of Southern and Western culture, it does help to reveal the crucial change that has been taking place in the United States. That is the decline of a peculiarly American form of deference. The important role played by the Northeastern Establishment for more than a century and a half was to give an educated and relatively cultured class a decisive role in American policy-making. As I have urged, that class was not in fact recruited simply from the Northeast, but it was either educated in Northeastern universities and law schools or came largely to conform to standards of behaviour set in the Northeast. Tacitly, Americans long deferred to that class.

Since the 1960s, however, that pattern has been seriously jeopardized. The partial eclipse of the Northeast within the political system, which had been predicted for a century or more, has actually taken place. The change can be illustrated if we compare the group of advisers surrounding President Kennedy in the early 1960s with the aides surrounding President Nixon only ten years later. Kennedy's men, such as McGeorge Bundy and Arthur Schlesinger, corresponded, almost to the point of exaggeration, to the older American political élite, Harvard-educated and strongly Europhile. By contrast, the men who staffed the presidential office under Nixon were more often Westerners. But not only that, their background was not so much a conventional legal one, as a background in advertising and public relations. It is hard to resist the conclusion that the resulting difference in political culture had something to do with the Watergate crisis. For one can say, at the very least, that men like Haldeman and Erlichmann had less concern with legality and more with marketing or public relations than is desirable in a constitutional order.

True, the continuing influence of Northeastern educational establishments, law firms and the culture they represent should never be underestimated. Their ability to subdue the populist inheritances of Presidents such as Carter and Clinton, who came out of the Southern culture not of tidewater Virginia but of the 'backwoods', has proved remarkable. But recent struggles to contain populist impulses have made the purveyors of traditional Establishment culture in the United States more aware than ever before of the fragility of the norms and behaviour which have, on the whole, characterized American federal government in our times.

Is it fanciful to suppose that awareness of that fragility has contributed to American political leaders' enthusiasm for the project of creating a United States of Europe? Perhaps not. To have an enlarged European polity with constitutional arrangements similar to those of the United States, and openly proclaiming the same liberal democratic values, must be an attraction for those who feel, at least occasionally, that they are walking on thin ice at home. The prospect of a federal Europe offers them a kind of consolation, a potential liberal democratic solidarity.

There is an additional consideration urging American leaders of the old school in the same direction. The shift of population and wealth South and West within the United States has coincided with an increasing inflow of Asian immigrants, the first significant inflow of non-Christian populations into the United States. The new economic clout of the Western states joined to the sympathies and traditions of these non-European immigrants has helped to divert American attention away from Europe and towards the Pacific basin. To some extent that development is probably irresistible and is even a good thing, correcting what might be called traditional Waspish myopia.

But the development could go too far. If it were to do so, it would raise questions not only about European relations with the United States, but also about the future character of American political culture. It would raise especially the question of language. I have argued that the commanding role of English in the past has been a necessary condition of sustaining the culture of consent which underlies American federalism. The diversity of recent immigration into the United States will probably safeguard that role. But there is an exception. The scale of Spanish-speaking immigration, legal and illegal, into the Southwestern states does raise a wholly new threat to English. For, of course, such states share a border with Spanish-speaking Mexico. Recent controversies in California, Arizona and other states about giving Spanish a status co-equal with that of English have begun to bring this question into public view – not least in the public schools.

Lurking behind the question of a common language is still another, even more difficult one. It is the question of religion, of the extent to which Judaeo-Christian beliefs, at least in a residual moral form, are also a necessary condition of sustaining a liberal democratic culture. Can the remarkable ability of American institutions to assimilate new immigrants to constitutional norms and a culture of consent survive without the help of the moral beliefs to which Christianity contributed? Is American life infinitely adaptable, with commerce and consumerism enough to sustain respect for individual liberty and encourage civic spirit? Unease about these questions has begun to invade American public life, adding perhaps to a still largely inarticulate wish that Europe might take a more vigorous part in the promotion of free institutions throughout the world.

Up to a point, that unease has been concealed by the growth of pressures for 'political correctness' in recent years. Yet what does political correctness amount to? It amounts to acknowledgement that shared beliefs – even if the beliefs shared are only that moral and social variety should be respected – are, ultimately, the only security for political stability and a culture of consent. The problem, however, is that political correctness breaches the walls provided until only recently by Christian moral beliefs. Those beliefs were interpreted as authorizing 'equal liberty'. But this was a liberty for individuals, a liberty offset by the duties which corresponded to the rights claimed. Political correctness, on the other hand, can involve pluralism moving beyond the confines of traditional liberalism – generating claims for 'group rights' which do not lay down any clear limits for moral variety. It is this character of political correctness which will, I think, cause increasing unease, and could unleash a moral backlash – a backlash which would be shaped by the populist culture of the South and West rather than by the nuanced liberalism of the Northeast. Yet even the latter is threatened by what amounts to an unprecedented separating of pluralism from liberalism, so that some of the claims being made and defended – on behalf of ethnic communities, for example – are no longer necessarily compatible with an individualist moral framework.

In effect, the claims of 'moral minorities' sometimes expand the meaning of pluralism beyond its traditional liberal democratic limits – threatening to replace liberal universalism with a new form of tribalism. My fear is that, in due course, this separation of pluralism from liberalism could create a deep and widespread revulsion which would reinforce the threat of populism in America. Then the 'moral majority' might return with a vengeance, a majority less constrained than in the past by the norms of liberal democracy and by the habits of the Northeastern Establishment.

It is not impossible that at some point a kind of European lend-lease or Marshall Plan in reverse will be necessary. Only this time the aid required will be moral rather than material. Despite what might be called a tarnishing of the American dream which has resulted from the growth of American economic and political influence, the advent of quasi-Empire, the United States has continued to be a beacon of democracy in a way that no existing European state can claim to be. That is because the Constitution of the United States is not just a design for the machinery of government. It is also an affirmation of beliefs. The beliefs affirmed are universal in their scope, involving claims to autonomy and respect which humans ought to enjoy as individuals. To that extent the American Constitution is, inescapably, a proselytizing document. It may be that, shorn as it is of overt metaphysical or theological assumptions, the constitution remains the most effective proselytizing agency for liberal democracy in the world.

However, as we have seen, liberal democracy is not without risk in the United States itself, as a consequence of social and economic changes there. Is it utopian to suppose that the emergence, sooner or later, of a formal constitution for Europe, a liberal democratic identity in Europe less closely tied to particular national traditions, might serve both to create another such proselytizing agency in the world and to reinforce American commitment to these values? Post-war American support for the European federalist project suggests that leading Americans do not think so. They may well be right. The French, at times, seem to understand and accept this ideological challenge, far more than the British.

If what I have argued about populist trends in the American polity and about an implied American wish to share responsibility for the cause of democracy in the world is correct, then an important question follows. What sort of relationship with the United States should a more integrated Europe seek to build? Should it be one which downplays idealism – that is, shared beliefs and aspirations – in order to avoid any appearance of the West 'ganging up' on the rest of the world? That might be the preference of those who fear, above all, the charge that Western imperialism, having left behind not only its political phase but even, perhaps, its economic phase, will now assume an ideological form.

Should Europe be content with *realpolitik* and assume that democratic liberty will follow economic development in the rest of the world almost mechanically? Or should Europe seek to reinforce American idealism, engaging with those features of the American polity which make it possible to present a common front in defence of human rights and representative government? Should a renewed Atlantic alliance between federal 'equals' try to establish that a liberal form of democracy prevails in the world? Such an alliance might have the benefit of offsetting populist pressures both within the United States and Europe, helping, in particular, the old Northeastern Establishment in the United States adjust to the movement of population and wealth South and West, while defending European values against an excessive straying of American attention towards the Pacific basin.

The problem, then, is to find a single European voice, a voice which can answer these questions. And that problem springs from the very different cultures associated with three forms of the European state. These cultures offer blueprints for different forms of a transatlantic relationship. They point to quite different directions of development. The British share with the Americans not only a language, but a culture of self-government and recent experience of Imperial responsibility throughout the world. On the other hand, the traditional British form of the state, with its aristocratic presuppositions, is a far cry from American federalism (though this may gradually change with the Blair Government's programme of devolution). In the past, the British political class has been embarrassed by the idealist features of the American political system and foreign policy, and has kept its distance from 'making the world safe for democracy'. Indeed, at times British foreign policy has seemed to make a virtue of cultivating relationships with the traditional ruling classes in areas like the Persian Gulf, testimony perhaps to the residually aristocratic character of the British state and the British political class. Here again the Blair Government's proclamation of an ethical foreign policy may represent the beginnings of a new British pattern.

The French pattern has long been different. At the ideological level the French have frequently displayed sympathy for American ideals and preoccupations. A kind of liberal (as distinct from Marxist) internationalism has bound together the two nations, a bond which extends back as far perhaps as the American Revolution itself, when France offered important aid to the British colonists. This ideological bond, a veritable republican fraternity, has remained important, surfacing again recently in shared concern about labour standards and welfare provision in the face of competition from low-wage, third-world economies.

The problems which undermine France's relations with the United States are instead linguistic and cultural. The last hegemony in Europe which France enjoyed was in the seventeenth and eighteenth centuries. It was even more a cultural than a political hegemony. The recollection of Europe as an area where French language and culture were widely accepted as the arbiters of taste has survived the development first of the British and then of the American 'empire'. That recollection makes the French, as we have seen, hypersensitive to the advantages of Europe's developing a separate identity and power base from that of the United States. It pulls the scales from French eyes whenever they inspect American motives and it prevents them from falling under the spell of that 'Anglo-Saxon' partnership which, in their view, puts Europe in thrall to America.

Now, a healthy scepticism about American motives is no bad thing in Europe. But the trouble is that the French attitude does not always stop at scepticism. It sometimes degenerates into a kind of paranoia or hysteria. The reason for this is, I think, that the subject of relations between Europe and the United States touches and reveals the least rational feature of the otherwise successful post-war strategy of the French political class.

The stumbling block for the French is the independent life which English as a language has taken on, a life independent of American economic and political interests. That is a development which the French cannot control, try as they may. And yet it is a development which they cannot really accept either. And so they try to deny it, at least in effect. But that, in turn, undermines the cosmopolitanism upon which French policy has always prided itself, for it reveals that French policy has been limited by unduly narrow assumptions about what constitutes culture – the culture to which others assimilated being, of course, French.

This 'irrationality' of French policy has had two dangerous consequences. First, it has led the French into dubious assumptions about a European identity and European interests. By defining that identity and those interests so much *against* Anglo-Saxon identity and interests, it underestimates the divisions both of sentiment and interest within Europe. The premise, then, of post-Maastricht French attempts to create a common European foreign policy and defence capability becomes dangerously unreal as a result. The débâcle of European policy in Bosnia, and the extent to which the beginnings of a resolution required American intervention, illustrated this only too well.

But the French make another, even more dangerous, mistake. Their frequently obstructive attitudes towards the United States, paradoxically, take American democracy too much for granted. They seriously underestimate the fragility of American democracy, in particular its populist as opposed to liberal potential. French policy does not even begin to address the need to strengthen liberal democratic influences within the United States. Nor does it sufficiently recognize the constructive potential of the alliance between Europe and the United States for reinforcing liberal democracy on both sides of the Atlantic. Yet, arguably, that has been one of the most important roles of NATO, almost as important as its role in deterring Soviet aggression in the post-war period.

France's partial withdrawal from NATO, its policy of non-co-operation in military matters after de Gaulle so decided in 1959, was symptomatic of the deep difficulties in France's relationship with the United States. It remains symptomatic of the suspicions France harbours about American policy and reveals what I have called French complacency about American democracy. The French desire to give Europe a clearer identity, with defence and foreign policies of its own, conforms superficially to the often expressed American wish to see Europe assume more of the 'burden of freedom' – in particular, by assuming a larger share of Western defence expenditure. In theory, that French vision of a European identity involves renewed partnership with America, but the trouble is that in practice the French convert partnership into rivalry, concentrating on areas where interests may conflict rather than those where they coincide – owing, probably, to insecurity about potential Anglo-Saxon domination. Rumours about French spying on American commercial secrets, in response to similar American 'tricks', are a case in point.

In some ways Germany now looks like being the most promising and stable partner for the United States in Europe. Sharing a federal system provides an ideological foundation for partnership, more important than might be supposed. Nor is Germany as worried by the international role of the English language and Anglo-Saxon culture as France. Yet there are also problems lurking in the German–American relationship. The passivity of Germany in foreign and military affairs, which marked the early post-war period, is now coming to an end. Germany's attention is increasingly drawn to its traditional hinterland in Eastern Europe, not least because of reunification and the re-siting of the capital to Berlin. As Germany regains confidence and the habit of self-assertion, its inclination to defend the interests of its own 'zone' will probably clash increasingly not only with the French inclination to rely on a Mediterranean zone, including Spain and Italy, as its base of power, but also with the American habit of regulating the West's relationship with Russia. Germany may be tempted one day to make its own arrangements with Russia.

A federal Europe would, at least in the near future, be hard pressed to reconcile such different attitudes towards the United States. In turn, the United States might find itself increasingly tempted to take up the traditional preference of British foreign policy – that is, trying to maintain a balance of power in Europe, if need be by playing one country off against another. But with European countries joined more closely in a federal union, that policy would become far more problematic. For a federal Europe, endowed with a unified decision-making procedure in foreign and military affairs, could more easily be dominated by attitudes which identify the United States as a competitor rather than a partner, even if those attitudes were by no means universal in Europe.

Much the best safeguard against this threat to the quality of relations between Europe and the United States is political idealism. It is for both sides to become clearer about a shared moral inheritance, about the core of moral intuitions which underpin liberal democracy. For the only form of Western imperialism which remains legitimate is ideological. We will be judged by our beliefs and our determination to act on them – beliefs which, because they require, within limits, tolerating behaviour that we do not favour, are more complex in their application to any society than merely rule-bound codes. These beliefs distinguish modern Western liberal democracy from traditional societies as well as from populist democracy or vulgar utilitarianism. That is why 'liberal' and 'democratic' matter equally in European and American self-descriptions. But if we are to be true to the moral intuitions of our tradition and offer a compelling model to the rest of the world – compelling morally, that is – we first have to overcome a widespread misunderstanding of the nature and development of our own tradition. Only that combination can create the culture of consent which is the last and most soundly based Western claim to superiority in civilization.

10

Europe, Christianity and Islam

Europe can do what it ought to do for itself and for the rest of the world only if it is secure in its own identity. Asking about the moral identity of Europe is, therefore, no secondary matter or mere afterthought. For unless a coherent identity presides over the process of European integration, that process will, sooner or later, lead to disorder. The habits and attitudes required to sustain new European institutions depend, finally, upon some shared beliefs.

Such a moral identity presupposes a story, a story we can tell ourselves about the origins and nature of our beliefs. And such a story *is* available. Europeans have only to pick up the pieces of their past in order to become aware of important moral continuities. Yet there is a snag. The pieces of our past lie scattered around us. But we seem afraid to pick them up and assemble them. Why is that? There are at least two reasons. One is the survival, beyond its time, of anti-clericalism in Europe. The other is a more recent phenomenon, the development of the outlook described as 'multiculturalism'.

Even in the United States, where there has long been a clearer, simpler story to be told – a narrative less obscured by anti-clericalism than in Europe – things have begun to change. The multiculturalist outlook, converted into a political weapon by increasingly self-confident minorities, is blurring the self-understanding of American liberalism. To see that, it is only necessary to look at the confusing pattern of Supreme Court decisions over matters such as positive discrimination. In Europe, where residual anti-clericalism and multiculturalism sometimes enter into a marriage of convenience, matters are worse. As a result, the moral identity of Europe has become problematic.

If we want to understand the distinctive constitution of Europe, we must go back to its religious foundations. For the moral beliefs which Christianity fostered still underpin civil society in Europe, the institutions that surround us.

At first glance this may seem an odd claim. For today the most striking thing is that Europeans live in a world in which no model of character, no conception of how we ought to criticize and shape our own wants, is deployed coercively. We not only lack any institution seeking to coerce private conduct – for which we should be grateful – but we also lack many traditional social pressures, whether deriving from patriarchal families or a monolithic public opinion. Moreover, in a rather bizarre way, the multiplication of wants which has accompanied the democratization of society and growth of market relations has combined with modern technology to bombard us with knowledge of all this. We are constant witnesses to the fracturing of our own characters.

In Europe, public discussion about how we ought to conduct ourselves has at times come to seem powerless, if not irrelevant, to the variety of human behaviour. About the latter we are now so much better informed, and so much more frank than in the past, that it seems to amount to an insurmountable obstacle to any attempt to defend a model of human character. For of course we not only know and discuss more openly the variety of human behaviour, we are also far more sophisticated about its sources – drawing, as we can, on an empiricist tradition which has analysed the social and psychological 'causes' of behaviour. Equipped with knowledge of the mechanisms of behaviour, it is tempting to take the view that outside the range of legal obligations required to protect individual choice and market relations, any attempt to put forward a model of human character, and of the moral obligations corresponding to it, would be futile. Wants are simply too diverse. The pursuit of one set of desires or values points to a model of character which cannot be reconciled with the model of character implied by the pursuit of other desires or values.

When seen against this background, the habits of thought associated with what I have called economism and its philosophical underpinning, utilitarianism, begin to look like a world-weary ratification of basic features of the modern Western world. Encouraging economic growth seems the best means not only of easing social conflicts, conflicts of distribution, but also of accommodating human diversity. It is probably no accident that, since the mid-eighteenth century, utilitarians have more or less openly insisted on the social formation of wants and doubted the autonomy, even at times the existence, of the self.

Of course, the great utilitarian philosophers from Hobbes and Hume through John Stuart Mill were not only anti-clerical but anti-religious. Now what is the most fundamental goal of religion? It is to govern the human will, to direct intentions and, through them, actions. So it is by no means cynical to suggest that the utilitarian account of the self as a mere bundle of desires or wants, with the will defined simply as the desire that precedes action, corresponds, in part, to a wish to destroy religion's empire over the will. If the human will does not exist, at least in the sense required by traditional Christian thought, what becomes of that empire? Seen in this light, the equivocal account of the self put forward by utilitarian philosophy looks convenient, to say the least.

The failure of utilitarianism to address a will in which it does not altogether believe stands in sharp contrast to the mainstream of liberal thought represented by the great German philosopher, Immanuel Kant. For Kant, liberalism was first and last about the will. The central principle of his moral philosophy was an attempt to provide a criterion for framing intentions, a criterion for morality properly so-called, which turned on the possibility of universalizing intentions. 'Act so that the rule of your conduct can be adopted by all rational agents.' It is tempting to see in this Kantian dictum a secularizing of the central norm of Christian ethics – that to 'love God with all your heart and mind' requires 'loving your neighbour as yourself'. Like Christianity, Kantian liberalism identifies the greatest need of humans, as self-conscious beings, as the need for a rule of conduct, the means of governing oneself as a free and responsible agent.

Modern economism's failure is that it does not face up to this question of self-government or address the issue of what is required to make the empire of the will legitimate. For the utilitarian maxim that pleasure or happiness should be maximized fails to acknowledge the need to govern the empire of the will. It provides instead an aggregative criterion for public decision-making, a criterion which is defective because it does not provide for the claims of justice. But that failure over justice reflects, in turn, utilitarianism's failure to distinguish between persons as separate and autonomous agents, as rational agents who need a rule by which to regulate their own wills. Utilitarianism merely aggregates satisfactions, looking upon society as a kind of *collective* self. It does not mark out or respect the differences between persons, their need for autonomy.

Two utterly different approaches to the idea of human equality emerge here. For utilitarians, as we have seen, everyone must count for one and no one for more than one in calculations of utility. But why is that? Why should not some count for six and others for minus one? Such unequal valuations have, after all, been the rule in most human societies. Yet utilitarianism provides no satisfactory answer to the question of why everyone should count for one and no more. In a sense, as we have just seen, it has no concept of the person at all. Taking people simply as equal units for the incidence of pleasure and pain will not do. For that confuses humans as separate physical bodies with humans understood as rational agents equally worthy of respect. It confuses fact and value.

The early utilitarians prided themselves on rejecting what they saw as the 'absurd' metaphysical assumptions of Natural Law theory and its religious sources. Attributing natural rights to individuals was condemned by Bentham as 'nonsense on stilts'. But the truth is that utilitarianism's commitment to equality was parasitic on the Christian Natural Law tradition it rejected. Bentham's insistence on equality for purposes of calculating utility and maximizing happiness depended implicitly on the principle that all natural persons should be the bearers of equal basic rights. And it was the norms of the Christian Natural Law tradition which had generated that principle in Europe.

So we come back to the idea of equality. We must now look more closely at its connection with Christian belief. For unless we do so, we shall not understand the nature of modern democracy, its sources and its dilemmas.

In looking at both the idea and the practice of democracy in the ancient world, we found that it was intimately bound up with the assumption of 'natural' inequality, that is, with the belief in irreducible differences of status. Citizenship was a privilege. Citizens of a *polis* shared equally in that privilege, it is true. But, taken together, the citizens constituted a privileged caste. They owned the *polis* and the public weal. Citizens were on parade before their inferiors, who included women, foreigners and slaves. The idea of humans as such, as rational agents deserving equal liberty and respect, simply was not present.

Nor was it originally present in Judaism. The Jewish God's relations with his own people made them a privileged group, the 'chosen people'. However refined Jewish reflections on the nature of God's will became, especially with the prophets in the later centuries BC, they did not really achieve an unequivocal universalism. Though pregnant with the possibility of moral development, Judaism remained primarily tribal in its outlook. It did not concern itself consistently with the human species as such.

It was the arrival of Christianity which accomplished that moral revolution. In that way Christianity provided the moral foundations of modern democracy, by creating a moral status for individuals – as children of God – which was eventually translated into a social status or role.

Christianity itself can be understood as an amalgam of Judaism and elements of Greek philosophy. In the Hellenistic period, some Greek philosophers had begun to speculate about a 'human' nature which underlay different social conventions. But their speculation was, in a sense, directed at demonstrating their own rational superiority, their ability to rise above the local and parochial. To that extent, it was a reassertion of the assumption of natural inequality. These philosophers' speculations did not have any radical moral import. They were not designed to challenge or undermine the 'aristocratic' beliefs and practices of the world of the city-state – though they may indeed have been influenced by the weakening of the city-state and the advance of the Roman Empire.

Difficult questions in the sociology of knowledge surround the advent of Christianity. But it is hard not to notice the parallel between a Mediterranean increasingly governed from one centre and the sudden movement towards monotheism in the first centuries of our era. What Christianity did, in effect, was to combine the abstracting potential of later Hellenistic philosophy – its speculations about a universal or human nature – with Judaism's preoccupation with conformity to a higher or divine will. By combining the assumption of human equality (the 'equality of souls') with belief in the need to discover the divine will, a new relationship became possible, a relationship with divinity which was radically personal rather than tribal. The result was the emergence of the individual, first as a moral status, and, many centuries later, as a social status or role.

The assertion of fundamental human equality ceased to be merely a speculative stripping away of the accretions of social convention and instead indicated the need for a moral response to the individual freedom implied by equal standing in the eyes of God. Jesus's injunction that 'the kingdom of God is within you' (as proclaimed and interpreted by the early Church) was designed to invoke such a moral response, to create an individual will. In that sense one can say that the Christian idea of God provided the ontological foundation for the individual, first as a moral and then as a social status or role. The interiority of Christian belief – its insistence that the quality of personal intentions is more important than any fixed social rules – was a reflection of this. Rule-following – the Hebraic 'law' – was downgraded in favour of action governed by conscience. In that way, the Christian conception of God provided the foundation for what became an unprecedented type of human society.

We can see this if we consider the imagery which we in the residually Christian West still rely upon when understanding the social world. We imagine every individual as having, by nature or right, his or her own access to truth, his or her own ground of being. Each of us is deemed to have a freehold in reality, a plot of truth to which we have direct access. Our access to the nature of things is presumed to be through conscience and personal judgement rather than through membership of any group. And this is crucial. For the Christian God survives in the assumption that we have access to the nature of things *as individuals*. That assumption is, in turn, the final justification for a democratic society, for a society organized to respect the equal underlying moral status of all its members, by guaranteeing each 'equal liberty'. That assumption reveals how the notion of 'Christian liberty' came to underpin a radically new 'democratic' model of human association.

If we want to understand the difference which Christianity has made to the world, we could do worse than fall back on a distinction made by Karl Marx in understanding the history of class conflict in Europe. Marx distinguished between a 'class in itself' and a 'class for itself'. By that he meant that a class could exist objectively – identified by its occupation, for example – without having any consciousness of itself as a class. A primary example of that in European history was the peasantry in the Middle Ages, a class that lived dispersed, local and ignorant, a class which lacked even a term for describing itself. In that way the peasantry differed, Marx argued, from the townspeople or bourgeoisie. For the latter gradually became conscious of themselves, and of their interests, through struggling against their feudal over-lords.

If we apply this distinction to the role of Christianity, it can be said that Christianity took humanity as a species in itself and sought to convert it into a species for itself. Thus, the defining characteristic of Christianity was its universalism. It aimed to create a single human society, a society composed, that is, of individuals rather than tribes, clans or castes. The fundamental relationship between the individual and his or her God provides the crucial test, in Christianity, of what really matters. It is, by definition, a test which applies to all equally. Hence the deep individualism of Christianity was simply the reverse side of its universalism. The Christian conception of God became the means of creating the brotherhood of man, of bringing to self-consciousness the human species, by leading each of its members to see him or herself as having, at least potentially, a relationship with the deepest reality – viz., God – that both required and justified the equal moral standing of all humans.

That framework of ideas can plausibly be described as the original constitution of Europe. It was this conception of the proper relationship of humans to each other and to their God that led St Augustine to distinguish between the City of God, which embodied these norms, and the City of Man, which did not. In that way Augustine recognized and celebrated the deeply subversive character of Christian beliefs – the way their universalism and individualism distinguished Christianity from all forms of localism and tribalism. Augustine identified the creation of humanity as a species for itself as a God-given task for Christians – a call upon their wills which, drawing upon Jewish beliefs, transformed the merely speculative universalism of Hellenistic philosophy into a militant church on earth.

These Christian beliefs became the crucible out of which Europe was created. The process can be seen more clearly in Western than in Eastern Europe, because the collapse of the Western Roman Empire left the Papacy as the unequivocal, sole spokesman for Christian universalism and individualism. Drawing on the inheritance of Roman Law, the papacy began to create a system of law for Christians founded on the assumption of moral equality. Of course, that system did not emerge overnight. Nor did it ever prevail completely. On the contrary, the barbarous social conditions and the habits of patronage of the German invaders of Western Europe gave rise to a feudal system which turned on the assumption of inequality, on relations of superiority and deference understood as a birthright. But in the longer run feudalism (which was assailed on many fronts) could not survive in Christian Europe, the norms of which rested on the contrary assumption of moral equality. That is why, after ancient slavery disappeared, it was replaced by a form of subjection, serfdom, which itself proved to be only transitory.

The Christian Church could not help but undermine permanent forms of subjugation in society. Its constituent moral beliefs worked against such forms, even when the Church had to acquiesce in social practices such as slavery or feudalism. It is no accident that the freeing of slaves was accounted an important virtue in the early Church or that slavery in its ancient form had virtually disappeared by the tenth century. Nor is it an accident that the Church remained the means of social advancement open to all, even at a time when feudal society was dominated by the spirit of caste, of hierarchy and subordination. The Christian Church strove incessantly to establish that there is a moral law superior to all human laws – and, consequently, that the spiritual realm, the realm of thought, ought not to be and indeed *cannot* be subject to the secular realm. Force cannot establish right. The claims of public power cannot obliterate the private sphere, the claims of conscience, when the latter are properly understood.

These are the primordial truths on which Europe was raised – slowly, painfully, fitfully, incompletely. They are the truths which originally endowed Europe with a kind of constitution, a sense of the limits of the legitimate use of public power, limits established by moral rights. For centuries in the West, the papacy was the instrument for asserting and defending that constitution. It was the instrument of universalism and individualism, the instrument of values which eventually created in Europe (even if partly as an unintended consequence) an unprecedented kind of society – what we can properly call a democratic society, for it is founded on the principle of civil equality. Yet our understanding of this role of the Christian Church has suffered from the fact that the Church became identified with the stratified society based on privilege which it had, at the deepest level, played a crucial role in destroying.

After struggling for centuries to shape European beliefs and practices, the Church was, alas, accustomed to moral hegemony, to its own privileged role in society. Even though it carefully refrained from employing physical force itself, it had learned to 'co-opt' the secular arm, and thereby, at times, enforce its own doctrines. In that way, the Church violated the 'Christian liberty' which many of its deepest thinkers – even for a time St Augustine – had always understood as ruling out coercion in matters of belief. There could be only one result. From the sixteenth to the eighteenth century, growing numbers of European intellectuals turned the moral intuitions generated by Christianity against the Church itself. In that way the central tenet of European liberalism – the principle of 'equal liberty' – emerged, and Christian moral beliefs henceforth took on a new secular life. In this new life they were increasingly distanced from Christian theology, often indeed generating a fierce anti-clericalism.

Drawing out the implications of belief in the moral equality of humans – what was by the eighteenth century more often described as their 'natural' equality – became a crucial part of the movement towards a new type of society founded on civil equality. Yet, as this movement developed and gained confidence, it found the Church, in some of its long-established practices and habits of mind, an obstacle and even a foe. That is why anti-clericalism became the dominant moral and intellectual fact in Western Europe by the eighteenth century. The vision of equal liberty, which the Church had in fact nourished, was then turned against the Church itself.

Today this must not be allowed to obscure the fact that what I have called the original constitution of Europe – the foundation provided by the egalitarian norms of Christian morality, with their implications for the role of conscience and a private sphere – differed from the religious foundation of most human societies even at the outset. It differed because it was universalist in outlook. In that way Europe differed from ancient Israel, the Greek city-state, Japanese Shinto, and from all essentially tribal deities. European norms were defined ultimately in terms of the rights and obligations of individuals rather than the special characteristics of groups.

The original constitution of Europe was never particularist. The Roman Church, its doctrines and magistracies, prevented that. The controversies and struggles which marked medieval Europe about investiture, about the relations between the religious and secular authorities and the role of moral law, were symptoms of this distinctive constitution. Of course the original constitution of Europe was never written. Whatever their other disagreements and struggles, the feudal nobility, national monarchies and independent communes of medieval Europe were united by a distrust of papal power – by the attempts of some Popes to make explicit and systematic a system of norms which would have presented the papacy as a final court of appeal in a European *Rechtsstaat*. That is certainly how the most lucid and ambitious medieval Popes understood their calling. What are often described as the 'theocratic' pretensions of Innocent III should be seen as the attempt to create a legitimate pan-European legal order – an order which recognized and protected certain moral rights against secular powers, of whatever kind.

But this has a strangely familiar ring. The attempt to circumscribe all governmental power by a rights-based theory of justice is the most striking thing about the American Constitution. Entrenched rights and the judicial review which developed from them give that document a universalist character, which has left its mark on the idiom of American nationalism – 'God's country'. The moral intuitions which shaped the drafting of the American Constitution were deeply individualist and Christian in origin. But then American liberalism was much less distorted by the anti-clericalism which the power and privileges of the Church had aroused in Europe by the eighteenth century. The result was that 'New Europe' was able to endow itself with a constitution which the social and intellectual conflicts of Old Europe had made almost impossible.

The universalism of the Declaration of Independence and the Constitution give the American polity its evangelical character. That universalism captures the character of European civilization more successfully perhaps than any political document that Europe itself has produced. For moral equality and human brotherhood are simply two sides of the same coin. That coin is one that was struck by Christianity.

Why does this matter today? It matters because we have discovered that our most basic habits of thought – distinguishing between the religious and the secular, between public and private spheres, as well as recognizing that while conformity can be enforced, truly moral conduct presupposes choice – have their origins in the Christian culture of Europe. The fact that they have outgrown their origins and indeed often been invoked to restrict the role of the Christian Church can be misleading, perhaps even dangerously so.

That is because of the upsurge of multiculturalism. No doubt recent immigration into European nations and the United States has resulted in the emergence of far more varied societies. That, in turn, has stimulated the development of new forms of liberal thought, forms which take more seriously the import of ethnic and religious cultures, the role of group identities. Implicit or explicit in these new forms of liberal thought is the suggestion that traditional liberalism concerned itself merely with the skeleton of the human body and ignored its flesh – that its abstract concern with individual liberty and human rights prevented it from feeling the real textures of social life, the variety of human experience. On this account, the loyalties and prejudices which are inseparable from belonging to and identifying with some group are neglected by traditional liberals, with the result that liberalism is unable to account for the way in which such values and commitments constitute different forms of life, forms which cannot be combined.

No one has expressed this point of view more regularly or delightfully than Oxford's Isaiah Berlin. Berlin argued against the superficiality of any view of life that assumes that all good things, all desirable values, can be combined without loss. Drawing on German Romantic philosophy of the later eighteenth century, Berlin insisted on the self-creation of man – that men and societies develop a particular character by pursuing one value over others, by coming to embody that value at the expense of others. These values, he argued, are themselves incommensurable. There is no objective or rational framework in the world – 'out there', so to speak – which can be appealed to in order to settle such radical differences of valuation and self-definition. We make choices, individually and collectively, and those choices determine our characters. That capacity for self-transformation is, moreover, the most distinctive thing about the human species.

This celebration of differences of character and culture is, at first glance, attractive and persuasive. It is also, of course, topical. Probably that is one reason why Isaiah Berlin's version of liberalism, his value-pluralism, has received so much attention latterly. For it ministers to the sensibility of Western societies which (not least because of massive immigration since the Second World War) have become far more diverse and more aware of their diversity.

Hence the theme of respect for variety has acquired a new resonance in the West – a resonance magnified, no doubt, by the decline of church attendance and formal adherence to Christianity. Less aware than formerly of shared religious beliefs or doctrine, people in the West see themselves as, and perhaps really are, more hospitable to a range of beliefs and practices. But here we must be careful. Are we as 'free' of Christianity as we suppose? There is much evidence that we are still subject to its moral sway. Take, for example, the powerful emotions raised in Europe by the sight of radical racial discrimination, emotions directed recently against South Africa for its Apartheid system. Belief in the moral equality of humans – and in that sense individualism – seems to have reached a new high-water mark. The belief that individuals should be free, under law, to lead their 'own' lives accounts for the European attempt to make respect for human rights the test of political legitimacy throughout the world.

Unfortunately, the idealism which springs from the belief in moral equality can also result in sentimentality and confusion. That is the threat posed today by the growth of multiculturalism. For there is a dangerous ambiguity about this apparently hospitable point of view. It can, in fact, camouflage a retreat from moral universalism. It is not tough-minded enough. It does not really provide an adequate framework for resolving conflicts between groups or individuals. Indeed, it cannot guarantee, out of its own normative resources, that we shall continue to live in a society of individuals, a society in which norms make 'the individual' the organizing social role, the fundamental status. That is the danger in a point of view which assumes that individuals are 'always there' – that they are, so to speak, natural facts rather than social artefacts. By ignoring the way particular moral beliefs or norms are the necessary condition of an individualist society, that assumption introduces a dangerous ambiguity.

We can see this ambiguity even in Isaiah Berlin's writings. For, if we look closely, Berlin's vision obscures the difference between two forms of pluralism. One is a vision of social groups or cultures, each defined by and expressing its own values. The other is a vision of individuals choosing to pursue different values within a framework of law which protects individual freedom but also sets clear limits to such freedom – that is, a vision of 'equal liberty'.

Evidently these visions are not the same. They may come into conflict. For there is nothing in the pluralist vision of groups or cultures growing and flowering like exotic plants in an exuberant garden which necessarily provides for or protects individual choice. The danger facing us therefore is of well-meaning but confused pluralist thinking which moves back and forth between these alternative visions, without noticing or drawing attention to the differences between them.

The crucial difference is this. A pluralist vision of *individuals* flourishing rests on the assumption of human equality – on those originally Christian assumptions about the brotherhood of men and the unity of the human race which slowly gave birth to liberalism as a social and political doctrine. So one form of pluralism presupposes both moral universalism and the principle of equal liberty, which make it possible to protect individuals from arbitary interference and social pressures, pressures often deriving from ethnic or religious solidarities. The other form of pluralism provides no such guarantees.

We do not have to look far to see what follows from the difference between these two forms of pluralism. It emerges in the model of human association characteristic of each. The model of association fostered by the Christian and liberal assumption about moral equality is that of voluntary association – of association which springs from an internal act of adherence, from a free act of will.

This has been the case to such an extent that Christian and liberal norms have always had difficulty with assessing the claims of the human family, often treating it primarily as a preparation for adult freedom – a view which can perhaps be traced back as far as Jesus's radical pronouncement on the need to reject family ties when the service of God, in conscience, requires it. That norm of voluntary association also explains why the notion and metaphor of contract have played such a large part in modern liberal political thought. Clearly, introducing the notion of contract amounts to invoking conscience and choice against merely inherited ties of kinship or status. That is how the Christian assumption about moral equality, which decisively shaped modern liberalism, has been and remains a radical challenge to many traditional societies.

By contrast, the second form of pluralism privileges inherited or natural attributes as the basis of association – whether language or ethnic identity, skin colour, sexual orientation or mere geographical location. Often the very 'givenness' of these sources of association is taken to be evidence of their greater strength and durability, when compared to the allegedly precarious and vulnerable basis of associations founded on adhesion by the individual will. So the implication of the second form of pluralism is that personal identity and social order are better secured by involuntary forms of association than by voluntary forms of association.

That assumption is not only very dubious but dangerous. For it threatens the whole project of self-regulation and its modern political extension, representative government. The idea of self-regulation – as opposed to playing out a prescribed social role, merely following rules laid down by one's inherited status or 'nature' – is the creative source of the project of a society regulating or governing itself. Without the first idea, the second is hardly intelligible as a moral imperative – becoming at best the means of defending a superior social position, as in the case of the citizens of an ancient city-state.

There is a deep and necessary connection between the assumption of moral equality, the belief that every human has the potential for rational autonomy and the prospects of self-government for any society. In the absence of that assumption it is not clear that a society is capable of self-government, of sustaining free institutions in the longer run. That assumption has not only given European societies an unprecedented dynamism, but led to the invention of representative

government – the form of government now so widely imitated throughout the world. That assumption retains a radically subversive potential
whenever it comes into contact with non-European societies in which
inequality remains the 'natural' assumption, condemning many
humans to ties of dependence rooted in kinship or social status.

Invoking conscience and choice against involuntary forms of association and subordination can plausibly be described as the genius of
European civilization – the moral logic which has brought into question
one traditional difference of status and treatment after another, a
scrutiny which has cast doubt on whether birth, wealth, gender or
even sexual preference are morally relevant grounds for treating people
differently.

This analysis of the moral distinctiveness of Europe makes it tempting
to suggest an approximate date for the emergence of a European moral
identity. The date I have in mind falls in the reign of Charlemagne.
We are told that in AD 792 Charlemagne, wishing to secure the
allegiance of his subjects and to restore a stable empire for 'the Christian
people', asked for an oath of allegiance from every man. What is
startling about his action is that he expected the oath to be sworn not
only by freemen but by some slaves as well! Such a request would have
been inconceivable in antiquity, a world in which slaves could be
defined as 'living tools'. In 802 Charlemagne asked for another oath,
this time requiring that it be taken by 'all men' over the age of twelve,
apparently extending the range of self-assumed obligation. (Certainly
the language of his edicts pointed in that direction – with phrases
such as 'every Christian person' and 'absolutely everyone, without
exception'.) Charlemagne's oaths implied that slaves too had souls, a
moral capacity which made their oath and loyalty worth having. The
moral norms associated with the term 'the Christian people' were thus
already working a fundamental revolution in minds – a revolution
which foreshadowed the end of ancient slavery, even when many
vestiges of it survived in the Carolingian Empire.

The difference between the two forms of pluralism is thus of fundamental importance. If we want to see how the difference emerges today
in an issue of public policy, we have only to consider the question of
whether public or state support for Islamic schools is acceptable. On
the grounds of diversity, hospitality and respect for variety there would

seem to be a great deal in favour of such state support. But there is a snag. If – and of course this is a crucial assumption – Islamic schools teach the radical subordination of women, if they teach that daughters must obey their fathers at whatever age, and that sisters are subordinate to brothers, do we really want public funding of such schools? For such funding amounts to a kind of endorsement of views which most of us find abhorrent, views which run directly contrary to our intuitions of justice.

Obviously the issue that emerges is one of individual liberty – the rejection of a form of permanent subjugation. It has been the genius of the Christian and liberal assumption about moral equality that it has generated over the centuries a profound critique of such forms of subordination.

The reason why it is so important to distinguish between these two forms of pluralism is that liberalism, properly understood, imposes strict limits on variety. These are the limits required by justice. What has, in our time, become a widespread association of liberalism with 'permissiveness' and 'indifference' is thus quite mistaken. Curiously, the second form of pluralism – the form which celebrates cultural variety rather than protecting individual choice – is more vulnerable to these charges. In that way it has more in common with utilitarianism than with classical liberalism. Just as we saw that utilitarianism does not really offer any principle for criticizing wants or preferences, so the second form of pluralism, in approaching different types of society, is only equivocally individualist. Some of its proponents may, as we have seen, take the individual for granted as an organizing social role. They may be in favour of individual liberty. But their framework of ideas does not safeguard such a role or such liberty.

The liberty of groups is not the same as the liberty of individuals. Respecting the beliefs and practices of a particular group, if that is understood as ruling out any interference in their ways, can indeed be described as respecting the 'liberty' of that group. But that liberty may involve an assault on or suppression of individual liberty. It may even rule out the norms and practices which are needed to sustain the individual as a social role. Certainly, the second form of pluralism does not draw attention to or make clear what those norms are. It avoids the difficult questions raised by the premise of moral equality, by the belief that all humans share an underlying equality of status and the claims, in justice, which follow from that. In that way, the second form of pluralism avoids the issue of universalism versus particularism.

Yet the issue cannot be avoided. Either one believes in basic human rights, in some version of natural law, or one does not. There is no middle ground.

It is just such a middle ground, however, which Isaiah Berlin tried to occupy. And here we may find indirect evidence for the Christian sources of individualism, of the intuitions of justice associated with modern liberalism. Berlin's Jewish heritage may well explain why he remained ambivalent in the face of individualism. For Judaism, in its traditional form, was particularist rather than universalist in outlook. Tribal claims might understandably have greater resonance for an intellectual Jew, for someone sensitive to the otherness of his own tradition. Yet European Jews live in a Christian or, more accurately, a post-Christian world. The universalist norms incorporated in Christian beliefs about God and man have infiltrated modern Jewish thinking to an extent which perhaps few Jewish intellectuals realize. Liberal or reformist Judaism can, indeed, be seen as an amalgam of Jewish and Christian norms. But even in this reformist variety modern Judaism does not openly confront the question of universalism versus particularism. It does not explore the way certain underlying beliefs are a necessary condition of the individual as a social role – the way that a Christian ontology underpins the premiss of moral equality, and thus lurks in the background of any society founded on civil equality, what I have called a democratic society.

Modern Judaism instead tends to treat the premiss of moral equality as a shared cultural inheritance – for that removes the need to explore carefully the sources of a belief which sits uneasily with the particularist heritage of Judaism. This throws some interesting light, I think, on the plight of Jewish intellectuals in a post-Christian world, in particular on the version of liberalism put forward by a thinker such as Berlin. For there is a striking coincidence between the equivocations of modern Judaism in the face of liberal universalism and the equivocations in Berlin's thought. The idiom which Berlin adopts makes it almost impossible to distinguish between the calls for variety and self-expression by individuals and for variety and self-expression of religious, ethnic or national groups. But of course the two are not the same. And they can easily come into conflict.

There are, after all, two utterly different ways in which ethnic and religious groups may live together. One is exemplified by North African cities during the later Middle Ages. In those cities, Muslims, Christians and Jews lived side by side, often showing considerable *de facto* tolerance of one another's beliefs and practices. But at the same time these groups kept largely to themselves. Nor was that all. The terms on which they co-existed were set finally by the most powerful group – rather than by law. At best, the weaker groups could rely upon established conventions, upon the 'good manners' of the conquerors. But at the end of the day their security and ability to practise their own beliefs depended entirely on sufferance. There was no accepted public framework of belief which could be invoked to defend their autonomy, no legal framework of individual rights, no genuine liberalism.

In becoming liberal, Isaiah Berlin, like many modern Jewish intellectuals, absorbed more of Christianity than he supposed. The commitment to equal liberty is wonderfully insidious. To see that, we might look at another historical example. The strong Catholic Nationalist movement in France in the years before the First World War – a movement which threw up talented writers like Maurice Barrès – often called into doubt the loyalty and patriotism of Jews, socialists and free-thinkers. Would these groups rally to the defence of France in case of need? Or were they at best *déraciné*, at worst foreign agents? Observing Jews and others rally to the Republic after 1914, making the same sacrifices as French Catholics, Barrès' attitude changed. It was not that the war turned these groups into Catholics, let alone unconditional nationalists. But the equal liberty guaranteed by Republican institutions seemed to provide the framework for a national coalition capable of defending France and perhaps contributing to the enrichment of French culture. As a result, Barrès' nationalism itself became more diluted, less intransigent. What had happened? The sight of groups whose loyalty to France he had initially doubted deciding that the framework of rights provided by Republican institutions was now so integral to their own identity and interests that they could not but fight for France, was deeply instructive. It suggested that the extreme form of nationalism represented by the *Action française* – a nationalism which would jeopardize the civil liberties of these groups by restoring the monarchy and re-merging Church and State – was now self-defeating. Liberal nationalism offered more hope for France than reactionary nationalism.

This historical example is of particular interest today when considering the future of Muslims in Europe and Europe's relations with the Muslim world. Is something like this 'insidious' infiltration of liberalism taking place among Muslims in Europe? Or are they coming to define their identity and interests in a fundamentalist way that is incompatible with liberalism?

The future of Europe is intimately joined to the future of Islam. That is not only because of the large Islamic communities that have developed in European states – in France numbering more than four million – but also because of the possibility that the nations of North Africa and the Middle East might one day be dominated by Islamic fundamentalism. There is today a desperate need to understand the nature of that fundamentalism. For the foreign relations of a unified Europe could easily become a hostage to this radical religious movement. It could be crucial to Europe not only because of the proximity of these states, several of which are oil-rich, but also because a fundamentalist revolution in these states could result in tens of millions of Westernized Arabs seeking to enter Europe as refugees.

If my account of the relationship between Christianity and liberalism is correct, then Islam poses an interesting problem. Islam, like Christianity, is formulated in a universalist idiom. In that way Islam resembles Christianity rather than Judaism. Both are religions of 'the book' and appeal to humans as such rather than as members of any particular society. Indeed, Islam may have learned to couch its appeal in this way through its early contacts with Christianity.

But the differences between Christianity and Islam are also remarkable. Islam emphasizes the 'equal submission' of believers to Allah's will rather than 'equal liberty' under the Christian God (a commitment which the early Church's need to distinguish itself from Judaism strengthened). Thus, Islam did not draw quite the same conclusions from the premise of moral equality. Its emphasis is rather on strict conformity to certain rules, to religious law. Rule-following rather than the rights of conscience is its hallmark. And, to that extent, it is tempting to suggest that Islam has more in common with Judaism than with Christianity (something which recent studies of Islam's origins reveal and which Islam's need to distinguish itself from Christianity makes plausible). The Islamic conception of religious law and of the role of mullahs does not clearly set out or protect the rights of conscience. This may, at least in part, be due to the fact that Greek philosophy and Roman Law did not enter into the composition of Islam in the way they did of Christianity. Islamic universalism lacks abstractness – an abstractness which Greek philosophical speculation about human 'nature' as opposed to 'convention' bequeathed to Christianity. Nor did Islam ever acquire a concern with *dominium* or 'rights' from Roman Law in the fashion of Christian Canon Law. Thus the idea that moral equality entails autonomy, respect for the rights of conscience, did not become a central feature of Islam. For that reason it could not generate what has become so central to the beliefs and practices of Christian Europe – the distinction between public and private spheres, between the secular and the sacred. It did not generate anything like the foundations of Western liberal thought. In fact, both religions continue to bear important marks of their origins. For Christianity, in its first few centuries, spread primarily by means of persuasion, whereas Islam spilled out of the Arabian peninsula and spread by the sword.

This provides, I think, the key to understanding Islamic fundamentalism. Islamic fundamentalism is a reaction against Western liberalism – a reaction which derives from the fact that, behind liberalism, Islam perceives Christianity at work. In a sense, Muslims are better placed than Europeans to perceive the connection between Christian moral beliefs and modernism in its many forms. For, more than many Europeans, Muslims may see the connection between the Christian emphasis on individual conscience and modernist commitments to economic, political and social liberty. To understand the Muslim reaction, it is only necessary to consider the recent controversy sparked by publication of Salman Rushdie's *Satanic Verses*, a book which many Muslims consider offensive to their religion and wish to see suppressed.

The most poignant aspect of the debate unleashed by the Islamic response to *Satanic Verses* is the moral confusion it has revealed in the West, especially in Europe. Under the impact of multiculturalism, the Christian or post-Christian nations are confused about their moral identity to an alarming extent. And that confusion has, in turn, two important consequences. First it makes the West a less effective defender of its own values than it ought to be. And, second, it prevents the West from understanding what is happening throughout the world at the most important level, the level of belief.

We have become unused to considering belief as the source of social and political change. The influence of Marxism, together with the market mechanism generated by that 'civil society' endorsed by liberalism, has drawn attention instead to events at an economic level. There is a widespread, if only tacit, assumption that when examining the world, economic developments, especially the spread of market relations, provide the key to all other developments. It is assumed that economic changes provide the key to social, political and intellectual changes.

But closely tied to the West's failure to understand both itself and others is the form of self-description which it frequently invokes. Western spokesmen – including quite often the clergy themselves – describe contemporary Western societies as 'secular and materialistic'. By that is meant not just that most Western people have ceased to be regular church-goers, but that Western societies are no longer grounded in shared beliefs. The implication is that what holds them together now are shared interests arising from consumer wants and the radical interdependence springing from an advanced division of labour. The pursuit of wealth, it is held, has replaced belief as the cement of society in the West.

Yet that widespread view – whether presented dolefully by churchmen and defenders of a lost 'community' or presented with satisfaction by those who have not entirely lost confidence in science and progress – is not only wrong, it is dangerously wrong. Of course, the problem of identifying the character of the Western tradition and finding a core of shared beliefs is complicated by Western individualism. The political and social vocabulary of the West apparently makes it possible to devalue belief as the source of social order by way of its distinctions between the state and civil society, the public and private spheres, ritual behaviour and truly moral action.

At first glance these Western notions seem to point to an irreducible plurality of beliefs or values as the distinctive feature of 'Westernness'. On that reading, pluralism, tolerance and even scepticism emerge as the intellectual attributes of the modern West. If these attributes are to be called beliefs at all, they must be described as negative beliefs, in contrast to the positive beliefs of other cultures.

However, we are now in a position to see that such an analysis misses something. It misses the fact that Western distinctions between the state and civil society, public and private spheres, mere conformity and moral conduct, are themselves derived from Christian assumptions. That is, they rest on a framework of assumptions and valuations which can be described broadly as individualist and which correspond in crucial respects to the framework of Christian theology. The assumption that society consists of individuals, each with an ontological ground of his or her own, is a translation of the Christian premiss of the equality of souls in the eyes of God. That fundamental equality of status which Christianity postulates became, especially through the Natural Law tradition, the means by which Western thinkers from the Middle Ages into the modern period drew an increasingly systematic distinction between the person as a moral agent and the social roles which such persons happened to occupy. Thus, a primary role shared by all equally was distinguished from secondary roles such as those of father, servant or woman.

The birth of the individual was, to that extent, a Christian achievement. Over centuries, the 'individual' was gradually translated from a moral criterion into a primary or organizing social role – the role which, in fact, organizes any society founded on civil equality, the role which gradually undermined the caste distinctions of Western feudalism, and remains a threat to ascriptions of permanent inequality of status anywhere.

Thus, Christian ontology provided the foundation for what are usually described as liberal values in the West – for the commitment to equality and reciprocity, as well as the postulate of individual freedom. These commitments are primary and foundational, whereas Western tolerance, pluralism and even scepticism are derivative and secondary. In that sense, Western culture is no different from any other. It is founded on shared beliefs, and when it fails to acknowledge or defend such beliefs its identity is eroded.

It is the privileging of equality which creates a sphere or role for individual conscience. For the premiss of equality operates to exclude not only permanent inequalities of status but also ascriptions of authoritative opinion to any person or group within society. Freedom thus becomes a birthright or 'natural' right, because no one is deemed to have, *ab initio*, the right to command actions or impose opinions by virtue of his or her intrinsic identity. That is what a society of individuals *means*.

And here we find the connection with what is most distinctive about the Christian conception of deity. For it is hardly too much to say that, in relation to other major traditional faiths, Christianity interiorizes God. It postulates a relationship with God which is prior to and becomes the criterion for any public expressions of faith. In that sense Christianity is not a social group identifying and worshipping itself in quite the way Durkheim attributes to all religions. For the social group which emerges from Christian premisses consists of individuals, of free and equal agents. Christianity thus provides the moral justification for the social role of the individual, who is presumed to have independent access to the deepest truth *qua* individual. That justification, in turn, fosters the idea of legitimate human associations as being those which are based on consent.

Evidently, the interiorizing of God is the source of subsequent claims made for conscience and a sphere of choice protected by rights. In consequence, the premiss of moral equality, claims for conscience and insistence that respect for human rights become the criterion of legitimate association are inextricably bound up together. They form a *Gestalt* which is distinctive of Western civilization and which has done more than anything else to make Western societies innovative and progressive.

That is the kernel of truth embedded in the Protestant version of Christianity – the kernel which makes it plausible to claim that Protestantism, for all its aberrations, is a more self-conscious form of Christianity than Catholicism. That kernel of truth triumphed at the Second Vatican Council and has thus finally led the ancient body of the Church to take its stand in favour of human rights – acknowledging, implicitly, the intrinsically individualist character of Christian thought. Catholic traditionalists who claim that, as a result, Rome has become infected with Protestantism are not entirely wrong. What such traditionalists fail to acknowledge, however, is that Vatican II saw the basic Christian *Gestalt* purged of assumptions and attitudes heterogeneous to it.

There is a striking resemblance between traditionalist Catholic arguments and criticisms which have recently been levelled against liberalism in the name of 'community'. Critics such as Alastair MacIntyre and Charles Taylor have argued that liberal ideas – by which they mean especially the framework of equality and reciprocity, resulting in individual rights being given priority to any conception of the good life – subvert that sharing which is indispensable to 'true' community. These critics of liberalism develop lines of arguments which are both methodological and substantive – though often they fail to distinguish between the two levels of argument. They argue that human agency, indeed the very idea of human action, presupposes a language and rules – that is, a social context. Consequently, it can be said that individual decisions and actions are radically dependent on a social context (or community) and cannot take place in a vacuum. That is indeed true. But it is not a decisive objection to liberalism. For when liberalism is viewed historically as itself constituting a tradition and mode of discourse, it can be seen as the matrix of our own liberal type of society.

The unhistorical, apparently traditionless mode of argument characteristic of much liberal thought since the seventeenth century has, alas, contributed to this confusion. When the matter is viewed historically, however, the sources and development of the liberal conception of community are complex and fascinating. In that story Christianity has played a crucial part. Indeed, a strong case can be made that the concept of an individual right against others or against society as a whole – what is sometimes called a 'subjective right' – found its first formulation in medieval Canon Law.

What recent critics of liberalism really seem to be objecting to is the liberal conception of community as an association of individuals rather than as some more permanently integrated set of social roles. But, at this substantive level, they are faced with a dilemma. For the type of society or social solidarity which they appeal to may require an articulation of roles incompatible with the premiss of moral equality common to both Christianity and liberalism. Yet it is in the name of Christianity that MacIntyre and Taylor mount their onslaught against liberal individualism. And one strongly suspects that they would have to rely ultimately upon liberal premisses of equality, reciprocity and liberty to choose between the various communities and ethics displayed on the stage of world history.

There is, then, a deep connection between Christianity and liberalism. The former provided, historically, the normative foundation for the latter. It is unfortunate and even dangerous that the West is so little conscious of the connection. For it cuts Western culture off from its roots, and sometimes weakens both its ability and inclination to defend its own values.

But not only that. Ignorance or merely vague awareness of the connection between Christianity and liberalism can put the West into a false position *vis-à-vis* other faiths and cultures. It opens the West to the charge of hypocrisy.

For there can be little doubt that the rhetoric of human rights amounts to a pared-down version of liberalism in much the same way as liberalism can be seen as a purged, secularized form of Christianity. If so, then the superb spread of the language of human rights throughout the world in recent decades, to the point where it has become almost a universal culture, should also be recognized for what it is – the ultimate and least resistible form of Western influence, something which must appear to defenders of other faiths as the last form of Western imperialism.

When Westerners see that emphasis on human rights spreading throughout the world, but interpret that spread as merely a matter of 'common sense' or 'obvious' human values or a 'neutral' framework for adjudicating international disputes, they deceive themselves more than they deceive the defenders of other religions and cultures. Thus, by failing to understand the extent to which Western societies continue to rest on shared beliefs, the West also fails to understand the degree to which its beliefs are now subverting the rest of the world. The Rushdie affair should have made the West more conscious of how Christian its moral intuitions remain.

Only when the connection between moral equality and the claim of equal liberty is understood is there a secure basis for self-government in any society. Only then can representative or free institutions send down the deep roots they need to survive. In that respect it is striking that the northern Protestant nations of Europe have, by and large, more durable traditions of self-government than the Catholic south. The importance of Vatican II lay not least in the reconciliation between the Roman Church and liberalism to which it contributed. The Vatican's espousal of the defence of human rights then removed a serious moral obstacle to the consolidation of representative government in the predominantly Catholic nations of Europe.

If the connection between moral equality and the claim of equal liberty is not understood or accepted, then the moral foundation for a democratic society and representative government remains incomplete. That is why the future of Islamic societies is both fascinating and troubling. It seems likely that the difficulties Islamic nations have repeatedly encountered in trying to establish representative government – truly free institutions – derive ultimately from such a moral cause. When the connection between moral equality and equal liberty is denied, it is not possible to distinguish clearly between mere conformity of behaviour and truly moral conduct. That confusion, in turn, plants the seed of tyranny.

It has been the glory of Europe that it has created and, at least intermittently, defended that distinction. The future influence of Europe in the world – as well as its ability to create free pan-European institutions – will depend upon its becoming more conscious of that moral inheritance.

II

Political Moderation and Social
Diversity in Europe: The Future

Different forms of the state have created very different political cultures in Europe. The question now facing Europe is whether these cultures can be combined successfully and, if so, how rapidly. For two great threats loom on the horizon if integration is over-rapid. The first is political, a threat to moderation in Europe. The second is social, a threat to diversity in Europe, something which has at times been described as the prospect of 'Americanization'.

Let us consider each in turn.

Since the earliest post-war moves towards greater military, economic and political co-operation in Western Europe, some have argued that a federal state for Europe, a United States of Europe, ought to be the goal. But it is only since the mid-1980s that developments in the European Union have really begun to raise serious doubt about the future of the nation-state as we know it. This doubt is not only the result of the cumulative impact of regulations imposed on the nation-states by Brussels. It is even more the result of the drive towards monetary union and a single foreign and defence policy for Europe.

In that drive the French have taken the lead, providing a constant impulsion. That impulsion is, I have argued, the delayed French response to German reunification – an event which aroused great fear among the French political class, fear, not least, of France losing the hegemony in Europe which it has enjoyed since the foundation of the European Economic Community and subsequent French veto over British entry into the EEC.

When abandoning their previous preference for a *Europe des patries*, a Europe of nation-states, in favour of 'ever closer political union', the French political class or élite fell back on its own culture, the culture created by the unreformed model of the French state. It fell back on a culture which traditionally fostered bureaucratic power, prizing knowledge, efficiency and consistency above democratic accountability or consent.

The paradox, then, is that Europe since the mid-1980s has been propelled towards a federal state by a national political class which does not really admire or pursue the values intrinsic to federalism – the formal dispersal of authority and power, checks and balances, and maximizing popular participation in the political process. Behind the French call for political control over the new European Central Bank lurks rather the model of a unitary state, a concentration of authority and power which is anathema to the values of federalism.

It is true that some European nations continue to speak a 'purer' language of federalism, notably the Germans and the Dutch. But that language no longer carries conviction throughout Europe, where public opinion, dazed by the speed with which monetary union is being imposed, and uncertain about its implications, has a growing sense that the élites of Europe have left public opinion far behind in the pursuit of this new project – and that power in Europe will be centralized, whether the peoples of Europe want it or not. A new kind of historicism or doctrine of historical inevitability has thus been born.

That is why the idealism associated with European construction during much of the post-war period is now draining away. That idealism was probably bound to suffer some sort of crisis anyway, as the generations that experienced the Second World War and were preoccupied with preventing anything like its recurrence gave way to generations which lacked direct experience of that war and its consequences. But the élitist turn taken by European construction since the Single European Act, and the Maastricht and Amsterdam Treaties, is in danger of making that crisis of idealism far more serious and prolonged than it would otherwise have been.

Indeed, European élites today are in danger of creating a profound moral and institutional crisis in Europe – a crisis of democracy – which may even call into question the identity of Europe. For, whatever the underlying French design may be, the public case for Europe is now being made almost exclusively in economic terms. In their pronouncements, the élites of Europe have fallen victims to the tyranny of economic language at the expense of political values such as the dispersal of power and democratic accountability. Increasingly, we find ourselves worshipping at the altar of economic growth rather than citizenship.

It is as if the economic model of democracy put forward by Joseph Schumpeter and his followers fifty years ago has become a self-confirming hypothesis. Democracy in Europe *is* in danger of being reduced to a competition between élites (alias parties) who manipulate consumer preferences in the fashion of companies. In the absence of a shared language and a Europe-wide public opinion, the appeal to democracy often becomes self-serving. Decisions taken in Brussels are opaque, the result of bureaucratic in-fighting and a lobbying process which puts a premium on special access and money. National identities and the civic traditions associated with them are being held of little account compared to the advantages of economic integration and rationalization. In that way, alas, the market has begun to usurp its function.

But when the market usurps its function it also calls into question its own justification. For there is an important sense in which the final, decisive justification of the market system is itself democratic – that it empowers individuals, dispersing rationality, choice and responsibility, in contrast to a command economy.

A democratic state and a free market system ought, ultimately, to serve the same ends. But that classical liberal alliance of state and market can be corrupted in two different ways. It can be corrupted through an exaggeration of the claims of politics – as both the fascist and communist experiences of mid-twentieth-century Europe reveal. When that happens, economic relations become a mere appendage of the state and its ideology, the means by which those who exercise state power impose their preferences.

But the classical liberal alliance can also be corrupted when the claims of politics are minimized while those of the market are inflated – when the 'freeing' of market forces and economic rationalization contribute to a downplaying of constitutional safeguards and thereby open the way to a centralization of political power. For the neo-capitalist habit of invoking the 'laws' of the marketplace *can* undoubtedly serve to draw attention away from such centralization. Britain experienced a minor version of that phenomenon under

Thatcherism. But today it is Europe which is in danger of seeing that perversion of a market system become a major perversion.

To the extent that European liberal democracy is perceived as acquiescing in this tyranny of economic categories – and becoming the 'fellow traveller' of centralization – it will put its own credentials at risk. It will begin to resemble the thin veneer for other more sinister forces that Marxism has always claimed it was. Then the way will be open for more extreme movements of the right and left to seize the label 'democratic' and use it for their own purposes.

For that is the great political danger posed by the rush to monetary union and political integration. Over-rapid integration risks discrediting the liberal democratic centre of European politics, both the centre-right and the centre-left. In nearly all European countries, the parties of the centre have presented a common front over the project for monetary union and further integration. But in doing so, they have deprived centrist voters of any real choice, leaving opposition to the single currency, for example, as a vote winner, real or potential, for the extremes. The ratification of the project by the German Bundestag in 1998 illustrated this only too vividly. After some dithering, the Social Democratic opposition voted with the Christian Democrats, to give an overwhelming majority of deputies in favour of monetary union. But at the time opinion polls showed that nearly two thirds of German voters were opposed to the project, preferring to retain the mark. By leaving public opinion so far behind, the German political class – prompted by the French – has run the risk of creating, sooner or later, a reaction in Germany. That reaction could even involve the Germans coming to see recent moves towards integration as amounting to the imposition of a new Versailles Treaty on Germany, a new national 'humiliation'. This is especially likely if the widespread rumours about President Mitterrand having channelled French funds to reinforce Chancellor Kohl's position and party prove to have any substance.

Of course, it is the duty of a democratic political class to give a lead. But it also has a responsibility to carry opinion with it. When it does not take the latter duty seriously enough, it finds itself exposed to challenges from movements which put 'nation' or 'class' above the claims of liberal democracy. Worse still, nationalist xenophobia and class resentments may coalesce, and a kind of unholy alliance of the right and left may begin to nibble away at the recent liberal democratic consensus in Europe, which the fall of Communism at first seemed to make impregnable. There is some evidence that this has been happening in Germany, where the former Communist Party has exploited East German veneration for the mark, in tacit alliance with right-wing Bavarian politicians who have almost a National Socialist pedigree.

In France, too, the drive towards a single currency could work to the advantage of the political extremes. Dissenting voices among the Gaullist and Socialist Parties have been kept at bay, leaving both the centre right and the centre left apparently solid behind the policy of monetary union. Yet doubt about the extent of public support – doubtful not least because of the refusal to hold a referendum after the wafer-thin majority supporting the Maastricht Treaty in an earlier referendum – has created an opportunity for the both the National Front and the Communist Party to pose as the spokesmen of France's 'true' interests, interests defined, implicitly, in terms of anti-immigrant racism and class-conscious anti-capitalism.

By allowing an élitist strategy for rapid European integration to shape the image of liberal democracy in Europe, to the point almost of constituting it, Europe's centrist politicians may unwittingly be fostering the things which are most antithetical to liberal democracy – xenophobic nationalism and economic autarky. Recent developments in Austria – with the far right-wing (some would say almost neo-Nazi) Freedom Party entering into a coalition government – could be a harbinger of things to come.

If too wide a gap between élites and public opinion opens up and is allowed to persist, then the causes championed by élites – even if constructive or admirable – are likely to be discredited. The American Supreme Court learned that lesson during both the 1930s and the 1960s. In the former period, justices had fallen behind public opinion in the face of the economic crisis of the Great Depression. Their traditional concerns with limiting the power of central government and preserving federalism began to look irrelevant to the nation's needs. Conversely, in the 1960s and 1970s justices found that the spate of civil rights decisions which followed the desegregation decision of 1954 had cumulatively brought liberalism itself into disrepute – associating it with contempt for localism and the family, especially with the reliance on 'busing' to achieve racially and socially 'balanced' schools. The ways in which the Supreme Court has since then trimmed its sails and made concessions to public opinion are not a sign of weakness. Rather, they are a sign that the Court recognizes that its strength comes from a powerful hold over public opinion, and that if it pursues policies inimical to this hold over opinion, it may undo its chief support.

The élites of Europe – ostensibly the champions of a post-Marxist, liberal democratic consensus – are putting that consensus at risk by opting for a policy of over-rapid integration. They risk confirming suspicions in the public mind that they represent no one so much as themselves, that they are creating a Europe which benefits an administrative and political élite at the expense of national identities and established civic loyalties. Yet those identities and loyalties could return with a vengeance if a world economic crisis intrudes or, even, if serious economic dislocation results from a single currency – say, a spiralling of unemployment in some countries, with consequent demands for protectionism and job-creating interventions in the market. For such demands will sit uneasily with the system presided over by a deflationary European Central Bank which has deprived national governments of control not just over monetary but also over fiscal policy.

No doubt that is one reason why the French have been insisting that the European Bank should be subject to 'political control'. But what exactly does this mean? It is far from clear that the political control prized by the French has much to do with democracy in Europe. If the past behaviour of the Brussels Commission and its decisions are anything to go by, political control might suggest rather a kind of power-brokering in which the prize often goes to the most determined and persistent country or lobby, regardless of the formal rules which are supposed to govern the decision.

Many of those who have been sceptical about European political integration and critical of the growing power of Brussels have been inclined to interpret pressures for unification as emanating chiefly from Germany. Some have even seen the project as little short of an attempt to create a Fourth Reich, a more benign and managerial but none the less German-dominated Europe. This interpretation is, I think, deeply mistaken. If the stubborn pursuit of any national advantage is to be identified behind pressures for unification it is that of France rather than Germany. The French political class has been far more skilful than that of Germany or, indeed, than that of any other major European nation. Behind the formal rules which govern the decision-making process of the European Union, the French have imposed their will to an extraordinary extent.

A tell-tale sign of that French success has, as we have seen, been the budgetary outcome in Europe. Despite France being one of the largest and richest member states, the French have managed to avoid becoming significant net contributors to the Union's budget – while Germany, Britain (despite the rebate won by Mrs Thatcher) and even Holland pay more into the budget than France! This is not mere chance.

Other examples might be cited. Take the issue of state subsidies to ailing industries or firms, subsidies which Brussels officially frowns upon. The French and, to a lesser extent, the Germans have come close to flouting the rules. Behind the scenes pressure has meant that the Commission has had to acquiesce in massive French subventions to rescue Air France and Crédit Lyonnais, while the German Government has continued to subsidise generously its coal-mining industry.

Too often, the impression given by Brussels decisions is that the rules are for some but not others. This can affect foreign and military as well as domestic affairs. Thus, the German Government brought great pressure to bear in order to secure for Croatia – which it clearly regards as a client state – more favourable terms of trade than those available to other Eastern European nations. By the same token, the French often fall back on the argument of national security in order to prevent major French companies falling subject to foreign ownership. Privatization in France has thus been subject to stringent political control.

Such power-brokering behind the scenes, in contempt of the formal rules, is not the way to create a culture of consent in Europe.

The habit of exercising administrative power which marks the French élite – and the extent to which that power is exercised to protect what are deemed to be French interests – emerges blatantly in French protectionism. For of all the members of the European Union, France strikes the visitor as the most protectionist. And the means of protection adopted must usually be administrative rather than legal, informal rather than formal. The symbiotic relationship between the French state and important sectors of French industry survives, despite Brussels' obligation to enforce competition and remove state subsidies. The Colbertian tradition dies hard. Indeed, the way in which members of the French administrative élite move between public and private sectors helps them to elude formal constraints. When the neo-liberalism of the Brussels Commission comes up against French *étatist* habits, Brussels usually gives way. Just as French state control of major industries has been protected, so has the range of products displayed on the shelves of supermarkets in France. France remains an internal market to a startling degree. The same pattern can be observed on the roads, where French-made cars predominate. Altogether, the extent to which the French continue to consume their own products sometimes gives France an almost pre-war aspect.

The informal means by which the French market remains closed, despite formal European Union rules to the contrary, is reinforced by the attitudes and habits of French farmers and wine growers. Fear of competition from Spanish or Italian producers often leads to demonstrations and barricades, the interruption of normal traffic on the roads and the railways. All too often such demonstrations degenerate into violence as well. The fact that an important part of the French balance of payments surplus derives from agricultural exports, which far exceed imports, counts for little with French farmers. It is almost as if they considered competition intrinsically unfair.

Evidently these are not the attitudes and habits required by the rule of law. Rather, they are the survival of a pattern established in pre-revolutionary France, when the peasantry – faced with an arrogant, unresponsive and remote state-machine – simply assumed that the law was made by and on behalf of others. If decision-making in Brussels comes to be perceived in the same way, associated with power-brokering by élites in contempt of the formal rules, suspicion of the law could become generalized across Europe – destroying the degree of consent sustained by existing national political cultures. For the sad truth is, that it is easier to destroy a culture of consent than to create one. And however sad that truth may be, we cannot afford to avert our eyes from it.

Nothing better illustrates my argument than the struggle surrounding the appointment of the first Director of the new European Central

Bank. As we have seen, Germany and all the member states of the European Union had thrown their support to a Dutchman, Wim Duisenberg, with the exception of one state – France. France stood out against all the others, insisting that its own candidate be elected and threatening a veto on Duisenberg's election. The French were moved neither by considerations of legality – the Amsterdam Treaty had stipulated that the election should not be a contest between national candidates – nor by solidarity. For the Franco-German axis was abandoned when the Germans supported the Dutchman Duisenberg. French obstinacy revealed both the importance which France attaches to dominating European Union appointments, and its habit of doing just that.

In the foreground was France's argument that the Central Bank should, after all, be subject to political control – that Europeans should not merely be at the beck and call of irresponsible bankers. But when that French position was probed, it was clear that the 'control' in question was not a matter of increased democratic accountability but rather of responsiveness to French interests and demands. The French were interested in constructing a chain of command, rather than ensuring that the formulation of fiscal and monetary policy become part of an open political process. The unashamed stubbornness of French negotiators testified to the fact that at times they approach European decisions more as a power-game than as creating a 'transparent' authority across Europe, something like a European *Rechtsstaat*.

No doubt all European nations are ferociously self-interested. But the peculiar French role in the creation and operation of the European Union, the habit of dominating its decision-making, has resulted in a fusion of the ideas of 'French interest' and 'European interest'. The survival of the Common Agricultural Policy in the face of so much trenchant criticism and opposition is itself testimony to the vice-like hold of the French administrative class on European policy. That class has come to use the idea of Europe in a way that rules out categorically any conflict between French national interest and European interest. Were those two ideas now to be prised apart, it is by no means clear how the French political class or the French people would react.

This may become a problem sooner rather than later. For, by accelerating the transfer to power to Brussels, the French have created an instrument of government which can be turned against them. For example, the European Commission could become more consistent and ruth-less in its application of free-market ('Anglo-American') rules to France than it has been hitherto. Then Europe, which the French have seen as the means of combating Anglo-American influence, might suddenly become – in French eyes – just another instrument of that influence. Administrative power inspired by the French state might come to threaten the French state itself. Then the often-repeated French belief in 'mastering' the marketplace in the name of social justice, cultural standards and the integrity of the rural landscape would be put at risk.

How would the French react? It is far from clear. But French idealism about Europe – that idealism which has been so important in the creation of the European Union – might become the victim. And that would be a tragedy for Europe as a whole. For, while I have been saying rather hard things about French habits of government, I do not want to be misunderstood. The French have more to give to Europe than any other country, *because they believe in Europe as a cultural and a moral undertaking.* Sustained by their extraordinary success in transforming France since the end of the Second World War, the French political class has acquired the conviction that Europe can be modern and still be Europe – that European values and practices can more than hold their own in competition with those of the United States, offering higher standards to the world in education and design, quality of life, public transport and fidelity to the environment. That conviction is extremely precious, even to the point of justifying French predomi-nance in Europe. But it is a conviction which France should seek to spread by example and persuasion, rather than by the over-rapid accumulation of power in Brussels. For that power may one day be turned against the French vision of Europe, with incalculable conse-quences for French opinion.

Nor is it only a question of the French reaction. If the over-rapid pursuit of political integration has the effect of discrediting liberal democracy in Europe, that will also have a profound effect on relations between France and Germany. A close relationship between these nations has provided the backbone of European construction since the 1950s. Yet, when inspected closely, it is clear that France has been the dominant partner, providing the will and defining the objectives for Europe. How will these two nations react if disillusionment with the

European project as an 'élitist conspiracy' creates a resurgence of nationalism? What seems most likely is that France, after flirting with a right-wing alternative, will turn towards the left, while Germany will turn towards the right – not least, with the impulsion of public opinion in the provinces which previously formed part of the Germany Democratic Republic and have had only minimal experience of the disciplines required for representative government.

Such developments would create a serious threat to European unity. For the German right might easily come to interpret recent German acquiescence in the French design for Europe as the kind of humiliation which requires redress. Of course, there is no need to suppose that the search for redress would turn into a nineteenth-century revanchist military strategy. But there is reason to suppose that a right-wing Germany facing a leftist France might decide that it was no longer comfortable with the kind of Europe that had been constructed – that differences over currency, national debt, immigration, industrial and foreign policies made it more attractive for Germany to pursue an 'independent' policy. That independent policy might well involve Germany seeking in a more concerted way to create its own sphere of influence in Eastern Europe.

If we have learned anything from our exploration of the problems which the project for a federal Europe must overcome, it is that the rule of law is only reliable and durable when it is rooted in popular habits and attitudes. For that reason, the problems facing law-givers are very different from those facing economists, bankers and industrialists. The creation of new wants is the key to economic growth. But it is not that difficult to create new wants. The history of economic development in the West testifies to that. By contrast, inculcating the rule of law and creating a culture of consent is a far more precarious undertaking – for such things depend upon the degree of self-control a society is able to generate and sustain.

Recourse to violence is a litmus test of failure. I have argued that recourse to violence is characteristic of national cultures which have been shaped by a bureaucratic form of the state – a form of the state which encourages its subjects to assume that public power is being exercised in the interests of others. It is also the nature of such cultures that the rule of law is identified more with fiat than with consent, with statute imposed by and enforced from above, rather than with law understood as the distillation of popular attitudes and habits. Historically, that has marked a profound difference between the Roman Law tradition of continental Europe and the Common Law tradition of the Anglo-Americans. Neither the development of representative government on the continent nor the ascendancy of statute over custom in Common Law countries has entirely effaced the difference.

That difference makes it important not just to assess the contents of proposals for political unification in Europe, but also to inspect their source. For it is likely that a project which issues from countries with a Roman Law tradition – countries in which the rule of law is associated more with the central imposition of rules than with the formalizing of popular attitudes and habits – will reflect the bias of that tradition. It is also likely that such a project will underestimate the importance of public opinion, as against the strategies of élites, and fail to appreciate the length of time needed to change popular attitudes and habits.

And so it is. The bias of the current project, which issues from France and an *étatist* political culture, reinforces what is already the dominant bias of our age – an economic point of view which assumes that because market incentives can be changed in a relatively short time-span, the behaviour appropriate to those incentives can be moulded from the centre, almost at will.

Yet the culture required by the rule of law is not like that. The stuff of that culture is far less tractable than consumer behaviour. That is why the marriage of economism and *étatisme*, which marks the present rush towards European integration, poses a serious threat to democracy in Europe.

Let us now turn to the relationship between democracy and social diversity in Europe. In order to think clearly about the implications of democracy in Europe in that respect – especially if such thinking involves comparisons with the United States – we have to overcome an initial difficulty. That is the difficulty raised by talking about recent social changes in Europe in terms of 'Americanization'. There are, of course, sometimes good reasons for describing social changes in that way. But there are also bad reasons for doing so – that is, reasons which do not stand up to critical examination. For 'Americanization' is now bandied about so freely that it is in danger of losing any clear meaning.

We can only make headway if we distinguish several distinct meanings of Americanization, to be sure that we know what we are talking about.

Two widespread uses of the term seem to me especially likely to result in misunderstanding, if what we really want to think about is democracy in Europe. The first is the prestige of American modes, styles and products which result from the United States being the richest and most important nation in the world today. That 'top-dog' appeal is of course very powerful and by no means unprecedented – at different earlier periods of history something like that glamour attached to French modes in the seventeenth and eighteenth centuries and to British modes in the nineteenth and early twentieth centuries. Power and wealth do amount to a kind of aphrodisiac. Exposure to them, perhaps especially with young people seeking ways to find something better and to distinguish themselves from their parents, does create explosive ammunition for change. That role for imitation in social life accounts for an important part of human history, and is unlikely to be reduced when communication and the media have become instantaneous and global. None the less, it is important to distinguish the prestige of American modes – what Gore Vidal likes to call the impact of America's 'Empire'– from the democratization of European society.

A second and closely related but separable use of Americanization refers to the constant pressures, which some see as insidious, of American commerce in the world market. American self-interest, in the form of the pursuit of the 'almighty' (a religious slip, if ever there was one) dollar, is real enough. And the extent to which vigilance against monopoly or quasi-monopoly is required, especially when commerce has now invaded communications, knowledge and cultural output, should never be underestimated. But American commercial pressures, and even the vulgarity which used to be associated with American products in Europe, should not be confused with democratization.

No, if we are to think clearly about the impact of democracy in Europe, we must not forget that what we should have in mind are the issues – the moral, intellectual and social issues – raised by a basic change in the structure of European societies. What is crucial is the increasingly 'middle-class' character of European societies, with the status differences, which had their origin in feudalism, eroding to the point of disappearance. That is, the original castes created by feudalism, the aristocracy and peasantry, have now collapsed into a new intermediate or 'bourgeois' condition. It is the consequences of the disappearance of a highly stratified or structured society which provide the real subject matter for reflections about democracy in Europe. Must this change in the structure of European societies result in their homogenization, in a 'suburban' uniformity which develops at the expense of social diversity?

Here, discussion of Americanization *does* overlap with discussion of democratization in Europe. And the reason is clear. The United States was the first society to experience the circumstances of and grapple with the problems raised by this revolution in the structure of society. It was the first Western society in which a middle-class condition became the predominant one – a society in which not only was prosperity widely spread, but the status differences which had survived feudalism in Europe had largely disappeared.

It is that similarity in social condition which has underpinned the influence of America on Europe since the end of the Second World War. In grasping the importance of that similarity of social condition, the instincts of the mass of people in European nations may cut more deeply than the instincts of their élites. For while the latter have worried – understandably – about the threats to traditional 'high culture' posed by products and modes associated with the United States, the peoples of Europe have often seized on those products with little or no reluctance. Why is that? It is because American products and modes are entirely free of any association with social subordination – free of the cues and codes which, until recently, sustained relations of superiority and deference in European life. Thus, it is no accident that American products and modes have made the least profound impact on the country in which upper- and lower-class manners have survived most markedly, the United Kingdom – and that despite a language shared with the United States!

The defining condition of the American economy and society – its middle-class condition – induces neither contempt for the marketplace nor fear of it. Where a more stratified European society used to induce very different attitudes towards the marketplace – a contemptuous upper-class view of the market as a poodle and a fearful lower-class view of the market as a devouring monster – the characteristic middle-class and American attitude is to view the market as a bedfellow, something which can interfere with sleep, but which none the less provides major consolations.

The assumption that everyone is more or less in the same position *vis-à-vis* the market has governed American life and shaped American responses to the problems posed by a middle-class or democratic society. The ability to imagine yourself in everyone else's situation – a kind of social transparency – has shaped not only the design of American products, but also American culture and humour. At bottom, that is what now constitutes its attraction for Europeans, who are being initiated into a similar social world. Yet that kind of social transparency does entail a degree of uniformity. It entails the need to appeal to consumers (in the broadest sense) who have the same basic range of experience, whose wants, needs and even fantasies can be said to have a 'standard' character.

Undoubtedly, that extent to which a democratic society subjects everyone, even those cushioned by the ownership of capital, to the pressures of the marketplace contributes to a standardizing or homo-genizing of outlook. It is easier to enter the minds of others who are subject to the same pressures. If one side of the coin is vulnerability, the other side is sympathy born of familiarity. In that way, the dis-appearance of a highly stratified or aristocratic society does mean that the human passions are excited by a more uniform set of social conditions. And that, in turn, can be said to raise the question of the future of social diversity or pluralism in a democratic Europe.

It has been argued that pluralism – a prolonged competition of values and institutions – has been the defining characteristic of European civilization, what sets Europe apart from other civilizations. The nineteenth-century French historian, François Guizot, pointed out that whereas most world civilizations fell under the domination of one value and institution relatively early in their history, Europe remained the scene of an intense, often bloody, competition between the claims of aristocracy, democracy, monarchy and theocracy. What set Europe apart was that none of these was able to triumph completely, so that civil society in Europe developed as a sphere in which the state set the ground rules for the peaceful interaction of individuals and associations whose values were by no means uniform – so that, apart from the rule of law, there was no official creed, no enforced set of beliefs and practices.

If this analysis is correct, then an important question raised by the democratization of European society is whether pluralism – a competition of values and institutions – is now at risk. Will market relations and a commercial ethic submerge all of these traditionally competing elements, narrowing the range of values on offer and gradually destroying the European past? In the end, that might leave European society scarcely different from that of the United States, a democratic society without a past in the sense that it was democratic from the outset and lacked the legacy of class conflict that has marked European history.

Europe has long laboured under the disadvantages of its history. For there is no doubt that the legacy of class-consciousness and of class conflict has made the achievement of representative government and a devolved form of the state a far more protracted, uncertain matter than the development of American federalism. But that is not the whole story. For, on the other hand, Europe has enjoyed an immense advantage. Here, the democratic principle has been hedged around by memories, instincts and manners which had their origins in a more stratified society – memories, instincts and manners which give a richer, more complex texture to European societies.

The danger of premature federalism in Europe – of the rush to political integration which turns federalism into little more than a mask for a unitary superstate – is that it could put at risk the complex textures of European societies. For these textures have developed in alliance with particular nation-states endowed with distinctive political cultures. It is far from clear that they could long withstand the sudden subordination of those states to a centralized rule-making agency which pitched its action at the level of a common denominator. In that way Europe could suddenly lose much of its own history. Or, rather, it might find itself lumbered with the disadvantages of its history, a residue of class hatreds, without its advantage, pluralism.

How does this traditional pluralism impinge on Europe today? It impinges in a subtle way. In each European nation, the transition from aristocracy to democracy involved a different kind of amalgam of the original elements of European society – feudal aristocracy, the self-governing cities or communes, royal power, and the Church, whether Catholic or Protestant, Gallican or ultramontane. Those different amalgams have, in turn, left their marks on the political cultures of each nation, giving each what 200 years ago would have been called its own *genius*. Thus, Dutch democracy has been oligarchical and confessional, German democracy decentralized and paternalist, French democracy bureaucratic and at times populist, Italian democracy communal and even anarchical, and so forth.

These differences are not superficial. The strength of democratic sentiment and its ability to resist oppression is, in each of these countries, tied to a particular bias. The history of Europe, the formation of these nation-states, survives in their distinctive political cultures.

To attempt to change those cultures too rapidly – subjecting them to rule from a single centre in fact, even if not in theory – would risk destroying the different forms of civic spirit which exist in Europe today. Even if that weakening of the nation-states coincided with a partial 'liberation' of the regions of Europe, the loss to democracy could be enormous, perhaps crippling. For, as we have seen, the European regions do not for the most part have civic traditions which can rival those of the nation-states – a fact which is hardly surprising, since their identities are often survivals from late feudal Europe.

The attraction of federalism, properly understood, for Europe is that it should make possible the survival of these different national political cultures and forms of civic spirit. But that can be the case only if federalism is approached gradually. For one of the pre-conditions of successful federalism is a consensus on which areas of decision-making belong to the centre and which ought to be reserved for the periphery. *Today in Europe there is no such consensus.* The establishment of a European Senate, charged with overseeing that question and the work of a European Court, creating a common jurisprudence, could gradually help to create such a consensus. But it cannot be created overnight. Nor can a Europe-wide political class, able to defend such a consensus and make the exercise of governmental power accountable, spring up suddenly.

These are not matters for a few years. These are matters for decades, probably for generations. Federalism is the right goal for Europe. But Europe is not yet ready for federalism.

A Brief Bibliography

In this book I have been more concerned to be provocative than informative. For the tendency of arguments about Europe's future to remain in the shallows is not only depressing but dangerous. I am convinced that only if deeper issues are identified and seriously addressed can federalism in Europe become either plausible or attractive. So what I have attempted to do is to raise at least some of the more difficult questions – to suggest what we ought to be thinking *about* rather than what we ought to be thinking.

Readers will not find here a detailed history of post-war moves towards European integration, that is, an account of the origins and development of the European Union; nor will they find a detailed analysis of the institutions of the European Union, the prerogatives and duties of the Council of Ministers, the Commission, the European Parliament or the European Court of Justice.

For such matters, readers will have to look elsewhere. Where should they look? A few books suggest themselves. The *Penguin Companion to European Union* by Timothy Bainbridge with Anthony Teasdale (Harmondsworth, 1995) is a very useful guidebook organized by topics. For the economic story, nothing is better than the *Economics of the Common Market* by Dennis Swann, 7th edition (London, 1992). *Development in the European Union*, edited by L. Cram, D. Dinan and N. Nugent (London, 1999), provides an overview of the development of European institutions, policies and outstanding issues. More theoretical – not always with advantage – is the approach in *European Integration and Supranational Governance*, edited by W. Sandholtz and A. Stone Sweet (New York, 1998).

What will probably become the standard set of readily accessible studies on different aspects of European integration is the *European Union Series* being published by Macmillan, under the general editorship of N. Nugent, W. Patterson and V. Wright. Several volumes which have already appeared are especially helpful. One is *Ever Closer Union?: An introduction to European Integration*, by Desmond Dinan (London, 1999). Another is *Understanding the European Union*, a concise introduction, by J. McCormick (London, 1999). Still another is *France in the European Union* by Alain Guyomarch, Howard Machin and Ella Ritchie (London, 1998). If anything, this subtle and interesting study might at first glance seem to underplay the extent of French influence on the formation of European institutions and policies. But careful reading dispels that impression.

For a more jaundiced and polemical but fascinating account of the inner workings of the Brussels Commission, particularly in connection with the creation of a common currency, readers should at least sample *Europe's Rotten Heart* by Bernard Connolly (London, 1995).

In what follows, I have first of all provided a chronology of the main events in the development of the European Union as an *aide-mémoire*; then I have indicated the more important sources or suggested further readings for each chapter.

Main Events in the development of the European Union

1951 Treaty of Paris creates the European Coal and Steel Community (the Schuman Plan).
1957 Treaty of Rome creates the European Economic Community (with effect from 1 January 1958).
1963 De Gaulle vetoes British entry into the EEC.
1966 The Luxembourg compromise on voting (*de facto* national veto).
1968 The customs union fully operational.
1973 Accession of the UK, Denmark and Ireland to the EEC.
1979 Direct elections to the European Parliament.
1981 Accession of Greece to the EEC.
1986 Accession of Spain and Portugal to the EEC.
1987 The Single European Act comes into effect.
1990 Reunification of Germany.
1992 The Maastricht Treaty on European Union signed (effective on 1 November 1993).
1993 Completion of the Single Market.
1995 Accession of Austria, Finland and Sweden to the EU.
1997 The Amsterdam Treaty.
1999 The launching of the euro.

1: Democratic Liberty on a Continental Scale?

Montesquieu (Charles Louis de Secondat, Baron de la Brède et de Montesquieu), *The Spirit of the Laws* (1748), edited by by A. Cohlar, B. Miller and H. Stone (Cambridge, 1989). For secondary works, see especially R. Aron, *Main Currents of Sociological Thought*, vol. I (London, 1974); M. Richter, *The Political Theory of Montesquieu* (Cambridge, 1977); and J. Shklar, *Montesquieu* (Oxford, 1987).

Alexis de Tocqueville, *Democracy in America*, Introduction by A. Ryan (London, 1994). For secondary works, see especially R. Aron, *Main Currents of Sociological Thought*, vol. I (London, 1974); L. Siedentop, *Tocqueville* (Oxford, 1994); G. Pierson, *Tocqueville and Beaumont in America* (New York, 1938); A. Jardin, *Tocqueville* (London, 1988); and C. Lamberti, *Tocqueville and the Two Democracies* (New York, 1989).

James Madison's contributions to *The Federalist Papers* include especially Numbers 10, 14, 18, 19, 20, 32, 39, 44, 51 and 63. See, for example, *The American Constitution For and Against, the Federalists and Anti-Federalist Papers*, edited by J. R. Pole (New York, 1987); and L. Banning, *The Sacred Fire of Liberty: James Madison and the Founding of the Federal Republic* (Ithaca and London, 1995).

Henri de Saint Simon (Comte de Saint Simon), *Selected Writings on Science, Industry and Social Organisation*, edited by K. Taylor (London, 1975). See also Frank Manuel, *The New World of Henri de Saint Simon* (Cambridge, Mass., 1956).

2: Where are our Madisons?

This chapter develops arguments I first put forward in a short article: L. Siedentop, 'Where are our Madisons?', *Financial Times*, 16 October 1992.

The principle of subsidiarity has been defined as 'a modern Catholic social teaching, first articulated by Pope Pius XI in *Quadragesimo Anno* (1931), that the best institutions for responding to a particular social task are those that are most proximate to it', *The HarperCollins Encyclopaedia of Catholicism* (New York, 1995), p. 1227.

Margaret Thatcher, *The Downing Street Years* (London, 1993).

On utilitarianism, see J. J. C. Smart and B. Williams, *Utilitarianism: For and Against* (Cambridge, 1973); A. K. Sen and B. Williams, *Utilitarianism and Beyond* (Cambridge, 1982); *Utilitarianism and its Critics*, edited by J. Glover (New York, 1990); and H. L. A. Hart, 'Between Utility and Rights', in *The Idea of Freedom*, edited by A. Ryan (Oxford, 1979). For a more refined form of utilitarianism, see J. Griffin, *Well-being: Its Meaning, Measurement and Moral Importance* (Oxford, 1983).

For rights-based liberalism, see especially J. Rawls, *A Theory of Justice* (Cambridge, Mass., 1971) and *Political Liberalism* (New York, 1993); R. Nozick, *Anarchy, State and Utopia* (Oxford, 1974); and R. Dworkin, *A Matter of Principle* (Oxford, 1985) and *Law's Empire* (London, 1986).

For communitarianism, see especially A. MacIntyre, *After Virtue* (London, 1981); C. Taylor, *Sources of the Self* (Cambridge, 1990); M. Walzer, *Spheres of Justice* (New York, 1983); and M. Sandel, *Liberalism and the Limits of Justice* (Cambridge, 1982).

For discussion of the debate between liberals and communitarians, see W. Kymlicka, *Liberalism, Community and Culture* (Oxford, 1989); and S. Mulhall and A. Swift, *Liberals and Communitarians* (Oxford, 1992).

3: The Dilemma of Modern Democracy

Alexis de Tocqueville, *The Ancien Régime and the Revolution*, Introduction by H. Brogan (London, 1976); B. Moore, *The Social Origins of Dictatorship and Democracy* (London, 1984).

Fustel de Coulanges, *The Ancient City: A Study on the Religion, Laws and Institutions of Greece and Rome* (New York, reprinted 1980).

Benjamin Constant, *Political Writings*, edited by B. Fontana (Cambridge, 1988).

For the classical republican tradition, see Jean-Jacques Rousseau, 'On The Arts and Sciences', in *The Discourses and Other Early Political Writings*, edited by V. Gourevitch (Cambridge, 1997); J. G. A. Pocock, *The Machiavellian Moment* (Princeton, 1975); and Q. Skinner, *The Foundations of Modern Political Thought* (Cambridge, 1978).

François Guizot, *The History of Representative Government* (London, 1852).

R. Tuck, *Natural Rights Theory* (Cambridge, 1979).

Bernard de Mandeville, *The Fable of the Bees, or Private Vices, Public Benefits*, edited by Phillip Harth (Harmondsworth, 1970).

S. Lukes, *Individualism* (Oxford, 1973).

4: How Britain has Lost its Voice

This chapter develops arguments that I first put forward in the following articles: L. Siedentop, 'The Impotence of the British Middle Classes', *The Spectator*, 30 December 1978; L. Siedentop, 'Mr Macmillan and the Edwardian Style', in *The Age of Affluence*, edited by V. Bogdanor and R. Skidelsky (London,

1970); and L. Siedentop, 'Thatcherism and The Constitution', *The Times Literary Supplement*, 26 January 1990.

The Age of Affluence, edited by V. Bogdanor and R. Skidelsky (London, 1970).

Thatcherism, edited by R. Skidelsky (Oxford, 1988).

V. Bogdanor, *Devolution in the United Kingdom* (Oxford, 1999).

5: Why Constitutions are Important

Here again I am developing arguments I first put forward in: L. Siedentop, 'Political Theory and Ideology: the case of the state', in *The Nature of Political Theory*, edited by D. Miller and L. Siedentop (Oxford, 1983).

K. Dyson, *The State Tradition in Western Europe* (Oxford, 1980).

J. Gough, *Social Contract: A Critical Study of its Development* (Westport, Conn., 1958).

H. J. Abraham, *Freedom and the Court: Civil Rights and Liberties in the United States* (Oxford, 1998).

François Guizot, *The History of Civilization in Europe*, edited with an introduction by L. Siedentop (Harmondsworth, 1997).

For other perspectives on nationalism, see E. Gellner, *Nations and Nationalism* (Oxford, 1994); and D. Miller, *On Nationality* (Oxford, 1995).

6: Three Forms of the State

This chapter develops arguments I first put forward in a short article: L. Siedentop, 'Models for Maastricht', *Financial Times*, 13 August 1992.

Those who wish to pursue a detailed study of comparative government might consult the following texts: S. E. Finer, *Comparative Government* (London, 1970); G. Sartori, *Comparative Constitutional Engineering* (London, 1997); and R. Hague, M. Harrop and S. Breslin, *Comparative Government and Politics* (London, 1992). The finer points of constitutional theory can be pursued in: M. Vile, *Constitutionalism and the Separation of Powers* (Oxford, 1967); and G. Marshall, *Constitutional Theory* (Oxford, 1980).

The following works discuss recent democratization in France: V. A. Schmidt, *Democratizing France: The Political and Administrative History of Decentralization* (Cambridge, 1991); *The End of the French Unitary State? Ten Years of Regionalization in France, 1982–1992*, edited by J. Loughlin and S. Mazey (London, 1995); and *Developments in French Politics*, edited by P. Hall, J. Hayward and H. Machin (London, 1990).

For an interesting discussion of the threat to the separation of powers from an American perspective, see Aubry Smith, 'Executive Branch Rulemaking and Dispute Settlement in the World Trade Organization: a proposal to increase political participations', *Michigan Law Review*, 94, p. 1267 (1996).

7: Creating an Open Political Class

Joseph Schumpeter, *Capitalism, Socialism and Democracy* (London, 1961). A condensed version of Schumpeter's argument can be found in his article 'Two Concepts of Democracy', in *Political Philosophy*, edited by A. Quinton (Oxford, 1967).

To sample several forms of reaction to the so-called revisionist or market-based model of democracy, see the following: J. Plamenatz, *Democracy and Illusion*, an examination of certain aspects of modern democratic theory (London, 1973); J. Lively, *Democracy* (Oxford, 1975); and C. Pateman, *Participation and Democratic Theory* (London, 1975).

For the national budget contribution figures released by the German government, see *The Financial Times*, 17 September 1998. For the figures subsequently released by the Brussels Commission (*Financing the Rueopean Union*), see *The Financial Times*, 8 October 1998. Despite some differences between the two, the basic profile remains the same.

For Mitterrand's initial reaction to German reunification, see the interesting interview with historian Joseph Rovan in *Le Figaro*, 10 November 1999.

8: Europe and the Global Market

For what I have called Capitalist Triumphalism, the most obvious source is F. Fukuyama, *The End of History and the Last Man* (London, 1992). For Capitalist Catastrophe Theory, at least two authors should be consulted: J. Goldsmith, *The Trap* (London, 1994); and J. Gray, *Enlightenment's Wake* (London, 1995) and *Endgame* (London, 1997).

On the relationship between Protestantism and capitalism, see Max Weber, *The Protestant Ethic and the Spirit of Capitalism* (London, 1930); and R. H. Tawney, *Religion and the Rise of Capitalism* (London, 1938).

Fustel de Coulanges, *The Ancient City* (New York, 1980).

The quotation from François Guizot can be found in his *Histoire de la Civilisation en France* (Paris, 1840), vol. I, pp. 325–6. See also his fascinating chapter comparing the Roman and the medieval municipality in the same work, vol.

IV, pp. 259–76. Of course, the question of the relationship between Christianity and the end of ancient slavery has generated an enormous literature, which goes far beyond my concerns in this chapter. However, readers might profitably consult a recent post-Marxist account of the transition from antiquity to feudalism which does not underplay the role of the Church: G. Bois, *The Transformation of the Year One Thousand: The Village of Lournard from Antiquity to Feudalism* (Manchester and New York, 1992).

9: Europe and the United States

Alexis de Tocqueville, *Democracy in America*, Introduction by A. Ryan (London, 1994).

Louis Hartz, *The Liberal Tradition in America* (New York, 1955).

For the historical background to American populism, readers cannot do better than consult several works by Richard Hofstader: *The Age of Reform: from Bryan to F.D.R.* (New York, 1955); *The American Political Tradition* (London, 1962); and *Anti-Intellectualism in American Life* (New York, 1963).

For social change in the United States and its political implications, see, for example, J. Bass and W. De Vries, *The Transformation of Southern Politics* (New York, 1976); and M. Kazin, *The Populist Persuasion* (Ithaca and London, 1995).

10: Europe, Christianity and Islam

Emile Durkheim, *The Elementary Forms of the Religious Life* (New York, 1995). I first broached some of the ideas in this chapter in an article called 'Liberalism: the Christian Connection', which appeared in *The Times Literary Supplement*, 24 March 1989.

For discussion of Charlemagne's use of oaths, see especially Edward Jones, *The Origins of France* (London, 1982), pp. 165–6; also R. Collins, *Early Medieval Europe 300–1000* (London, 1999), pp. 306–8. For the language of Charlemagne's capitularies, see P. King, *Charlemagne: Translated Sources* (Kendal, 1987), passim.

Probably the most relevant works by Isaiah Berlin are his *Four Essays on Liberty* (London, 1979); *Vico and Herder* (London, 1976); and *The Roots of Romanticism*, edited by Henry Hardy (London, 1999). For a genial account of Berlin's life, see Michael Ignatieff, *Isaiah Berlin* (London, 1998). A more extensive account of Berlin's liberalism, especially his 'value pluralism', can be found in John Gray, *Berlin* (London, 1995).

Index

Made in the USA
San Bernardino, CA
08 May 2017